21

WAYS TO FINDING PEACE AND HAPPINESS

Overcoming Anxiety, Fear, and Discontentment Every Day

JOYCE MEYER

New York   Boston   Nashville

Unless otherwise indicated, all Scripture quotations are taken from THE AMPLIFIED BIBLE (AMP). THE AMPLIFIED BIBLE, OLD TESTAMENT, copyright © 1965, 1987 by The Zondervan Corporation. THE AMPLIFIED NEW TESTAMENT, copyright © 1954, 1958, 1987 by The Lockman Foundation. Used by permission.

Scripture quotations marked KJV are taken from the KING JAMES VERSION of the Bible.

Scripture quotations marked NKJV are taken from THE NEW KING JAMES VERSION. Copyright © 1979, 1980, 1982 by Thomas Nelson, Inc. Used by permission. All rights reserved.

Scripture quotations marked NIV are taken from the HOLY BIBLE, NEW INTERNATIONAL VERSION®. NIV®. Copyright © 1973, 1978, 1984 by International Bible Society. Used by permission of Zondervan Publishing House. All rights reserved.

Scripture quotations marked TLB are taken from THE LIVING BIBLE © 1971. Used by permission of Tyndale House Publishers, Inc., Wheaton, Illinois 60189. All rights reserved.

Faith Words
Hachette Book Group USA
237 Park Avenue, New York, NY 10169

Visit our Web site at www.faithwords.com

Printed in the United States of America

Originally published in hardcover by Warner Faith as *In Pursuit of Peace: 21 Ways to Conquer Anxiety, Fear, and Discontentment.*

First Trade Edition: May 2007

10 9 8 7 6 5 4 3 2 1

The Faith Words name and logo are trademarks of Hachette Book Group USA.

LCCN: 2006939834
ISBN 978-0-446-58150-9 (pbk.)

CONTENTS

Part 3
BE AT PEACE WITH OTHERS

INTRODUCTION

The first forty years of my life, I lived without the blessing and benefit of peace; therefore, I can say from experience, life without peace is *miserable*. One cannot enjoy life without first having peace. Without it, we live in turmoil—always worried, anxious, and upset about something.

I came to a point in my life of being so hungry for peace that I was willing to make whatever changes were necessary in order to have it. As a result of that decision and the investment I made during the following years, I now enjoy a life of peace that often passes understanding. In other words, I enjoy peace *during* the storms of life, not just when the storms don't exist. I am not saying that I have arrived at a state of perfection in my pursuit of peace, but I have made a lot of progress. As the apostle Paul said in Philippians 3:12, I have not arrived but I press on.

There were times in my life when I could be peaceful if everything was going my way, but since that seldom occurred, I rarely had peace. Now I have learned to change what I can change, accept what I cannot change, and regularly seek wisdom to know the difference. What I can do, I do with God's help; what I cannot do I turn over to Him so He can work. This leaves me free to enjoy my life.

A life of frustration and struggle, a life without peace, is the result of trying to do something about something you cannot do anything about. The apostle Paul said, "Be anxious for nothing, but in everything by prayer and supplication, with thanksgiving, let your requests be made known to God; and the peace of God, which surpasses all understanding will guard your hearts and minds through Christ Jesus" (Philippians 4:6–7 NKJV).

Once we realize we are struggling with something and feel upset, we need to start praying and immediately turn the situation over to God. You and I are not called to a life of frustration and struggle. Jesus came so we could have righteousness, peace, and joy (see Romans 14:17). He said, "The thief comes only in order to steal and kill and destroy. I came that they may have and enjoy life, and have it in abundance (to the full, till it overflows)" (John 10:10). The Word teaches us to "search for peace (harmony; undisturbedness from fears, agitating passions, and moral conflicts) and seek it eagerly. [Do not merely *desire* peaceful relations with God, with your fellowmen, and with yourself, *but pursue, go after them!*]" (1 Peter 3:11, italics mine).

Simply desiring peaceful relations is not enough. We're to pursue peace with God, peace with ourselves, and peace with our fellow man. In this book, I will share with you many things within these three areas of relationships that needed to change in order for me to enjoy peace.

If you sincerely want a life of peace, you will need to be willing to change too. Peace does not just come; we have to pursue, crave, and go after it. Walking in peace must be a priority, or we will not make the effort needed to see it happen. I spent years praying for God to *give* me peace and finally realized He had already provided peace, but I had to *appropriate* it.

Jesus said in John 14:27, "Peace I leave with you; My [own] peace I now give and bequeath to you. Not as the world gives do I give to you. Do not let your hearts be troubled, neither let them be afraid. [Stop allowing yourselves to be agitated and disturbed; and do not permit yourselves to be fearful and intimidated and cowardly and unsettled.]" We will refer often to this verse throughout this study.

We can see that Jesus has already provided peace, so now we must take action and stop responding to unpleasant things by being upset. Being upset certainly does not change anything, but it does make us—as well as the people around us—miserable.

Jesus made the statement recorded in John 14:27 after His death and resurrection and prior to His ascension into heaven. There were many things He could have taught His disciples, but He chose to talk about peace. This fact alone reminds me of how important peace is. What a tragedy it would be if we spent our lives without peace when it was available all the time.

Some people don't have peace with God because they are not born again and need to trust Jesus Christ to be their Savior. But some, even Christians, still lack peace because they have not responded to the leading of the Holy Spirit simply to do what is right. They don't have peace because they are living in disobedience or they have built up a bad habit of worrying over the years. And some people don't have peace because they are mad at God. Perhaps they prayed for something and it didn't happen. Perhaps somebody else got what they wanted. Perhaps somebody they loved died, and they don't understand why, or they were praying for a healing and didn't get it.

There are many, many reasons why people don't trust God, but in order to enjoy peace, we must learn to trust Him in all things. We must trust that God is totally and completely just, which means He always makes wrong things right if we continue to lean on Him. The Bible says we know "in part." I believe God has an individual plan for everyone. God is perfect; He never does anything wrong. We don't know everything, and we're not ever going to know everything. Sometimes we make ourselves unhappy because we don't *trust* enough.

We always want God to change our circumstance, but He's more interested in changing *us* than He is our situation. A lot of people have faith to ask God for deliverance *from* something, but they don't have enough faith to take them *through* anything.

Job said, "Even though He slay me, yet will I trust Him" (see Job 13:15). If we're asking God for something and don't get it, then we have to believe God knows more than we do. We need to trust God beyond what we see and beyond what we know. We cannot have peace without that trust in God.

We tend to think that the persons with the greatest faith are the ones who get the miracles. I'm not really sure about that, myself. We make so much out of miracles when they happen. We think, *Oh, what great faith they have! They got a miracle.* But I think the ones with the greater faith are the ones who *keep their peace* even when they don't get the miracles they wanted. I think the greater faith is in those who have to walk it out and decide to love God anyway. The people who don't get everything they're asking for, and who might not understand why, but yet continue to love and praise God, are truly trusting God. They stay in church, give their tithes and offerings, and stay full of peace. That is remarkable faith, in my opinion.

Thomas wanted proof that Jesus really had risen from the dead. He said he would not believe unless he could see in Jesus' hands the marks made by the nails and actually put his fingers into the nail prints and put his hand into Jesus' side. Jesus allowed Thomas to do so but told him that those who believed without having to see were blessed and happy and to be envied (see John 20:24–29).

We all would enjoy a miracle breakthrough every time we had a need, but we should have enough faith to stay the course if God chooses to take us on the long, hard route.

If you are ready to do whatever you need to do to enjoy a life of peace, this book is for you. I cannot promise that all your unpleasant circumstances will change, but I sincerely believe you can have and enjoy peace no matter what your circumstances are if you are willing to learn how to respond to people and situations the way Jesus did.

I pray that the Holy Spirit will enlighten you and grant you revelation as you press toward a life of peace. The book includes twenty-one ways you can do this. Even after you have completed the book, I suggest you read it often to remind yourself of the principles of peace. If you find you are slipping back into old ways (something we all do at times), go back over the principles and see where you have begun to backslide. I pray this will be one of those books you can use the rest of your life to help you maintain peace, which I believe is one of the most important benefits and blessings that God has given us.

Part I

BE AT PEACE
WITH GOD

*Therefore, since we are justified (acquitted, declared righteous, and given
a right standing with God) through faith, let us [grasp the fact that we]
have [the peace of reconciliation to hold and to enjoy] peace with God
through our Lord Jesus Christ (the Messiah, the Anointed One).*

—The apostle Paul, *Romans 5:1*

TRUST THE LORD OF PEACE

God wants us to enjoy life and see good days. In fact, God's Word tells us to *search* for peace, and seek it eagerly (see 1 Peter 3:11). We are not to merely *desire* peaceful relations with God, with our fellow men, and with ourselves, but we are to pursue and go after peaceful relationships!

The first way to find peace is in learning to trust God through a relationship with Jesus Christ. Jesus is the Prince of Peace. We cannot have peace with God, others, or ourselves without His lordship in our lives. The Bible says that Jesus is our wisdom from God (see 1 Corinthians 1:30). His Word teaches us how to live properly. He doesn't just give us wisdom—He *is* our wisdom. Through trusting the Prince of Peace and having a personal relationship with Him, we actually have indwelling wisdom from the Lord's presence in us.

If we would get still long enough to let that wisdom rise and minister to our minds, we wouldn't do so many foolish things. Too many times, we react through our emotions and we don't pay any attention to the wisdom in our hearts. We tend to make decisions according to our thoughts rather than living by discernment and according to what the Holy Spirit is placing in our hearts. Consequently, we get ourselves in trouble.

I believe that Jesus is everything we need in any situation. He is sufficient to meet the need for every circumstance that we will ever face. So, we certainly must learn how to go to Jesus for much more than just salvation or a ticket into heaven. We need to take Him as our everything in life, including as our Prince of Peace.

JESUS GOVERNS OUR LIVES

Isaiah 9:6–7 says, "For to us a Child is born, to us a Son is given; and the government shall be upon His shoulder, and His name shall be called Wonderful Counselor, Mighty God, Everlasting Father [of Eternity], Prince of Peace. Of the *increase of His government and of peace there shall be no end*" (italics mine).

The government that is upon the shoulders of Jesus is not a political government; the verse is referring to the governing of our lives. We are not supposed to be running our own lives. In fact, we are not capable or qualified to run our own lives. Not one of us is intelligent enough to know what is best. That is why we should be thankful for God's interference.

I like the promise that there will be no end to the increase of His government and peace. The more His government increases in my life (the more He governs my life, my thoughts, my conversations, my decisions, and my actions), the more peace I am going to have.

Peace doesn't come from success and money and promotions and feeling good about everything in life. We find peace in the kingdom of God, which is righteousness, peace, and joy within us. Being right with God, knowing we are right with God, and doing the right thing out of knowing who we are in Christ is a process, but it leads us to peace, and peace leads us to joy.

And if we don't have righteousness, peace, and joy, then we are not enjoying the kingdom of God as we should. Sometimes we may need to take a vacation from all the other things we look for and instead seek the kingdom. Matthew 6:33 says, "Seek (aim at and strive after) first of all His kingdom and His righteousness (His way of doing and being right), and then *all these things* taken together will be given you besides" (italics mine).

We work and struggle and strive at "all these things," such as food and clothing and position in society. But what we should be doing is searching out God's kingdom; we should seek Jesus and His government in our lives. Colossians 1:10 says, "That you may walk (live and conduct yourselves) in a manner worthy of the Lord, fully pleasing to Him and desiring to please Him in all things."

BE A DISCIPLE OF JESUS

Jesus said, "If anyone would come after me, he must deny himself and take up his cross and follow me" (Mark 8:34 NIV). If we want to have peace, we have to stop following other voices; we must be God pleasers, not man pleasers, and we must choose to follow Jesus on a daily basis.

For many years, I was in a church that gave me a great foundation about salvation, but I never learned much past that. I had many problems in my life, but I wasn't getting any victory over any of them. I certainly didn't know how to pursue or go after peace. Satan distracted me by getting me involved with many activities that did not produce good fruit in my life.

I was not taught to study God's Word myself, and because I didn't know the Word of God, I wasn't aware of the many deceptions that can grossly mislead people. For example, before I was in ministry I worked at an office where a coworker studied astrology. At the time, the things she talked about seemed to make sense (because I had no knowledge of God's Word on this subject). She believed the position of the planets and stars directed her life. She said there were even optimum times to get a haircut to have the best results.

Today, advice is easy to obtain from psychics, tarot card readers, sorcerers, and people skilled in divination who would like to run people's lives. They may give information that seems to make sense, but it will not produce lasting peace in a person's life. As I look back at those early years of being a believer, I am sad to say that nobody in my church told me not to follow these voices of deception. No one warned me that the Bible clearly says those who practice these types of things will not enter the kingdom of heaven (see Revelation 21:8). We are to follow God, not psychics, astrologers, mediums, tarot card readers, or any such thing. God's Word actually says that these things are an abomination to Him. To enjoy peace, we must be led by the Lord of Peace.

To be a disciple of Jesus means to study His teaching, imitate His life, and correctly analyze the Word of Truth (see 2 Timothy 2:15). We will have God's power to live our lives well if we devote our attention to God's Word and allow Jesus to transform us by following the peace that He alone can give.

Peace is our inheritance from Jesus, but we have to choose to follow Him daily. Colossians 3:15 teaches us that peace is to be the "umpire" in our lives, settling every issue that needs a decision. To gain and maintain peace in our hearts, we may have to learn to say no to a few things.

For example, if we don't feel peace about something, we should never go ahead and do it. And if we don't have peace *while* we are doing something, then we shouldn't expect to have peace *after* we have done it. Many people marry others they didn't have peace about marrying, and then they wonder why they don't have peace in their marriages. Many people buy expensive items they didn't have peace about buying, then continue to lose their peace every month when they have to make payments on them.

I want to repeat the text I used previously because it is vital to living life well. Colossians 3:15 says to let the peace from Christ "rule (act as umpire continually)" in our hearts. The presence of peace helps us decide and settle with finality all questions that arise in our minds. If you let the Word have its home in your heart and mind, it will give you insight *and* intelligence *and* wisdom (see v. 16). You won't have to wonder, *Should I or shouldn't I? I don't know if it's right. I don't know what to do.* If you are a disciple of Christ, He has called you to follow peace.

Dave, my husband, and I were trying to make a decision on a large purchase we needed to make. We called some of our board members from the ministry and presented the need to them, asking, "What do you think?"

They all gave their opinions, but as I listened to them I knew suddenly that I didn't have peace about going forward with the plan. We have learned by experience to wait if we don't have peace for something. Everyone agreed to wait on God to give us all peace before we proceeded.

I was out shopping recently and went into a children's clothing store. It was one I had not been in for perhaps a year or more. I saw some items that I thought would be perfect for two of my granddaughters. They were little pink shirts with rhinestone hearts on them. It was Valentine's Day and I wanted to give them something, so I called my daughter to check on their clothing sizes before making my purchase.

She said, "I cannot believe this! I was in that shop last night, looking at those exact shirts, but I didn't have peace about spending any money. I really wanted to buy them for the girls but felt I needed to honor God by not doing something I did not have peace about." Then she said, "Mom, I believe God is blessing me because I obeyed Him." She was very excited.

Letting her girls receive the shirts as a gift was much more fun than purchasing them. Had she disobeyed what she felt in her heart and done what she did not have peace about, she probably would have been uncomfortable in her spirit, perhaps even miserable. We both got to be part of a miracle because she chose to follow peace!

Following the Lord of peace may mean that you have to make some adjustments in your life. You may not be able to do everything your friends do. You may not be able to buy everything you want.

You may not be able to have something just because a friend, or a sister or a brother, has one. You may have to wait. But I believe that peace is the most important, the most valuable thing we can have. If we follow peace, we will end up living holy lives and thoroughly enjoying them.

Many people cannot hear from God because they have too much turmoil in their lives. Their insides are like a freeway during rush-hour traffic. They literally don't know how to be peaceful; it is as if they are addicted to turmoil. They keep things agitated and stirred up, seemingly on purpose. In fact, they get comfortable living in a state of chaos. It has become their normal state, even though in God's economy it is not normal at all.

It sounds strange, but when I started learning to be peaceful, I was *bored* at first! I was so accustomed to having something major going on in my life all the time that I wondered, *What am I supposed to do with myself?* Romans 3:17 says, "And they have no experience of the way of peace [they know nothing about peace, for a peaceful way they do not even recognize]."

That describes how my life used to be. I had no experience at all in enjoying a peaceful life; I did not even know how to begin. I had grown up in an atmosphere of strife, and it was all I ever knew. I had to learn an entirely new way of living.

But now I'm addicted to peace. As soon as my peace disappears, I ask myself how I lost it and start looking for ways to get it back. I am believing that as you read this book you will become so hungry for peace with God, peace with yourself, and peace with others that you will be willing to make whatever adjustments you need to make in order to have it. I am also believing that you will begin to follow peace at all times, because peace will lead you into the perfect will of God.

Jesus said that if we follow Him, He will give us peace (free of charge). In fact, He said He will bequeath His own peace to us (see John 14:27).

THE GOSPEL OF JESUS BRINGS PEACE

I want to see people love God's Word and put it first place in their lives. I believe there is an anointing on the Word; it has inherent power that makes positive changes in us. The Word of God is truth, and John 8:32 says, "And you will know the Truth, and the Truth will set you free." Truth sets us free from turmoil and leads us into a life of peace when we follow it.

The gospel of salvation through Jesus makes peace available to us *in all areas* of our lives. First Corinthians 1:21 says that when people failed to find God through earthly wisdom or by means of their own philosophy, God saved people through the preaching of salvation "procured by Christ." *Strong's Exhaustive Concordance of the Bible* says the Greek word translated as "save" in that verse is *sozo,* which means God "delivers, protects, heals, preserves, saves and makes whole" those who believe, trust in, and rely on Him.

We will experience peace in our personal lives when we stop trying to do so many things ourselves and just rely on God to deliver, protect, heal, and save us, as He wants to do.

And God will also lead us to peace in our relationships. Ephesians 2:14 is an awesome Scripture that says, "For He is [Himself] our peace (our bond of unity and harmony). He has made us both [Jew and Gentile] one [body], and has broken down (destroyed, abolished) the hostile dividing wall between us." Where there is no unity, no harmony, God Himself will break down and abolish the walls that divide people. He has broken down walls between so-called classes of people. He makes equal those who have higher education and those without any education at all. Somebody with a lot of money is no better to Him than somebody without money. The preacher is no better than the person who cleans the toilets.

The Lord loves each of us unconditionally. The hand of God uniquely created and personally designed each of us. That doesn't mean that we don't need some sandpaper to smooth our rough edges or polishing to make us shine. We all need to change and grow, but we can still be at peace about who we are without comparing ourselves with somebody else. We can stop thinking we are flawed because we are not like anyone else we know. We must have peace with ourselves before we can have peace with others.

I believe God wants you to have peace about where you are in your spiritual growth and to realize that you won't always stay the way you are. Anyone seeking God regularly is always changing, but we can enjoy where we are on the way to where we are going.

In the next chapter, I will share more about how we can surrender our will to God's leading. He doesn't want us to wait to have peace until we have all the things that we may want and desire or think are necessary to our lives. He doesn't want us to be jealous or envious of those who have the things we want and don't have, or those who can do what we can't do. He wants to prove to us that *He is* our peace.

God has an individualized, customized plan for your life. As you trust Him, He will bring it to pass in His timing, not yours. Waiting on God's plan and timing is wise because His ways are always best. He is the Lord of peace, and as you surrender your heart and life to Him, you will experience the peace that passes understanding.

MAKE PEACE THROUGH A SURRENDERED WILL

The apostle Peter challenged believers to find "every kind of peace and blessing, especially peace with God, and freedom from fears, agitating passions, and moral conflicts" (1 Peter 5:14). Surrendering our wills in order to maintain agreement with God is the foundation for all peace in our lives. God has a good plan for each of us, but when we go against His will by pursuing our own wills, we experience turmoil rather than peace. God is the source of all peace, and it stands to reason that He will not release peace to us unless we are following His ways and not our own. God desires for us to live free from fears and agitating passions, and He does not want us to be in bondage to immorality of any kind.

The Bible teaches that God will lead us by the presence of peace. Again, peace is the umpire in our lives that lets us know if we are in God's will or out of it. Ask yourself the following question, and be honest with your answer: Are you walking in God's known will to the best of your ability, or are there areas in your life in which you know you are not obeying God?

You will not experience peace if God is pulling in one direction and you are pulling in another; you will feel as if you are being torn apart. God will not force us to do what is right. He shows us what to do but leaves the choice to us. If we make right choices, we will reap good results that we can be happy with; if we make wrong choices, all we have is regret. Many individuals want their lives to change, but they don't want to do what God is showing them to do. If we are really serious about having change, we must follow God, no matter how difficult it is.

Carnality and God do not mix well together. We are called to walk in the Spirit, to be guided and willingly controlled by the Holy Spirit, who will lead us to make choices that make and maintain perfect peace.

We read in the book of Jonah how God told him to go to Nineveh and preach repentance to the people there. But Jonah did not want to, so he went to Tarshish, which, according to geography, is the exact opposite direction from Nineveh. Running from God does not help us to be at peace with Him.

What happens when we go in the opposite direction from where God has directed us? What happened to Jonah? When he boarded a ship and headed in his own direction, a storm arose. Many of the storms we face in life are the results of our own stubbornness, and nothing else. We may try to blame them on other things and people, but the truth is that in many instances, we have been disobedient to the voice and leadership of God.

The violent storm that came upon Jonah frightened the men on the ship, and they knew if something did not change, they would all die. They cast lots to see who was causing the trouble, and the lot fell on Jonah. They asked Jonah what he had done that made God so angry. He knew he had disobeyed God, so he told the men to throw him overboard in order to deliver them from danger. They did as he requested; the storm stopped, and a great fish swallowed Jonah. From the fish's belly (not a pleasant place), he cried out to God for deliverance and repented of his stubborn ways.

The fish vomited Jonah upon the dry land and in chapter 3, verse 1, we see that the word of the Lord came to Jonah a second time, and it was no different from the first time: God told him to go to Nineveh and preach to the people there.

No matter how long we avoid God's instruction, it is still there for us to deal with when we stop running. God's will makes us uncomfortable only as long as we are not pursuing it. In other words, we always know when something is just not right in our lives. Eventually we see that being *in* God's will, not *out* of His will, is what brings peace and joy to us. We have to surrender our own wills, because walking in our self-centered ways is what keeps us unhappy.

Running from difficult things never works long term. I know a woman who ran from everything in life that was difficult. She ignored things she needed to deal with, including abuse in her home. She lived in fear and actually had a very miserable life. She ultimately carried so much turmoil she had a complete mental and emotional breakdown, and she has never totally recovered. Pretending that her problems did not exist did not make them go away. They were there, pressuring her, all the time. God was trying to lead her to deal with her conflicts, but she would not trust Him enough to do so.

God never leads us anywhere that He cannot keep us. If God is leading you to deal with some unpleasant situation in your life, don't run from it. He promises to be with you at all times and never to leave you, or forsake you.

Surrender can be frightening when we first begin to practice it because we don't know what the outcome will be if we yield ourselves to God's will. However, once we have surrendered, and we begin to experience the peace that passes understanding, we learn quickly that God's way is better than any plan we could ever devise.

Not knowing exactly what will happen in the future, but trusting God to take care of us and enjoying peace, is far, far better than erroneously thinking we have life all figured out while continuing to live in fear and anxiety. To enjoy peace with God, we must become comfortable with not knowing what the future holds. There is no such thing as trust without unanswered questions. If God is leading you to do something difficult, just begin to take baby steps of faith, and after each one He will show you what to do next. We don't have to have an entire blueprint for the future; we don't need to have all the answers. All we need is to know the One who knows, and that is Jesus Himself.

We must realize that we are not nearly as smart as we think we are. God's Word advises us not to be conceited in our own wisdom and not to think more highly of ourselves than we ought. God has the answers; we don't. We need to seek Him, and He will lead us.

Proverbs 3:5–7 are some of my favorite Scriptures, and ones I have to return to frequently. They say, "Lean on, trust in, and be confident in the Lord with all your heart and mind and do not rely on your own insight or understanding. In all your ways know, recognize, and acknowledge Him, and He will direct and make straight and plain your paths. Be not wise in your own eyes." Notice we are told to "be not wise in [our] own eyes." To me that simply means we should not even think that we are smart enough to run our own lives. We need an attitude of humility that helps us lean on God for everything. An independent, I'll-do-it-myself attitude and dependence on God can't coexist.

Reasoning, struggling, and trying to figure out everything in life will steal our peace. God says to trust Him with all of our hearts and minds. I used to say I trusted God, yet I worried; therefore I did not truly trust Him. As I learned to keep my "ways" before God for alteration according to His will, He started guiding the events of my life, and the quality of it improved greatly.

GOD LEADS US BY PEACE

One of the major ways we hear from God is through peace. As I mentioned before, peace is our umpire in life. "And let the peace (soul harmony which comes) from Christ rule (act as umpire continually) in your hearts [deciding and settling with finality all questions that arise in your minds, in that peaceful state] to which as

[members of Christ's] one body you were also called [to live]"
(Colossians 3:15).

We are to follow peace. If our decisions and actions produce
peace, we know God approves and we are safe in going ahead. If
we don't have peace, we need to stop or at least wait. What we are
doing or considering may be wrong, or the timing may be wrong.

People do so many things they don't have peace about, and then
they wonder why they have big messes in their lives. If we follow
His Word, God has promised us that we will enjoy blessed and
peaceful lives. He also warns us that we will be miserable and live in
turmoil if we follow our own will and walk in our own ways (see
Deuteronomy 28:15-33).

I hear people say things like this all the time:

- "I know I shouldn't do this, but—"
- "I know I shouldn't buy this, but—"
- "I probably shouldn't say this, but—"

What they are saying is, "I know this is wrong, but I am going to
do it anyway." They have a check in their spirits, a little bit of an
uncomfortable feeling deep inside, a "knowing" that the action
they are taking is not right or good for them, but they won't surrender their wills to God's leading.

We have to learn to release our plans when we don't have peace
and wait to find God's good plan for our lives. When we sense we
are losing our peace, we should know that it means danger to press
on the way we are going. We really need to have a healthy fear of
not following peace. We should respect what God says in His Word
about peace being the umpire in our lives, and let peace make final
decisions for us.

Over the years, I have learned many things, but one of the
most significant is the importance of walking in peace and staying
in the rest of God. It is God's will for us to live free of upset and

frustration. He wants us to enjoy our lives, and we cannot do that if we don't have peace.

Do you enjoy a peaceful atmosphere most of the time? Do you keep your peace during the storms of life? Are you at peace with God? These are important questions. We need to take a "peace inventory," checking every area of our lives to see if we need to make adjustments anywhere. Jesus said, "My peace I've given unto you." If He gave us His peace, He wants us to walk in it and enjoy it.

We must resist the devil at his onset. The minute we sense that we are losing our peace, we need to make a decision to calm down. Even allowing ourselves to become upset places us out of God's will. To establish it in our hearts, let's look again at what Jesus said:

> Peace I leave with you; My [own] peace I now give and bequeath to you. Not as the world gives do I give to you. Do not let your hearts be troubled, neither let them be afraid. [*Stop allowing yourselves to be agitated and disturbed;* and *do not permit yourselves to be fearful and intimidated and cowardly and unsettled.*] (John 14:27, italics mine)

We can see plainly from this Scripture that Jesus has provided the peace, but we must appropriate it, not letting our hearts be troubled or afraid. We cannot just passively wait to feel peaceful. We are to pursue peace and refuse to live without it. As Jesus said, "Stop allowing yourselves to be upset."

In 1 Peter 3:10–11, the Bible teaches us that if we want to enjoy life and see good days, we should keep our tongues free from evil, we should do right and search for peace and harmony with God, with ourselves, and with our fellow man. These Scriptures have had a major impact on my own life, and I pray they will impact yours. They are core principles to enjoying peace in our lives.

What is life worth if we are at war in our relationship with God, people, and ourselves? Not much of anything, as far as I am concerned. As I mentioned, peace with God is the foundation for all peace in our lives. How can we be at peace with ourselves if we are not at peace with God, and how can we enjoy peace with other people if we don't have peace with ourselves?

There may be personal issues you need to settle with God before you can enjoy peace. God may have been dealing with you about certain things for a long, long time which you have been ignoring. Remember, ignoring God's will does not change it. You can go around the same mountains again and again, pass through storms, or find yourself in uncomfortable places the way Jonah did, but when all is said and done, God's will is still the same.

Do you sense a tug-of-war inside yourself about some issues in your life? If so, I encourage you to not spend one more day in turmoil. Face the issue, and give God the right of way. In other words, lay your ways down and adopt His ways. Make a decision to stop running and deal with any issues God may be placing before you. Are you doing something that is bothering your conscience? If so, that is God letting you know He is not pleased with that action or decision. Your conscience is actually intended to be your friend; it is a great blessing in life. It will keep you out of trouble if you learn to respect and listen to it.

When God has His will for our lives and we have other wills, life gets hard and uncomfortable. But we can have and enjoy peace by surrendering our wills to God's. God will not surrender to us; He is waiting for our surrender.

TRUTH LEADS US TO PEACE

We gain peace with God through facing the truth about the changes He is asking us to make. God never asks us to do something without giving us the ability to do it. Truth is not easy to face, but it is the avenue to peace. When we hide from, avoid, and evade God, we are usually running from His will for us.

A man once told me he had run from God's truth for so long he had finally run past himself. He meant that he had totally lost himself and any understanding of what God wanted for him. He was confused and miserable. He felt like a total failure, as if he had completely wasted his life. He was depressed, discouraged, and without vision for his future.

I don't think I have ever seen anyone who was more unhappy and pitiful than he was. Why? Because he had spent his life doing what he wanted to do, what he felt like doing, rather than walking in God's plan for him. He was reaping what he had sown, just as we all ultimately do.

I thank God for the ability to turn around and go in the right direction. That is actually what true repentance is. It is not just a feeling of being sorry, but also a decision to go in the right direction from now on. We get into trouble through making a series of wrong decisions, and we will get our lives straightened out by a series of right decisions. It took more than a day to get into trouble, and it will take more than a day to get out. Anyone who is ready and willing to make a real investment of time and right choices can see his or her life turn around for the better. God's mercy is new every day. He is waiting to give you mercy, grace, favor, and help; all you have to do is say yes to whatever God is requiring.

The miserable man I referred to did what was right for about two years, and his life really began to change. He had every opportunity to have a great life, but he did not "keep on keeping on." He eventually went back to his old ways.

Recently I talked with a Christian sister who was very depressed and felt as if she was on the edge of a nervous breakdown. As we talked, I discovered she had spent years not making right decisions and then found herself overwhelmed with the outcome of her own poor choices. She had not raised her children in church, and she said they were out of control and impossible for her to manage. She had been very difficult to get along with, and the result had been the loss of several friendships and family relationships. She certainly had serious problems, and I did not have an easy answer for her.

She wanted me to tell her what to do, so I seriously pondered before the Lord what I should suggest. All I could tell her was that she needed to start making right decisions, and eventually they would overtake the crop she was now reaping from her previous bad decisions. People usually want to overcome a lifetime of bad choices in a short period of time without much effort on their parts, or they want other people to deliver them from the messes into which they have gotten themselves.

I sincerely felt compassion for her, yet I also realized she had been a Christian for over twenty-five years and had spent much time (at least in the early years of her walk with God) studying God's Word and ways. I felt she knew better than to behave the way she had. When we lack knowledge, we often experience a "special grace" in our lives from God. However, once we have knowledge of God's Word, we become responsible to apply it to our lives, and I personally believe we reap what we sow much quicker as knowledgeable persons than as ignorant ones.

God wanted to work with this sister and help her. He would give her mercy and grace and another chance, but there really was no easy answer like the one she appeared to be seeking. We cannot do right a few times—we must continue on. Jesus said, "If ye *continue* in my word, then are ye my disciples indeed; and ye shall know the truth, and the truth will make you free" (see John 8:31–32 KJV).

Both the brother and the sister I have mentioned gained help in their lives through applying God's principles, but they did not maintain. They did not *continue* in the truth they had learned. Galatians 5:1 teaches us to stand fast in the liberties we have; that means to gain and maintain. It has helped me to realize that I will need to stand fast for the rest of my life.

We cannot get lazy and start letting things slip. Each time God convicts us of wrong behavior, we need to listen to Him. Anytime we lose our peace even slightly, we need to stop and find out what is wrong. That loss of peace is God letting us know something is not going the way He wants it to go.

We gain a right relationship with God through complete surrender to Him, and through repentance of all of our sins. We maintain it through *continued* right living: making right choices, honoring our consciences, and following peace. Being a successful Christian is a full-time job; we must be on guard all the time against the deceptions of Satan.

Just going to church for one hour on Sunday morning is not enough to maintain peace. We need megadoses of God's Word, prayer, and regular fellowship with God and other godly people in order to stand fast in God's will.

Peace with God is available to every person, but we cannot have it on our own terms. Surrender seems so frightening because we are not sure what God may require. Will we suffer? Will God ask us to do things we don't want to do or don't even know how to do? Will we ever get to have any of the things we want? We all have these questions.

We may not get things our way, but we can trust that God's way is better. God is a good God, and He said that He has good things planned for His children: "For I know the thoughts and plans that I have for you, says the Lord, thoughts and plans for welfare and peace and not for evil, to give you hope in your final outcome" (Jeremiah 29:11).

We should not be afraid of harm, because God is not an ogre, He is not mean. He is good. Everything good in life comes from God. He wants us to trust Him, and when we take a step of faith to do so, we will see the goodness of God manifested in our lives. The more we surrender, the better life becomes.

THE HOLY SPIRIT FILLS US WITH PEACE

In Acts 2:4, we see that believers were *all* "filled with the Holy Spirit," and later in Ephesians 5:18, we find the instruction to "be filled with the Spirit." One Scripture tells us what happened on the day of Pentecost, and the other is a command.

What does it mean to be filled with the Spirit? It does not imply a state of high excitement, or being perfect in all of our ways, nor is it a state in which we have no need for growth. It is having our entire personalities yielded to the Holy Spirit and being filled through and through with His awesome power *daily*. It is daily surrender; it is yielding to God's ways and plans for our everyday lives.

The following Scriptures are absolutely wonderful; I encourage you to meditate on them often.

May He grant you out of the rich treasury of His glory to be strengthened and reinforced with mighty power in the inner man by the [Holy] Spirit [Himself indwelling your innermost being and personality] . . . [That you may really come] to know [practically, through experience for yourselves] the love of Christ, which far surpasses mere knowledge [without experience]; that you may be *filled [through all your being] unto all the fullness of God [may have the richest measure of the divine Presence, and become a body wholly filled and flooded with God Himself]!* (Ephesians 3:16, 19, italics mine)

Just imagine having your personality filled with the Holy Spirit of the living God and being a body wholly filled with God Himself! The apostle Paul was a man filled with the Holy Spirit; he was also a man who had forsaken all to follow Jesus. Any area of our lives that we hold back from God is an area where we cannot be filled with His Spirit. I encourage you to open and surrender every room in your heart to God. Your time is His, your money is His, as are your gifts and talents, your family, your career, attitudes, and desires. He wants to be involved in every area of your life: how you dress, whom you choose for friends, what you do for entertainment, what you eat, and so on.

After conversion, Jesus is our Savior, but is He our Lord? Any area we claim as our own is one we have not surrendered to the lordship of Jesus Christ.

I lived a defeated life for many years simply because I was not fully surrendered. I had accepted Jesus as Savior; I had enough of Jesus to stay out of hell, but I had not accepted Him as my Lord, I had not accepted enough of Him to walk in victory. There is a difference. I lacked peace because I was still trying to manage my own life.

The blessedness of being filled with the Spirit is clearly visible in the change in the people's lives after Pentecost. Peter, for example, who had displayed great fear in not being willing to even admit that he knew Jesus, became a bold apostle who stood in the streets of Jerusalem and preached the gospel so fervently that three thousand souls were added to the church in one day. Complete surrender brings good change into our lives. Surrender to God actually opens the door to the things we desire, and yet we waste our own energy trying to obtain access to them our own way.

Realize that every act of obedience brings with it a corresponding blessing. Consecration, commitment, yielding, surrendering, obeying: all these words may sound frightening, but remember that fear is not from God. Fear is from Satan; he uses it to prevent us from entering God's plan for our lives. He uses fear to prevent progress. Each time we feel fear, we should recognize it as opposition from the enemy of our souls.

I share more about living a Spirit-filled life in my book *Knowing God Intimately*. I encourage you to read that book if you feel you need to surrender to the Lord in a deeper way. Being filled with the Spirit is like finding the "pearl of great price" that the following verses speak of:

The kingdom of heaven is like something precious buried in a field, which a man found and hid again; then in his joy he goes and sells all he has and buys that field. Again the kingdom of heaven is like a man who is a dealer in search of fine and precious pearls, who, on finding a single pearl of great price, went and sold all he had and bought it. (Matthew 13:44–46)

The kingdom of heaven, as God intended us to enjoy it, includes being wholly filled with the Holy Spirit. These Scriptures teach us that we must "sell all" to buy the pearl of great price. That simply means we surrender everything we now have in order to gain the one thing we truly need to enjoy kingdom living. The kingdom of God is righteousness, peace, and joy in the Holy Spirit (see Romans 14:17).

Perhaps as you read this book today, you realize you have something against someone. Perhaps God has dealt with you to give up some bitter attitude, but you have stubbornly held on to it, feeling justified in your anger. I tell you that if you will surrender that attitude, God will give you peace in the place of it.

You may spend many days feeling sorry for yourself or being jealous of what someone else has. God has asked you to lay aside those bad attitudes and be content. If you will do so, His peace and joy will fill your life.

People may have more possessions than you do, but they can never have more peace and joy than you do if you follow the leading of the Holy Spirit. It is not what we own that makes us happy and peaceful; He is our joy and our peace.

A CONSECRATED, DEDICATED LIFE RESULTS IN PEACE

God's Word instructs us to be vessels fit (consecrated) for the Master's use. To be consecrated is to be set apart for a special use, as these verses explain:

> But in a great house there are not only vessels of gold and silver, but also [utensils] of wood and earthenware, and some for honorable and noble [use] and some for menial and ignoble [use]. So whoever cleanses himself [from what is ignoble and unclean, who separates himself from contact with contaminating and corrupting influences] will [then himself] be a vessel set apart and useful for honorable and noble pur-

poses, consecrated and profitable to the Master, fit and ready for any good work. (2 Timothy 2:20–21)

To God, we are precious treasures. According to His great plan, we are vessels He has set aside for a special purpose. God wants to show His glory through us. He wants to use us to bring others to Himself. We are His representatives, His ambassadors here on earth. God is making His appeal to the world through His children (see 2 Corinthians 5:20).

To dedicate is to give, to offer to another, or to set aside for a purpose. If I were to say a room in my house is dedicated to prayer, that would mean I wanted that particular room used primarily for that purpose and not for other things.

I own some dresses that I use only for fancy parties. I have set them aside in a certain place in my closet and keep them inside garment bags for protection. This makes them special; they are not used for ordinary purposes but are set apart for special purposes. That is the way God views us; we are not to be used for the world's purposes, but for God's. We are in the world, yet Jesus tells us we are not "of" the world. Don't be worldly, adopting its ways and methods. Even after we have dedicated ourselves to God, we should rededicate ourselves to our real purpose, as the following verse encourages: "I APPEAL to you therefore, brethren, and beg of you in view of [all] the mercies of God, to make a decisive dedication of your bodies [presenting all your members and faculties] as a living sacrifice, holy (devoted, consecrated) and well pleasing to God, which is your reasonable (rational, intelligent) service and spiritual worship" (Romans 12:1).

It is not too much for God to ask us to dedicate every facet of our being. It is actually our worship and spiritual service. Under old covenant law, God required animal sacrifices to atone for sin. He no longer wants dead sacrifices; He wants us offering ourselves as "living sacrifices" unto Him for His purpose and use.

There is nothing we can offer to God that He has not first given us, so we are only offering what already belongs to Him anyway. In reality, we are stewards, not owners. Andrew Murray taught in his book *Consecrated to God* that if God gives us everything and we receive everything, then what comes next is very clear: We must give everything back to God again. God gives us a free will so we can freely and willingly give ourselves back to Him. He does not want robots, who have no choice, serving Him. He wants us to *choose* Him! What a privilege, what an honor to give ourselves willingly to Him.

Offer Him your mouth to speak through, your hands to touch through, your feet to walk through, your mind to think through. Dedicate every area of your life to Him, remembering that anything we give to the Lord He gives us back many times over, and we get it back in much better condition than when we gave it.

When I gave my life to the Lord, it was an absolute wreck. He has now given me a life that is wonderful and beyond imagination. Ephesians 3:20 states that He is able to do much more than we could ever imagine if we will give Him the opportunity.

God wants you to enjoy a life of peace, the peace that passes understanding, and it begins by being at peace with Him. This requires regular surrender, consecration, dedication, and a willingness to let God be in the driver's seat of your life at all times. But beware; you have an enemy who plans to make it difficult to surrender your life to God. Next, we will look at what God's Word says about that enemy.

KNOW YOUR ENEMY

If finding peace is a struggle for you, it is a sign that your enemy is working hard to keep you from receiving what is rightfully yours. Are you confused about who your real enemy is? According to God's Word, your enemy is not a person, or even circumstances— it is Satan himself. Knowing your enemy, and the weapons that God has given you to defeat him, is the third way to keep in perfect peace with God.

"For we are not wrestling with flesh and blood [contending only with physical opponents], but against the despotisms, against the powers, against [the master spirits who are] the world rulers of this present darkness, against the spirit forces of wickedness in the heavenly (supernatural) sphere" (Ephesians 6:12). We can never win our battles if we are fighting against the wrong source in a wrong way. The source of our troubles is Satan and his demons. We cannot fight him with carnal (natural) weapons, but only with supernatural ones that God gives us for the destruction of Satan's strongholds (see 2 Corinthians 10:4).

What exactly are these weapons? I believe the weapons God gives include His Word used in preaching, teaching, singing, con- fession, or meditation. Our weapons are righteousness, peace, and joy in the Holy Ghost, and we can and should use these against Satan, our enemy. Yes, peace is a weapon! The Bible talks about putting on the shoes of peace. Righteousness is a weapon! "By [speaking] the word of truth, in the power of God, with the weapons of righteousness for the right hand [to attack] and for the left hand [to defend]" (2 Corinthians 6:7).

Through faith in Christ we are placed in right standing with God. And by faith, we are covered with His robe of righteousness (see Isaiah 61:10 AMP). In other words, because we are trusting in Jesus Christ's righteousness to cover us, God views us as right instead of wrong. His righteousness becomes a shield that protects us from Satan. He absolutely hates it when a child of God really knows who he or she is "in Christ."

In and of ourselves, we are less than nothing; our righteousness is like filthy rags, for all have sinned and come short of the glory of God (see Isaiah 64:6; Romans 3:23). But we are justified and given a right relationship with God through faith.

"Therefore, since we are justified (acquitted, declared righteous, and given a right standing with God) through faith, let us [grasp the fact that we] have [the peace of reconciliation to hold and to enjoy] peace with God through our Lord Jesus Christ (the Messiah, the Anointed One)" (Romans 5:1). This Scripture teaches us that righteousness brings peace and joy. When we feel all wrong about ourselves, we do not have peace. Satan seeks to condemn us in order to steal our peace. Remember that Satan is your enemy, and you need to know that it is he who tries to make you feel bad about yourself. He works to steal your peace.

Satan uses people and circumstances, but they are not our real enemy; he is. He finds things and people through whom he can work and delights in watching us fight and war without ever realizing he is the source.

When Satan used Peter to try and divert Jesus from going to Jerusalem to complete the task God had sent Him to do, "Jesus *turned away* from Peter and said to him, Get behind Me, Satan! You are in My way [an offense and a hindrance and a snare to Me]" (Matthew 16:23, italics mine). Satan used Peter, but Jesus knew that Peter was not His real problem. He *turned away* from Peter and addressed the source of His temptation. We need to look beyond what we see or initially feel and seek to know the source of our problems too.

Usually we blame people and become angry with them, which only complicates and compounds the problem. When we behave in this manner, we are actually playing right into Satan's hands and helping his plans succeed. We also blame circumstances and sometimes even God, which also delights Satan.

Yes, we need to know our enemy—not only who he is but what his character is like. The Bible encourages us to know the character of God so we can place faith in Him and what He says. Likewise, we should know Satan's character so we do not listen to or believe his lies.

SATAN IS A LIAR

First and foremost, Satan is a liar, and Jesus called him "the father of lies" (John 8:44 NIV). All lies originate with him. He lies to us in order to deceive us. When a person is deceived, he believes lies. This is a terrible condition to be in, for one does not know that he believes lies. The lies are his reality because he believes them.

For example, I believed the lie from Satan that I would never overcome my abusive past. I believed I would always be tainted, second best, and soiled merchandise because of the things that had happened to me in my childhood. As long as I believed these things, I was trapped in my past. I could not really go forward and enjoy the future God had always planned for me (see Ephesians 2:10). I could not receive it because I was not aware of it. I believed what Satan said because I did not know what God had said.

I was miserable, hopeless, bitter, and in turmoil all because Satan was lying to me, and I believed his lies. When I began to study God's Word and His truth started renewing my mind, I knew Satan for what he is: a liar!

People who have had long-standing financial pressure are often convinced by Satan's lies that things will always be the way they are. The enemy tells them they will never have anything, never own a decent car or have a nice house. They believe they will never have enough, and so it becomes reality for them. We receive what we believe, whether what we believe is positive or negative.

God's Word says that He wants us to prosper (see Deuteronomy 29:9). It states we can and will be blessed in every way when we walk in God's statutes. Satan seeks to keep people hopeless. Hopelessness steals our God-given peace and joy.

Refuse to be hopeless. Be like Abraham, of whom it is said that although he had no reason to hope, he hoped on in faith that God's promises would come to pass in his life. As he waited he gave praise and glory to God, and Satan was not able to defeat him with doubt and unbelief (see Romans 4:18–20).

Satan Is a Thief

I often repeat John 10:10, which states that "the thief comes only in order to steal and kill and destroy." The passage is referring to Satan and his system. Just as God has a system that He encourages us to live by, and He promises blessings if we do, Satan has a system and his hope is that we will live by it so he can steal our blessings. Remember, he wants to prevent us from having righteousness, peace, and joy.

He steals through lying, and all of his tactics are connected in some way. They are all perverse in nature and the opposite of anything God would have for us. Satan steals from us through fear. Actually we receive from Satan through fear, just as we receive from God through faith. One might say that *fear is faith in what Satan says*. Fear threatens us with thoughts of harm or disappointment. Satan shows us a circumstance and then makes us afraid it will never change. God wants us to believe His Word is true even while we are still in the midst of the circumstances. Romans 8:37 says, "Yet amid all these things we are more than conquerors and gain a surpassing victory through Him Who loved us."

In God's economy, we must believe before we will see change or the good things we desire. Satan seeks to steal our vision and hope for the future. He tries to steal our sense of right standing with God through guilty feelings and condemnation, through self-rejection and even self-hatred. He steals our joy because the joy of the Lord is our strength, and he wants us to be weak.

Satan is a thief. He tries to steal every good thing that Jesus died to give us. Jesus gave us peace as our inheritance, but Satan does everything he can to rob us of it.

Recognize your enemy, know him, and stand aggressively against him.

SATAN IS A LEGALIST

You may already have deep furrows in your brow, trying to figure out what I could possibly mean by the statement that Satan is a legalist. This is what I mean: He pressures us to be perfect, to live without making mistakes, to never, never break any of the religious rules. When we do make mistakes—which everyone does—he then tries to make us feel condemned by our guilt because we have not followed all the rules and regulations.

What rules and regulations am I talking about? The ones some so-called religious organizations and systems impose. These include things like praying for certain amounts of time, doing good works, reading a certain amount of the Bible each day, observing religious holidays, and using various formulas that will supposedly give us God's approval.

When Jesus stated in Matthew 11:28, "Come unto me, all ye that labour and are heavy laden" (KJV), He was talking to people who were struggling while trying to live under the law, but who were always failing. There is nothing wrong with any of the rituals I have listed, and they are in fact good Christian disciplines. But if we view them as something we *have to* do to gain God's approval, rather than something we *want to* do because we love Him, they minister death to us instead of life. They become a burden rather than a joy. The Word teaches us that the law kills, but the Spirit makes alive (2 Corinthians 3:6).

Jesus had much to say about religion, and none of it was good. Why? Because religion in His day was, and often still is, man's idea of what God expects. Religion is man trying to reach God through his own good works. The Christian faith teaches that God has reached down to man through Jesus Christ. By placing our faith in Jesus Christ, we receive the benefits from the work He has done for us. His work, not our own works of religion, not following rules and regulations man prescribes, justifies us and makes us right with God, as these Scriptures confirm:

- For no person will be justified (made righteous, acquitted, and judged acceptable) in His sight by observing the works prescribed by the Law. (Romans 3:20)
- [All] are justified *and* made upright and in right standing with God, freely and gratuitously by His grace (His unmerited favor and mercy), through the redemption which is [provided] in Christ Jesus. (Romans 3:24)

Many might describe a Christian as "someone who goes to church." This, of course, is not a Christian. A Christian may go to church, but one does not *become* a Christian through church attendance alone. I can sit in my garage all day, and that won't make me become a car. A Christian is someone who has had his heart changed by faith in Jesus Christ. He has had a change in his moral nature (see 2 Corinthians 5:17). He is not just someone who has agreed to follow certain rules and regulations and observe certain days as holy.

Religion is filled with rules and regulations one must follow to be part of a certain religious group. Christianity, however, is agreeing to follow the leadership of the Holy Spirit entirely. We must remember that God has invited us into personal relationship and intimacy with Him through the death and resurrection of Jesus Christ. His invitation is not to be in a religious organization, where we strive to follow rules in order to gain acceptance and right standing with Him.

Religious rules and regulations steal peace and joy. They rob us of what Jesus died to give us. Through religion we become works oriented, rather than faith oriented. We pray because we are *supposed* to, rather than because we *want* to. We study the Bible because we are obligated; we have made it a rule. We have been taught that we *should,* so we do because we are *afraid not to.* We may do good works, but our motive is wrong if we do them to gain acceptance from God, rather than to reach out to someone in love because of what Christ has done for us. Religion causes us to live under the tyranny of the "shoulds" and "oughts."

Religion is the topic of discussion in John 9. The religious leaders were upset because Jesus had healed a blind man on the Sabbath. You see, with religious people, everything must be on the right day and done in the right way—their way. The results don't really matter as long as you follow their rules. If you don't follow the rules, they will not validate you.

The Pharisees interrogated the blind man over and over to learn exactly how Jesus did this work that gave him sight. They felt that Jesus must be a common sinner because He worked on a holy day.

Finally the man said, "I don't know all the answers to your questions. All I know is I was blind, and now I see." Then he asked the religious leaders if they wanted to be Jesus' disciples, at which point they became enraged and stormed at him (see John 9:27–28).

The Bible says the religious leaders sneered and jeered at the man's question. Isn't it a shame they could not rejoice with him? But then again, rejoicing with others is not what those types of people do. Enjoyment is foreign to them, and they want to make sure nobody else enjoys himself or herself either. Righteousness, peace, and joy are not part of their religious system. The man whom Jesus had healed had a very simple answer: "I was blind, and now I see." God intends Christianity to be simple, but religion and its systems can become very complicated and confusing.

I know many people who have struggled a lifetime to follow all the rules, and they still feel like failures. This is not God's will for His children. Again, Jesus said that He came that we might have *and enjoy* our lives (see John 10:10).

You might ask, "Doesn't God want us to be holy? Doesn't He want us to do good things?" The answer is yes, a thousand times yes. But we don't *accomplish* holiness through our good works. Christ Himself imputes holiness to us as a gift from God. We receive holiness by faith, not by good works. First Thessalonians 5:23 states, "And may the God of peace Himself sanctify you through and through." It is God Himself who will do it, we don't do it, and it is impossible for man to sanctify or make himself holy.

Jesus seriously chastised the religious leaders—the scribes and Pharisees—of His day. In Matthew 23, He called them "pretenders" and hypocrites because they demanded that others do things they were not doing themselves. He said they were play actors. They did good works, but their hearts were filled with wicked things. They paid their tithes and followed other rules, such as fasting, but they did not treat people justly and fairly. Jesus said they tied up heavy loads for others to carry but would not help bear the burden.

Like many others trying their best to serve God, I have experienced judgment and criticism from various people. Most of those people have been "religious" folks who actually don't know me at all. They assume and presume and accuse, but they never come to me in a loving manner to give me an opportunity to share anything about my life with them. They don't like anyone who does not do things "their way."

They are faultfinders who magnify every flaw they can find but never bother to examine or even mention any of the good fruit that has come from my ministry over the years. In Matthew 7:17–20, Jesus explained that we will know people by their fruit. He did not say, "Examine people, and if you find any fault at all, broadcast it to everyone you know, hoping to ruin their reputations." Faultfinders are angry with anyone who has prospered or succeeded. Their "ministry" becomes criticizing the ministry of others. This is a sad state of affairs. Jesus has called us to love Him and to love one another, not to be faultfinders in the body of Christ.

People like this have deeply hurt me in the past, as they have many others, but I must remember that even Jesus Himself was attacked by the religious people of His day. Satan attacks, hoping to get people to quit and give up. He wants to drain us and wear us out, but God gives us endurance and makes strong in Him.

Satan is the author of this legalistic system that sucks the life out of people. The Holy Spirit ministers life to people. The Holy Spirit adds to us, Satan steals from us. In John 10, Jesus was making reference to the scene regarding the man who had been born blind when He said, "The thief comes only in order to steal and kill and destroy. I came that they may have and enjoy life, and have it in abundance (to the full, till it overflows)" (v. 10). Remember that Satan is a liar, a thief, and a legalist. Don't be deceived by him any longer—know your enemy!

SATAN IS A TROUBLEMAKER

The word *trouble* in *Webster's II New College Dictionary* is defined in part as: "distress, affliction, danger or need; malfunction, to stir up or agitate; to inconvenience or bother." Needless to say, we all experience these things on a rotating basis.

When people accept Jesus Christ as Lord and Savior and begin to study His Word, when they make progress in any way, Satan launches an all-out attack against them. He wants to entangle people in trouble so they will focus on the wrong things. He wants us to focus on things we cannot do anything about, rather than growing in God.

Mark 4 illustrates what is called the parable of the sower. It tells us of four types of ground onto which someone sows seed. In this parable the seed is the Word of God, and the ground is the heart conditions of mankind. Verse 15 says, "The ones along the path are those who have the Word sown [in their hearts], but when they hear, Satan comes at once and [by force] takes away the message which is sown in them."

Verse 17 says that some have the Word sown in their hearts, but "they have no real root in themselves, and so they endure for a little while; then when trouble or persecution arises on account of the Word, they immediately are offended (become displeased, indignant, resentful) and they stumble and fall away."

Verse 19 says, "Then the cares and anxieties of the world and distractions of the age, and the pleasure and delight and false glamour and deceitfulness of riches, and the craving and passionate desire for other things creep in and choke and suffocate the Word, and it becomes fruitless."

We can see from these verses that Satan works diligently to cause trouble and bring distractions.

The Word teaches that Satan will attack us for a season, and if we pass all of our tests, if we endure the testing and remain firm in our faith, he goes away for a while and waits for another time to attack. Luke 4:13 confirms his tactics: "And when the devil had ended every [the complete cycle of] temptation, he [temporarily] left Him [that is, stood off from Him] until another more opportune and favorable time."

This verse refers to Jesus' temptation in the wilderness. Even Jesus Himself was not immune to Satan's being a troublemaker. The Bible never promises us a trouble-free life, but we do need to know who the source of our trouble is. It is Satan!

Hold your peace. Satan may be a troublemaker, but Jesus is your Trouble Solver. He is your Deliverer, your Hiding Place. These times of testing, too, shall pass.

Satan tries to cause trouble in virtually every area of our lives. He does not attack every area at one time, but eventually he gets to everything. He will bring inconvenience of every kind, and it seems the wrong thing never happens at the right time. Problems never come when we are ready to deal with them.

He may attack people in their finances, relationships, physical health, mind, emotions, job, neighborhood, or projects. The apostle Paul said there were times when he was abased and times when he abounded (see Philippians 4:12). In other words, he experienced good times and hard times, as we all do.

We recently invited four different men from four different parts of the country to be guests on our television show. These men were all involved in the restoration of morality in America. They were all praying for revival. Dave and I are also very interested in this, and we wanted to impact the nation with some special programming along these lines.

Two of the four men had major delays with their flights. One had a flight entirely cancelled and was very late, and another sat on the runway for two and a half hours without any real explanation except that it was raining. What was Satan trying to do? He didn't want them to come at all, but if they were going to come, he wanted them to be upset when they arrived.

Two out of four of our guests having this type of trouble is more than coincidence. Satan sets us up to get us upset! He wants to steal our peace because our power is connected to it. I have learned that my ministry does not have much effect if I am not ministering from a heart of peace, so I strive to stay in peace at all times. Satan tries to steal my peace, and with God's help, I try to keep it.

We can trust God not to allow more to come on us than what we can bear (see 1 Corinthians 10:13). Paul also said that during all those times, he had learned to be content (satisfied to the point where he was not disquieted or disturbed.) It sounds to me as if he always kept his peace, no matter what was going on in his life.

This is an example we should seek to follow. Paul actually told the believers to follow him as he followed Christ. He believed he was doing what Christ would do. Jesus is "the Way." When we follow Him, we always end up enjoying a great victory.

Nobody likes trouble, yet we all have it. Everybody gets upset about it, and it never does any good. It is time for change! Don't go around and around the same mountains all of your life—learn a different approach.

I spent years getting upset every time trouble came, and Satan prized my response. I was following his lead, not the leading of the Holy Spirit. My response gave Satan power over me. The outer storms of life have no real power over us unless we let them rage on the inside of us. We cannot always do something about how life turns out, but we can do something about our inner responses.

I know you have probably heard the statement, "Attitude determines altitude," and it is very true. A good attitude will take you farther in life than most other things. I had a bad beginning in life; Satan had brought trouble for me as long as I could remember, and I had a bad attitude. I was filled with self-pity, bitterness, and resentment. I was jealous of those who had experienced an easier life than I had.

Jesus taught me to have a good attitude. He said I could not be pitiful and powerful at the same time, and He let me know that I had to choose which path I would take. By the grace of God and the help of the Holy Spirit, I made the right choice, and although it has been a long journey, it has been worth it.

Remember that peace must be aggressively pursued. I am encouraging you to adopt a new attitude toward trouble. Remember that what the enemy means for harm, God intends for good, and all things work together for good to those who love God and are called according to His purpose (see Genesis 50:20; Romans 8:28).

THE WEARING-OUT TACTICS OF SATAN

Daniel 7:25 says that Satan seeks to wear out the saints of the Most High God. How does this wearing out take place? Often his work is barely noticeable, because he slowly tries to wear us down—a little here and a little there. Satan sends people to irritate us just as he did with the apostle Paul (see Acts 16:17–18).

A woman followed Paul and Silas, crying out that they were servants of the Most High God. This she did for many days. It annoyed Paul, it grated on him that she *continually* shouted the same thing all throughout the day. Paul finally turned to the woman and cast an evil spirit of divination out of her. Satan hopes we will just be aggravated and never deal with the situation aggravating us. He does this to wear us out.

Felix used his authority to postpone Paul's trial and keep him in prison. He wanted money from Paul, so he continued to send for him (see Acts 24:26). We know this went on for at least two years: Paul continued to argue about uprightness and purity of life, and Felix continued to prolong Paul's sentence without trial.

When people continue to be irritating, it has a different effect than someone who is irritating once or twice. In Judges 16:16, we see that Delilah pressed Samson *daily* until her deception worked, and he revealed the secret to his strength.

Likewise, Satan seeks to wear me out in various ways, but one of his favorite tactics is through trouble with employees—and not just one employee, but several in a row. For example, we might have to deal with several people who are initiating strife with other employees or remind people we have hired them to do specific jobs, not to run the ministry. Not too long ago, we had to deal with three issues concerning pornography in a ten-day period of time. That had never happened before, but suddenly we had three separate situations to confront.

You may be shocked to think that people working in a Christian ministry would have problems with something like pornography or commit such obviously disobedient acts, but they are tempted the same as everyone else, if not more so. Satan worked through their weaknesses and used them to drain me of much-needed energy.

I want you to pay particular attention to the fact that I said it had never happened before, and *suddenly* we had *three* issues with pornography at one time. That sounds like a wearing-out tactic of Satan to me. Satan not only attacked the people involved, but also the people who had to deal with the issue. He often works through other people to get to leaders of ministries. If Satan cannot get to you directly, he may try to work through the weakness of someone you know or love, hoping he can upset you through them.

Once we had a trusted employee steal from us. We had chosen him to help with a special financial project in which he had to count a lot of cash. We selected him because we "knew" we could trust him. Then five hundred dollars was missing, and at the same time, this man's wife was sharing how she had mysteriously found five hundred dollars in her mailbox at work. We questioned him, along with everyone else involved in the project, and of course, he denied any involvement. We had no proof and had to let the situation rest; however, we were convinced in our hearts he was the guilty party. A few months later, he and his wife quit working at the ministry and moved back to their hometown.

A few years went by, and one day we got a call from him, asking our forgiveness for stealing the money. I was glad for him because he could not have had peace with God until he told the truth and asked for forgiveness from God and us. This situation was most unfortunate for the man and his family, but Satan also used it to try to wear us out. It is draining when you trust people and find out they are dishonest.

These, of course, are isolated cases, and 99.9 percent of our employees at the ministry are quality people who walk in truth and integrity. But Satan does seek to find someone to work through to bring aggravation and trouble.

Another way he might seek to wear me out is through something I mentioned earlier: judgment from people in the world or the church who know absolutely nothing about the ministry, or the price we have paid to get from where we began to where we are today. People are jealous of the success of others, but they don't want to do what they did to get there.

I have to remind myself all the time that it is not my concern what people think of me; my concern is what God thinks of me. I will stand before Him, not anyone else, on Judgment Day. I want to have a good reputation because I know people cannot receive from me if their hearts are not open, but I cannot make myself responsible for what everyone thinks of me, and you cannot make yourself responsible for what everyone thinks of you.

It seems these situations also come in groups. A long time may go by without any occurrences at all, then suddenly it seems that the faultfinders and troublemakers come from every direction. Satan knows it takes more than one attack to wear us out, so he relentlessly comes again and again.

Satan seeks to wear out the saints by stealing our time, forcing us to deal with trouble that he starts. He actually would like us to spend our lives trying to put out the little fires he builds.

What is the answer? James 4:7 says we are to submit ourselves to God, resist the devil, and he will flee. We see that we have to *resist* the devil. When should we resist him, how long should we wait, how much should we put up with before coming against him? The Bible teaches us as Christians to be patient, but we are not to be patient with the devil. First Peter 5:9 shares a wonderful and most important principle; it says, "Withstand him; be firm in faith [against his onset—rooted, established, strong, immovable, and determined]." We are to resist the devil *at his onset*. I have benefited greatly over the years as a result of this Scripture.

When Satan attacks, we should immediately begin to praise God; in this way, we resist Satan. When he speaks lies, we should speak truth. The instant we sense an attack, we should draw near to God and pray. The Bible tells us to be alert for when we can practice prayer. Several times the Word of God instructs us to "watch and pray." This means to watch for things going wrong in our own lives or the lives of others and immediately pray—don't wait—*pray!*

Another way to resist Satan is to apply the blood of Jesus by faith to the situation. Just as the Israelites were delivered from death by putting the blood of a lamb on the lintels and door frames of their homes during Passover (see Exodus 12:1–13), so we can apply the blood of our Passover Lamb, Jesus, by faith and be protected.

Remind Satan of the cross on which Jesus totally defeated him; remind him that he is already a defeated foe and that you will not be deceived or deluded in any way. Let him know that you recognize that it is he who is coming against you and that you won't blame people, God, or life.

Satan wants us weak and worn-out; that way we have no power to resist him. He knows that if he gains a foothold, he can get a stronghold. As I said before, *resist the devil at his onset!* Be aggressive; don't wait to see what will happen. If you wait, you won't like it. Stir yourself up in the Holy Ghost, fan the embers of your inner fire, and don't let it go out during trouble. Remember that Jesus, the Victory, lives inside you—you have the Victory!

Matthew 11:12 teaches us that the kingdom of God has suffered violent assault, and violent men seize it by force. When we study the original Greek of this word *violent* (as defined by *Strong's Exhaustive Concordance of the Bible*), it reads more like this: "The kingdom of God has suffered violent attack, but the *energetic* take it by force." The *Amplified* version adds: They take it "[as a precious prize—a share in the heavenly kingdom is sought with most ardent zeal and intense exertion]."

Satan loves a lazy man or woman; he knows that our inactivity is victory for him. We are to resist Satan in the power of the Holy Spirit; if we do, we will trouble him instead of his troubling us. As one minister said, "Trouble your trouble."

You will trouble your enemy by keeping peace when he tries to bring you worry, fear, and dread. Read on to see how to overcome these common temptations.

DON'T WORRY ABOUT THE FUTURE

Worry, fear, and dread are classic Peace Stealers. Anxiety is a problem for many, if not most people, and it is a sure sign that they are not pursuing peace with God. These Peace Stealers are all things God tells us in His Word not to do, because all of them are a total waste of energy; they never produce any good results.

Worry can drain our energy, make us grouchy, and even make us sick. Worry has many negative side effects and none that are good. It is totally useless! We worry simply because we don't trust God. We worry because we think we can solve our own problems if we dwell on them long enough. We worry because we are afraid things in life won't turn out the way we hope.

The only solution to worry is total abandonment to God and His plan. Even when unpleasant things happen, which they do in everyone's life, God has the ability to make them work out for the good if we continue to pray and trust Him (see Romans 8:28).

TAKE LIFE AS IT COMES

Like most people, I resist things I don't like. One day the Lord said to me, "Joyce, learn to take life as it comes." That does not mean I am to lie down and become a doormat for the devil and people who would abuse me; it does mean there are many things that I can do nothing about, so it is pointless to fight them.

If we are traveling somewhere and suddenly find ourselves in heavy traffic due to an accident or bad weather, it doesn't do any good to resist it. Only time will change it. Worry will not change it, being upset will not change it, so why not relax and find some way to enjoy the time?

God has equipped us to handle life as it comes, but if we spend today worrying about tomorrow, we find ourselves tired and frustrated. God will not help us worry! Each day has enough for us to consider, we don't need to anticipate tomorrow's situations while we are still trying to live out today.

Jesus said, "So do not worry or be anxious about tomorrow, for tomorrow will have worries and anxieties of its own. Sufficient for each day is its own trouble" (Matthew 6:34). This is some of the best advice any of us will ever receive.

Ask yourself: What good does it do to worry?

Tell yourself: It does not do any good at all. It never solves the problem, it actually adds to it.

Most of the things we worry about are solved in time; sometimes they even solve themselves. Somehow an answer comes, and all the time we spent worrying was a total waste.

I have realized that when I worry, it is because I am really concerned about me. Worry is rooted in selfishness, just like so many other sins. Worry is a sin because it is not faith, and Romans 14:23 states that "whatever does not originate and proceed from faith is sin."

Usually when I worry, it is rooted in what I fear people will think of me, what people will say about me, what will happen to me, or what I am going to do. All of us worry about other people and what they will do or what may happen to them, but we can do less about them even than we can about ourselves. If we cannot even control our own destinies, how can we hope to control someone else's?

Worry definitely torments us. There is always, absolutely always, something to worry about unless we consciously choose not to.

Peace and worry do not cohabit together. If you intend to enjoy a life of peace, worry is one thing that you will have to give up.

The Lord wants us to be free from all anxiety and distressing care. He wants us to be free to serve Him without being "drawn in diverging directions" (1 Corinthians 7:34). He does not want our interests to be divided between Him and the things in this world we feel we need to worry about.

We should strive to keep our lives as simple as possible; it helps us to have fewer temptations toward worry. The more we are involved in, the more we face temptation to be concerned in new areas. I have discovered, for example, that the less I know, the less I worry. I was the type of person who wanted to be "in the know," but now I would much rather have peace.

Paul even went so far as to instruct people to consider remaining single in order not to have spouses they would have to please. He said "The unmarried man is anxious about the things of the Lord—how he may please the Lord. But the married man is anxious about worldly matters—how he may please his wife" (1 Corinthians 7:32–33).

It is certainly not wrong to get married, but Paul's point was that we should keep life as simple as possible so we are free to serve the Lord. Married or single, we should seek simplicity in our daily lives.

Let God Take Care of You

God wants to take care of His children, and He has promised to do so: "Casting the whole of your care [all your anxieties, all your worries, all your concerns, once and for all] on Him, for He cares for you affectionately and cares about you watchfully" (1 Peter 5:7).

We can either try to take care of ourselves, or we can trust God and He will do it for us. Psalm 55:22 says to cast our care on Him, and He will sustain us. The Holy Spirit is a gentleman, and He will not force His help on us. We must ask for it.

We can say that we trust the Lord, but He also wants to see the fruit of it. One of the ways we show our trust in God is by refusing to worry and be anxious.

Because of being abused in my childhood, I learned at an early age to take care of myself. Those I turned to for help had let me down; they disappointed me, so I vowed not to trust people. It took me a while to learn that God is definitely not like people; if He says He will do something, He never fails to do it.

I was thrilled to learn that God wanted to take care of me, but learning how to cast my care so He could do His job was a long lesson. It seemed so foreign to me not to worry about situations. I still need more growth in this area, but at least I'm not where I once was.

I admit that worry has been a problem in my life. I had many burdens at a young age and didn't know anything else to do except worry. I formed bad habits, and they have not been easily broken. It seemed I was literally addicted to worry and reasoning. I could not settle down and feel peaceful until I thought I had an answer to my situation. The main problem was that I always had some sort of situation; therefore, I rarely had the pleasure of being at peace.

If you are one of those people who seem to worry about everything, I want you to know that I know how you feel. I do believe the Lord can and will deliver you. There are biblical principles you can learn that will bring freedom from the bondage of worry. Retire from self-care! Make a decision to let God take care of you.

First Peter 5:6 says we are to humble ourselves under the mighty hand of God, so in due time He might exalt us. It says in verse 7, as we've seen, to cast all our care on Him, for He cares about us. These two verses together are saying that humility leads us into freedom from worry. We will worry as long as we think we can solve our problems, but humility says, "I need God, I need help."

Proud people are independent, but God requires us to be totally dependent upon Him. Habakkuk 2:4 teaches us that the soul of the proud person is not right within him. Part of the soul is the mind, and God does not consider our minds to be "right" when we are worrying. The just and righteous man lives by faith; he leans on God for everything.

First Peter 5:5 states that God resists the proud but gives grace (help) to the humble. Humble people know they are nothing without God, that they can do nothing of any real value without Him. I did not even begin to enjoy any measure of freedom from worry until I faced the fact that I was not able to solve my own problems.

If we know what to do, we should do it; if we don't, we should admit it.

MEDITATE ON THE WORD

If you know how to worry, you know how to meditate. It means to think of something over and over. Meditation on God's Word is one of the major ways you can find deliverance from worrying. Just as we once formed a habit of worrying (meditating on the problem), we can form a new habit of meditating on God's Word. Take portions of Scripture that comfort you, and roll them over and over in your mind. Do it on purpose!

As soon as you are facing a difficult situation that tempts you to worry, begin to confess and meditate on Scripture. In this way, you do warfare with the enemy of your soul (Satan).

When you begin to worry, go find something to do. Get busy being a blessing to someone; do something fruitful. Talking about your problem or sitting alone, thinking about it, does no good; it serves only to make you miserable. Above all else, remember that worrying is totally useless. Worrying will not solve your problem.

FEAR

Worry cannot exist without fear. We can fear things into existence. Fear looks into the future and imagines the worst that can happen. "Fear hath torment," according to 1 John 4:18 (KJV). Anyone who has experienced fear can say a loud *Amen* to that statement. Fear definitely torments!

Having revelation on God's love for us and placing our faith in that love is the only antidote for fear. We can relax and live free from worry and fear when we know that God is good and that He loves us. He loves us with a perfect, full, and complete love. He loves us unconditionally, which means there are never days—not even moments—when God does not love us. Knowing this helps us feel better about ourselves, and it also delivers us from tormenting negative emotions such as worry and fear.

God is on our side, and no matter what happens, He has promised never to leave us or forsake us. He said, "Fear not, for I am with you." Meditate on this Scripture until it becomes a reality in your life: "There is no fear in love [dread does not exist], but full-grown (complete, perfect) love turns fear out of doors and expels every trace of terror! For fear brings with it the thought of punishment, and [so] he who is afraid has not reached the full maturity of love [is not yet grown into love's complete perfection]" (1 John 4:18).

God loves you, and you can live without fear because He does. He has promised to take care of you, to meet your legitimate needs. I am not promising that God will give you everything you want. There are times when we want things that God knows would not be good for us. He promises in Luke 11 that if we ask for bread, He will not give us a stone; likewise, if we ask for a stone, He will not give us a stone when what we need is bread. God will always do what is best for us, and we need to trust that. That kind of faith leads us into lives of peace that passes understanding.

KNOW GOD'S CHARACTER

God is faithful, and because faithfulness is embedded in His character, He cannot fail us or let us down. Experience with God gives us experience with His faithfulness. We have needs, and He meets them time and again. He may not always do what we would like, but He does do the right thing. He may not be early, but He is never too late.

I have seen God come through multitudes of times during the years I have been serving Him. I can truly say, *God is faithful.* He has given me needed strength, answers that came just in time, right friends in right places, open doors of opportunity, encouragement, needed finances, and much more. There is nothing we need that God cannot provide.

God is good. Goodness is one of His many wonderful character traits. When something is part of an individual's character, we can expect him to respond in that way every time. God is not good only sometimes, He is good all the time. He is good to people who don't deserve it. He helps us even when we have done dumb things, if we will just admit our mistakes and ask boldly for His help. We can always ask God for help: "If any of you is deficient in wisdom, let him ask of the giving God [Who gives] to everyone liberally and ungrudgingly, without reproaching or faultfinding, and it will be given him" (James 1:5).

What good news! God will give us wisdom when we have trials—He will show us the way out. All we need to do is ask, and He will give without finding fault with us. Amazing! We don't have to be afraid that God will not help us because we have been weak or made mistakes.

Another one of His character traits is mercy. Mercy chooses to be good to people who, in reality, deserve punishment. His mercy is new every morning. I have always said that God makes a new batch of mercy daily because we used up all of yesterday's supply.

Study the character of God (I have a tape series available on the subject); it will increase your faith and help you not to worry or be fearful. Remember that fear is a demon spirit Satan sends out from hell to hinder our progress. Fear stops us and even drives us backward. It causes us to shrink back. Hebrews 10:38 says, "Now the just shall live by faith: but if any man draw back, my soul shall have no pleasure in him" (KJV).

The *Amplified* translation of that verse says if we draw back and shrink in fear, God has "no delight or pleasure" in us. This simply means that God is not delighted when, through fear, we are cheated out of what Jesus died for us to have and enjoy. We must keep going forward in God's plan and never fall back. Satan hates progress, and more than anything, he uses fear to prevent it.

I believe fear is the master spirit Satan uses to control people. It seems that so many of our problems are rooted in fear. The only answer to fear is to face it with courage. Courage is not the absence of fear—it is going forward in the face of it. Courage overrides fear; it refuses to bow its knee to it. The only acceptable attitude toward fear is: *I will not fear!*

To fear is to take flight or to run away. We are truly afraid if we run from what God wants us to confront. When the Israelites were afraid of Pharaoh and his army, God told Moses to tell them to "fear not; stand still and see the salvation of the Lord" (see Exodus 14:13).

We will never see or experience God's delivering power if we run from things in fear. Stand still, and see what God will do for you. Trust Him; give Him a chance to prove His faithfulness and goodness to you.

When fear knocks on the door, send faith to answer. Don't speak your fears; speak faith. Say what God would say in your situation—say what His Word says, not what you think or feel. The book of Mark relates an account of a woman who had been bleeding for twelve long years. She heard of Jesus and believed that He could help her. "For she kept saying, If I only touch His garments, I shall be restored to health" (Mark 5:28).

The very next verse says, "And immediately her flow of blood was dried up . . . and [suddenly] she felt in her body that she was healed." This woman received her miracle because of faith, but notice that her faith said something.

Whatever is in our hearts will come out of our mouths. Are you speaking fear or faith? Both can produce results. Faith produces positive results, and fear produces negative ones. Did the woman sense any fear? I believe she did. The Bible records that the crowds were so heavy that people pressed Jesus from all sides. I am sure the woman looked at those people and thought, *How am I ever going to get to Jesus? What if I cannot press through to Him?* The devil offers fearful thoughts of that nature.

But the woman made a choice: In the presence of fear telling her she wouldn't make it, she pressed on! She did not shrink back in fear, she pressed on, and that is exactly what God wants all of us to do. She pushed forward and kept speaking her faith, and she got her miracle.

Jesus told the disciples that if they had "faith [that is living] like a grain of mustard seed," they would *say* to the mountain, "Move," and it would move. He further said that with faith, nothing would be impossible to them (see Matthew 17:20).

We see that once again Jesus told us that faith *says* something. I ask again, what are you saying in your situation? When trouble comes, are you able to keep a good confession?

In Matthew 21:21, we find Jesus saying basically the same thing to the same group of men. He was reminding them that if they had faith and did not doubt, even if they *said* to the mountain, "Be cast into the sea," it would be done. The mountains mentioned in these verses refer to obstacles in our way.

Imagine having that kind of power! God wants us to have power, but He also wants us to have spiritual maturity. He would not allow us to use His power for carnal, personal desires. We are His representatives on earth, and our goal should be to see His kingdom come and His will be done on earth as in heaven.

During our trials and tribulation, during the times of what Paul called "abasing," we should hold fast our confession of faith in Jesus, wait patiently, and know that He will never fail us.

What we talk about has a lot to do with our level of personal peace. Why? Because Proverbs 18:20 teaches us that we must be satisfied with the consequences of the words we speak. The next verse adds, "Death and life are in the power of the tongue, and they who indulge in it shall eat the fruit of it (for death or life)."

We can encourage ourselves with our own conversation, or we can discourage ourselves. We can decrease and even eliminate our peace or increase it. I encourage you to be accountable for your words—they are powerful!

DON'T BELIEVE YOUR FEELINGS

God wants us to enjoy lives of peace. Jesus provided it, and we must aggressively pursue it and hold on to it. Second Corinthians 5:7 says that we walk by faith and not by sight; that means we do not make decisions by what we see or feel. We have to search our hearts, where faith abides, and live from there. The kingdom of God is *within* us, and we are to follow those inner promptings that lead to righteousness, peace, and joy in the Holy Spirit.

Feelings can mislead us and steal our faith more than any other single influence. The problem with feelings is that they are ever changing. We can feel one thousand ways about the same thing in thirty days. One minute we may feel like doing a thing, and the next minute we don't.

Feelings provoke us to say things that are unwise; we talk a lot about how we feel. Do you believe the god of your feelings or the God of the Bible? This is a question we must all ask ourselves. More than anything, people who come to me for help and counsel tell me how they feel. We should be telling each other what the Word of God says, not just how we feel.

Our feelings do not convey truth to us; Satan can use them to deceive and lead us astray. Emotions are unreliable; don't believe them. Respond with your heart, where the Spirit of God abides, and see if you then have peace. Check with your heart, not your emotions, before making decisions.

For example, I may meet individuals with whom, in the natural,

I would like to form relationships. They may have gifts or talents that I think would benefit my ministry. But the more I am around them, the more uncomfortable I become in my spirit about them.

I can sense strongly if people are phony or their motives are impure. I may not have anything natural to base my knowledge on, but the inner sensing will not go away, and I do not have peace about making alliances with them. I have learned to trust those promptings of the Spirit but to distrust emotional feelings. I may want to do something in my flesh but know in my spirit it is the wrong thing to do.

I remember one woman we hired at the ministry. This woman seemed to have strong gifts of leadership, and some of our key leaders wanted to promote her. I had a sense that something was not right but could find no natural reason for my feelings. We desperately needed good leadership, so I finally relented, even against what I sensed within, and agreed to put the woman in a place of authority.

She seemed to function in that position well for a while, so I assumed I must have been wrong. But after a period of time went by, we began to have complaints of her mistreating other employees. She was always very respectful to me and other people in authority, but to those under her leadership she was a different person.

A phony is a person who pretends to be one thing to one group of people but is quite another at other times. I know she had the ability to be respectful because she treated me well, but she abused people when she thought she could get away with it. I absolutely despise that kind of attitude.

More than anything, Jesus despised the phonies of His day. He rebuked openly and often those who behaved well when someone was watching them but who, inside, were devouring wolves. People can pretend for a while, but under pressure the real person always shows up. I realized later that I should have listened to those inner promptings. God was giving me discernment about the woman that would have prevented a lot of heartache and wasted time and money had I listened.

There are intuitive (spiritual) feelings we should respect, but most of our emotional feelings will lead us into trouble if we obey or follow them. Emotions will tell us to bow down to fear, when actually that fear will destroy us if we don't resist it. They tell us to give up on things that God intends us to finish or to purchase things we cannot afford and don't even need. Satan uses our emotions to wreck our lives. Not only does Satan come against us through our emotions, but he also wars against our thoughts.

Examine your thoughts and feelings carefully. Don't follow them unless you are sure they are conveying God's will.

LET PEACE BE YOUR UMPIRE

Paul told believers to let peace decide with finality every question that came up. We are to follow peace. If we will remember that, we will have lives we can really enjoy, not ones we just endure. I hate to see people with lifeless attitudes, people who are just going through the motions and enduring each day. I was one of those people for a long, long time, and I know from experience that we must press into peace and joy if we intend to have them. Satan definitely tries to steal the best in life. He is not enjoying himself and does not want any of us to enjoy life either.

If we would obey the teaching from Colossians 3:15, which says peace is to be the umpire in our lives, we would save ourselves unbelievable misery. We open the door for many difficulties in our lives through doing what we think or feel rather than following peace.

I've mentioned that, out of fear of being lonely, some people marry people whom deep down inside they don't have peace about. I married out of fear when I was very young, and it ended in divorce a few years later. As I have mentioned in my teachings, I felt like used merchandise because of my father's abuse. I was afraid that nobody would ever want me, so I married the first boy who showed interest in me. I think I knew it would never really work, but the fear of being lonely caused me to ignore the lack of peace I felt inside.

My first husband had lots of problems himself, and I know God was warning me that I would only get hurt more, but I took a chance. I gambled that maybe I could make a wrong decision and get right results. This, of course, was very foolish, and because of my decision I added another five years of torment and mistreatment to the ones I had already experienced. By the time my first marriage ended, I was twenty-three years old and could never remember being truly happy or having any real peace in my life.

It was not until I learned, many years later in life, to follow peace that I broke these negative patterns in my life. Peace is a wonderful thing; it leads us into many other blessings. We should be completely unwilling to do without it. As Psalm 34:14 states, crave peace, inquire for it, require it, and go after it! Don't let worry or fear steal your peace.

Don't Live in Dread

Dread is closely related to fear. We might say it is the forerunner to fear. I believe a lot of people dread many things and yet don't realize what a problem it is. We dread everything from getting out of bed to going to work, doing dishes, driving in traffic, paying our bills, confronting issues, and just about any little thing we can think of.

Why do we dread something we have to do anyway? Through the power of the Holy Spirit, we can enjoy every aspect of life. An unbeliever may not be able to avoid dread, but a believer in Jesus Christ can. We have supernatural strength and ability available to us. Unbelievers have to depend on their feelings, but we can go beyond feeling and live by faith.

How we approach any situation makes all the difference as to whether we will enjoy it. We will, of course, be miserable if we approach driving to work in traffic with a negative, complaining attitude. It won't do any good, because we must drive to work anyway.

It is actually extremely foolish to dread things we must do and know we will do. The main thing dread does is steal the peace and joy of life. It also drains us of energy and strength we need for the day.

God commanded the Israelites to "dread not," nor fear their enemies (Deuteronomy 1:29). Can something like traffic be an enemy? Yes it can, if we perceive it that way. Anything that we don't want in life, that hinders or aggravates us, we can perceive as an enemy. We are not to dread or fear anything—we are to live courageously and boldly.

Dread drains, faith energizes. Being negative drains us while being positive energizes us. Millions of people in the world today are tired. They see doctors who cannot find any real reason for their condition, so they tell them it is stress. Often we take medication for conditions that would be totally solved if we would eliminate worry, fear, and dread from our lives. If we will make a decision to approach every aspect of life, no matter what it is, with a pleasant, thankful attitude, we will see major changes for the better, even in our health.

The future is coming, no matter how much we fear or dread it. God gives us what we need for each day, but He does not give us tomorrow's grace or wisdom today. If we use today trying to figure out tomorrow, we feel pressure because we are using what we have been allotted for today.

Probably one of the greatest ways we show our trust in God is by living life one day at a time. We prove our confidence in Him by enjoying today and not letting the concern of tomorrow interfere.

It made a big change in my life when I began to gain insight from the Holy Spirit on this problem of dreading things. This truth about living one day at a time greatly increased my peace and joy.

I learned that it really was not the event I was facing that was so bad—it was dreading it that made it bad. Our attitudes do make all the difference in the world. Learn to approach life with an "I can do whatever I need to do" attitude. Don't say that you hate things like driving to work in traffic, going to the grocery store, cleaning house, doing laundry, changing the oil in the car, or cutting the grass. These chores are all part of life. Don't let the events of life dictate your level of joy. It is the joy of the Lord that is your strength. Be joyful that you are going to heaven, that you have someone who always loves you, no matter what. Look at and concentrate on what you do have, not what you don't have.

Everyone has to attend to some unpleasant details in life. We would not know what God's peace was if we never had any difficulty to go through. It is in these difficulties that we learn how valuable His peace is to us.

Some things are certainly more naturally enjoyable and easier to do than others, but that does not mean we cannot purposely enjoy the other more difficult tasks. We can choose to have attitudes of joy and peace. Usually, if we don't feel like doing something, we automatically assume we cannot enjoy it or have peace during that time, but that is a deception. We grow spiritually when we do difficult things with a good attitude.

I don't always feel like being nice and pleasant, but I can choose to in order to honor God. We live for His glory, not our own pleasure. Dreading things does not glorify God. He wants us to live aggressively, to be alive and face each day with courage. How would any parents feel if their children got up each day and said they feared and dreaded the day the parents had prepared for them? They would, of course, feel terrible. God is a parent—He is our parent. The psalmist David said, "This is the day which the Lord has brought about; we will rejoice and be glad in it" (see Psalm 118:24). Notice he said, "We *will* rejoice," not "We *feel like* rejoicing."

What Does the Future Hold?

The future holds a mixture of things we will enjoy and things we would rather do without, but both will come. In Philippians 4:11–12, Paul experienced abasing and abounding, but he also stated that he was able to be content in both, and we also have this option (and ability) as a gift from God.

Jesus promised us that in the world we would have tribulation, but He told us to "cheer up" because He had overcome the world and deprived it of power to really harm us (see John 16:33). Dreading hard times will not prevent them from coming, but it will make them even more difficult than they would have been. Make life as easy as possible; don't dread it. Face it with courage and say, "I will not fear, because greater is He that is in me than he that is in the world" (see 1 John 4:4).

No mortal really knows what the future holds, only God knows, and He does not usually tell us what it is. Why doesn't He reveal more to us about the future? Because He wants us to trust Him that everything will work out for our ultimate good, that all things work together to help accomplish His will for each of us. We may not know what the future holds, but we can be satisfied to know Him, the one who does know.

I spent some time today thinking about the future, and I realized that everything out there won't be something I will welcome with open arms. I will face things that I would rather not have to deal with, but I cannot stop them, so I may as well embrace and go through them with a smile on my face.

I am convinced of one thing: I may go through difficulties, but God also has wonderful things planned for me. He always balances things so we don't become discouraged and defeated by too many difficult days without good ones in between. Remember, God never allows more to come on us than what we can bear, but with every temptation He also always provides the way out.

I have noticed in my life that when I have truly had all I can take, something happens to relieve the pressure for a while. I get built up, rested, and have times of joy, then perhaps go another round with the trouble. When I feel I have reached my limit, I pray for good news, because the Bible says that good news nourishes us, it encourages us and strengthens us. Another Scripture says that David prayed for God to show him evident signs of His goodwill and favor (see Psalm 86:17); I also pray for that, and God always gives me what I need when I need it.

Remember, James 4:2 says we have not because we ask not. Ask God for good news—ask Him to encourage you. Too often in life, we go to people for encouragement or even get angry at them when they are not giving it to us. We should go to God because He is the God of all comfort (see 2 Corinthians 1:3).

We would not need faith if everything in life went the way we wanted. We would need no patience if we never had to wait for anything. Faith and patience work together to bring our break-throughs. While we are waiting, let us do so with joy and peace. This shows that we are children of God.

The whole world lives in fear and dread, but God's children should not. We are to behave differently from the people in the world; we should let our light shine. Just being positive in a negative circumstance is a way to do this. The world will notice when we are stable in every kind of situation.

Make up your mind right now that all of life does not need to make you feel good in order for you to face it with peace and joy. Make a decision that you will not dread anything you have to do. Do it all with a thankful attitude. There are people who are sick and diseased or perhaps in the hospital who would absolutely love to be able to move about enough to do what you may be dreading.

I never considered driving down the street to get a cup of coffee a huge privilege until after I had been hospitalized with breast cancer and had surgery. When I was released, I asked my husband to take me out for a coffee and a drive through a local park. It was amazing how much joy I felt.

I was doing a very simple thing that was previously available to me every day, yet I had never seen it as a privilege. When I had faced the possibility of death or long-term treatment for cancer and discovered I would not only live but was pronounced well, I suddenly loved life so much that very simple things brought extreme joy.

Our son went on an outreach with a team of people who go visit the homeless each Friday evening. After helping in this ministry, he called me and said, "If I ever complain again, please knock me down and then kick me for being so stupid!" He was appalled at himself for the things he had murmured about in the past once he saw by comparison how some people were living. We would all feel exactly the same way.

Those without a place to live would love to have a house to clean, while we dread cleaning ours. They would delight in having a car to drive, even an old one, while we complain about needing to wash ours or take it in for an oil change.

I am sure you are getting my point. We lose sight of how blessed we are most of the time, but we should work at keeping it in the front of our thinking. Be thankful you can do anything, and don't dread things you have to do.

Choose to bless God all the time, no matter what is going on, as David did: "I *WILL* bless the Lord at all times; His praise shall continually be in my mouth" (Psalm 34:1, italics mine).

PROSPERITY AND PROGRESS

God certainly wants all of His children to enjoy prosperity and progress, but once again I want to remind you that worry, fear, and dread can stop and hinder both of these. This verse says all that I am trying to say: "Then you will prosper if you are careful to keep and fulfill the statutes and ordinances with which the Lord charged Moses concerning Israel. Be strong and of good courage. Dread not and fear not; be not dismayed" (1 Chronicles 22:13).

The negative expectations of worry and dread hinder and prevent progress. Live courageously, live with faith, and keep a good confession.

Good things will not just fall on us; we must aggressively pursue them like the woman with the issue of blood pursued Jesus. She refused to take no for an answer, and she got her miracle breakthrough. We can have the same results if we press in and press on instead of drawing back in fear and dread. God will either give us a breakthrough, or at the very least He will give us grace to go through whatever we need to and enjoy our lives while we are doing it.

Recently a group of pastors asked me a question: Besides God Himself, what one thing had helped me get from where I started in ministry to the level of success I currently enjoy? I immediately said, "I refused to give up!" There were thousands of times when I felt like giving up, I thought about giving up, I was tempted to give up, but I always pressed on. I thank God for the determination He gives us.

Don't let life defeat you—face it with boldness and courage, and declare that you will enjoy every aspect of it. You can do that because you have the awesome power of God dwelling in you. God is never frustrated and unhappy. He always has peace and joy, and since He lives in us and we live in Him, surely we can attain the same thing.

Right now, as I am writing this portion of this book, I have a terrible backache. I did some new exercises yesterday and apparently strained some muscles, but I will not dwell on the pain and let it ruin my day. I have something to accomplish today, and by God's grace, I will do it. I will not worry that I might still have the same pain tomorrow or dread it if I do. Whatever we go through, God will always be with us. I choose to believe that Jesus is my Healer and that His healing power is working in my body right now!

When tempted to worry, Dave always says, "I am not impressed." He believes we should be more impressed by God's Word than our problems. He says if we don't get *impressed*, we won't get *depressed*, then *oppressed*, and ultimately perhaps even *possessed* by our difficulties. No matter what you are facing right now, God has a great life planned for you. It includes prosperity and progress in every area of life. It includes great peace, joy unspeakable, and every good thing you can imagine. Refuse to settle for anything less than God's best for you!

DON'T BE DOUBLE-MINDED

Double-minded, indecisive people are always miserable; they certainly don't enjoy peace with God. Nothing is worse to me than being between two decisions and not making either one of them. I am usually a very decisive person. At times in life I have made decisions too fast and made mistakes. I have also found that I can slip into being double-minded and indecisive if I am not careful.

I believe this is something the devil tempts all of us with at various times. He does anything that steals our peace because he knows that without peace, we are without power. We often don't make decisions because we don't want to make mistakes. But making no decision is still a decision *and* a mistake. Decide to decide! It will produce peace in your life, as long as you don't second-guess yourself and fall back into being indecisive once again.

Stick with your decisions unless you are definitely shown that they are wrong. Sometimes we find out whether a decision is right or wrong only by making it and seeing what happens. Making a wrong decision is not the end of the world, in most cases, and it is usually better than making no decision.

Some people do nothing most of their lives because they are afraid to commit to action. I hope you are not one of those people, but if you are, I want to help you. Please realize you need to start somewhere. Begin with smaller things, and work your way up to major decisions.

DON'T BE AFRAID OF WHAT PEOPLE THINK

Most of us would not mind making a mistake if we thought we could make it privately. It is not the mistake, but people knowing about it that bothers us. We are afraid of what people think, and yet their opinions cannot really harm us. Our indecision can.

Many people have destroyed their lives by being overly concerned about what others think. Saul lost his kingdom and the opportunity to be king because he cared so much about what people thought that he disobeyed God on more than one occasion.

We have all experienced having to choose between God and people. It really should not even be a contest, but somehow it always is—at least until we are delivered from the fear of man.

Can someone's *thoughts* really harm us that much? I think I have finally realized that if someone wants to judge me, he will find some way to do it, no matter what I do; therefore, I may as well follow my heart and get about enjoying my life.

We will be judged, criticized, and misunderstood at various times in life, and we really can't do much about it. Fear of people's thoughts about our decisions only prevents us from making progress. We decide nothing and then nothing happens, with the exception that we remain frustrated while going back and forth and being confused about what we should do.

Satan always threatens us with, "What if . . . ?" He shows us the most terrible thing that *could* happen, and it always revolves around our making a mistake. When needing to make a decision, we must remember that there is as much of a chance that we will be right as wrong.

We will never fulfill our destinies if we have undue concern over what people think. Let them think what they want. If they think wrong thoughts, they will pay the price by being miserable. Wrong thoughts can do nothing except produce misery. Many people blame their unhappiness and lack of peace on their circumstances when it really is rooted in their own lousy thinking.

People who can break free from caring about what other people think will instantly upgrade their level of living. They will increase their joy and their peace one hundredfold.

BE CONFIDENT

God wants us to live with confidence and approach life boldly. Being indecisive is neither. Make a decision today to start being decisive. It will never happen if you don't. It may be a bold move for you if you have spent a lot of your life in fear and indecision, but it is necessary if you really want to enjoy a life of peace. Indecision is not a peaceful place.

Put your confidence in Christ and who you are in Him, not in what people think of you. We cannot base our worth on what others have said or how they have treated us. People who are hurting will hurt others. If you have come into contact with people who are hurting, they may hurt or reject you. They may have transposed their pain onto you, when in reality you were not the real problem at all.

Know yourself! Know your heart, and don't wait for other people to dictate to you the truth about your value. Don't assume you are wrong every time someone does not agree with you. Believe that God's wisdom dwells inside of you. Believe you can make decisions. There is no point at all in believing something negative about yourself when it is just as easy to believe something positive—and it's certainly a lot more beneficial.

People who are indecisive are usually more passive in nature or insecure. They are fear-based and should be faith-based individuals. Is fear, or faith, motivating most of your actions?

A believer without confidence is like a jumbo jet sitting on the runway with no fuel in it. It looks good but goes no place. People who are indecisive are the same way. They may have all the qualities needed to be successful, but if they refuse to make decisions, they go nowhere and accomplish nothing. Progress begins with a decision.

BE COURAGEOUS

Courage is a vitally necessary quality if we intend to do anything worthwhile with our time here on earth. Leaders are not always, or even usually, the most gifted people, but they are people with courage. They step out when others shrink back in fear. They take bold steps of faith, they do things that to other people might even seem foolish or unwise, but they are willing to take a chance. They may be wrong occasionally, but they are right enough of the time that it doesn't matter.

I would rather try to do a lot and accomplish a little than try to do nothing and accomplish all of it. If I try nothing, I will accomplish nothing. The worst thing that can happen is I will be wrong, and that really is not the end of the world. After all, nobody is right all the time. I would rather take a chance on being wrong and trying to accomplish something than definitely be wrong because I have done nothing.

God expects us to increase, to be fruitful and multiply (see Genesis 1:28). He admires courage; in fact, He demands it from those who will work alongside of Him. The Lord told Joshua that he was to take Moses' place and lead the Israelites into the promised land. There was one stipulation: He had to be strong and of good courage.

Be strong (confident) and of good courage, for you shall cause this people to inherit the land which I swore to their fathers to give them. Only you be strong and very courageous, that you may do according to all the law which Moses My servant commanded you. Turn not from it to the right hand or to the left, that you may prosper wherever you go. . . . Have not I commanded you? Be strong, vigorous, and very courageous. Be not afraid, neither be dismayed, for the Lord your God is with you wherever you go. (Joshua 1:6–7, 9)

It doesn't matter what qualities or provisions we do not have, as long as God is with us. He is all we need. He makes up for anything we are lacking. God told Joshua, "As I was with Moses, so I will be with you" (Joshua 1:5). Moses was great because God was with him and he took courageous steps to do what God told him to do. The same thing would hold true for Joshua—and will be true for any one of us who follows God's ways in these areas. His way is not one of shrinking back in fear, but of going forward courageously in faith.

God's way is one of being decisive. We are not to make decisions so quickly that we don't give them proper thought and prayer. We should seek wisdom and be sure we are following peace. But once we have done all we can do to assure we are making a right decision, as far as we know, there is nothing else to do except be courageous and do something, lest we do nothing.

DECIDE BY YOUR HEART, NOT YOUR HEAD

A person who needs to have everything all figured out will not be courageous. People who do courageous things follow their hearts. They may not always fully understand why they feel courage, but they are bold enough to follow it. I am not suggesting we follow our emotions, which would not be good since they are rather unstable. But we should follow our born-again spirits, our hearts.

People who do bold things step out in faith even though they have no real proof they will even work. They make decisions by discernment. *Discernment* means to be able to grasp and comprehend what is obscure. It is the ability to see what is not obvious based on circumstances. A person might say he makes decisions by his "gut." This simply means he does what he believes is *right* even if he feels uncomfortable. Jesus Himself did not make decisions based on natural knowledge.

> And shall make Him of quick understanding, and His delight shall be in the reverential and obedient fear of the Lord. And He shall not judge by the sight of His eyes, neither decide by the hearing of His ears; but with righteousness and justice shall He judge the poor and decide with fairness for the meek, the poor, and the downtrodden of the earth (Isaiah 11:3–4)

We see from this Scripture that He did not decide "by the sight of His eyes," or the "hearing of His ears," yet He was of "quick understanding." If we follow our hearts, we can understand quickly what we could not learn by natural means in a lifetime. It is sad, but most people are afraid to operate in the supernatural realm; they want to understand everything in their minds.

One year a man was helping me do my income tax. When he observed that we gave 10 percent of our income to the church each year, he promptly told me that we were giving too much, that it was not necessary, and we should stop.

He was looking at our giving in the natural and could find no reason why we would want to do such a thing. We were looking at it according to our knowledge of God's Word. We understood spiritually what we were doing and believed that if we gave, God would always take care of us. I tried to explain God's principles on sowing and reaping to him, but he insisted that even if we wanted to give, it did not need to be that much, especially since we didn't have an abundance left over after giving to the church and paying our bills.

This is an example of a natural man not understanding the spiritual man. First Corinthians 2:14 explains that the natural man cannot understand spiritual things because they must be spiritually discerned. This simply means that spiritual things take place in the born-again spirit of the inner man, not in the natural mind.

This is one of the reasons God's Word instructs us to let peace be the umpire in our lives, deciding with finality everything that is questionable. If we could go two ways, which way do we go? What do we decide? We decide to do what we have peace in our hearts about, what we are comfortable with inside of us. God speaks and communicates to the heart of man, not necessarily to his head. We know God in our hearts. He dwells in our hearts.

This is the reason people who depend on their intellects have a difficult time believing in God. They don't see Him, they don't feel Him, and many of His principles don't make sense to their natural minds.

Naturally speaking, what sense does it make to tell people that they will have increase if they give away some of their money? It makes no sense at all. The Bible says that the first will be last, and the last will be first. That makes no sense to my mind, but I know by spiritual understanding that it means when we try to push ourselves forward into first place, we will end up last. When we wait on God to promote us, even if we start out last, we will end up first.

I am very grateful for discernment and spiritual understanding. I appreciate the fact that you and I, as believers in Jesus Christ, filled with His Spirit, can make decisions courageously because we can trust what is in our hearts.

If you have been having difficulty making a decision, try this: Let your mind rest. Don't be *thinking* about what you should do. Then see what is in your heart—what do you *know* inside that you should do? Whatever you have peace about, do that.

A person might want to purchase a new car but not have real peace about it. Emotional excitement is not peace. If you are confused, you are not in God's will. He is the Author of peace, not confusion. Satan wants you confused. It is really very simple: If you don't have peace, don't buy the car. If you do purchase it without peace, I can guarantee that later on you will be sorry that you did. You will either have purchased something that will not meet your needs, it will require a lot of maintenance, or it will create financial pressure.

We don't have to know why God is not giving us peace to do a certain thing; we just need to follow His leading. He is not obligated to explain, but we are obligated to trust Him.

THE DOUBLE-MINDED MAN IS UNSTABLE AND UNRELIABLE

In James 1, we find that when we need wisdom we should ask God for it, and He will give it—but we must ask in faith. We are not to waver, hesitate, or doubt. The person who does these things will receive nothing he asks for from the Lord. Why? If the man cannot settle on something and make a decision about what he believes, how can God give him anything? "[For being as he is] a man of two minds (hesitating, dubious, irresolute), [he is] unstable and unreliable and uncertain about everything [he thinks, feels, decides]" (James 1:8).

The double-minded man is unreliable and unstable. This is not a reputation anyone wants to have. I want people and the Lord to be able to depend on me, to know that I mean what I say and won't change my mind without a very good reason.

Paul told the Corinthians that when he said yes to them, it meant yes. He promised that yes would not end up being no (see 2 Corinthians 1:17–18). In other words, Paul was promising not to be double-minded. He was telling the church members that they could count on him to be stable, and he would keep his word to them.

Integrity is extremely important for every person, and especially for those who lead others. How could Paul expect to be respected if he was unreliable? He couldn't, and neither can we.

I want to be in relationship with people I can depend on, people I know who are decisive, stable, and reliable. I want to be able to trust people. Good relationships are built on trust. I was recently involved in an event that required people to sign up ahead of time, indicating whether or not they would be attending. We had nine hundred people say they were coming, and only seven hundred showed up. Very few of them made any effort to cancel or even communicate that they were not coming. The problem was twofold: First, they did not keep their word, and second, we had purchased and cooked meat for nine hundred, and since seven hundred showed up, we obviously had lots of meat left over.

This was inconsiderate on their parts and harmful to them spiritually because they didn't honor their commitment. This is a widespread problem today in our society. Most people don't think anything at all about saying they will do a thing and then changing their minds without any good reason, except they did not feel like doing what they said they would do. Their excuse is "I changed my mind."

The very least we can do when we have made a commitment and cannot or will not keep it is to make a phone call and say so. Don't just leave people hanging, not having any idea what happened.

Those who didn't attend the event I mentioned thought it didn't really matter. But it always makes a difference if we don't do what we say we will.

Our word is a verbal contract. This verse shows that God considers it to be a vow: "When you vow a vow or make a pledge to God, do not put off paying it; for God has no pleasure in fools (those who witlessly mock Him). Pay what you vow. It is better that you should not vow than that you should vow and not pay" (Ecclesiastes 5:4–5).

We should take these Scriptures to heart and view them seriously. Don't make commitments rashly without giving thought to whether or not you are prepared to follow through. I am sure that some of the two hundred people who failed to show up had good reasons for not doing so, but I am equally sure that most of them just plain didn't see the need to keep their word.

When we keep our word, even if it is inconvenient for us to do so, it shows good character. We should be concerned about our example because the world is watching those of us who claim to be Christians. They want to see if we are all talk, or if we are living what we are saying we believe.

I have witnessed people signing up for things and not showing up numerous times during my years of involvement with people in the church. I started out being shocked because I assumed church people could be trusted, but I quickly learned that just because someone goes to church, he is not automatically honest and truthful.

The ones who don't keep their word always have an excuse of some kind, but I don't believe they have peace. We cannot be double minded, unreliable, and unstable and enjoy peace at the same time. We may try to override the feelings of conviction about not keeping our commitment, but its presence nibbles away at the peace God wants us to enjoy.

One of the ways to maintain peace with God, with yourself, and your fellow man is to do what you say you will do. Once you have made up your mind, don't change it unless you have no other choice.

DON'T BE DOUBLE-MINDED, EVEN IN SMALL MATTERS

Although I am usually very decisive, I have been known to be double-minded about little things, like what to wear or where to go and eat. God showed me that even being double-minded in these things places pressure on me and robs me of available peace. I like my meals, for example, to be perfect. I think of one restaurant that has the salad I like, but then another comes to mind that has wonderful coffee. Then I remember the pasta dish I love at another one, and before I realize what I am doing, I have spent a half hour or more going back and forth in my mind and in conversation with others about where I want to eat.

It's so bad that it has become a family joke. My son says to me early in the morning, "You better start thinking now about where you want to go eat, so you have a decision by tonight when it is time to go." Or when I tell him to make a reservation at a restaurant for all of us, he might say, "I will check with you in two hours and see if the decision is still the same, so I won't have to change the reservation three times between now and then."

I am doing better, but I still find myself falling into the trap of being double-minded in this area simply because I want to get a perfect meal—and there is probably no such thing.

I have a large classic-movie collection and I often get double-minded about which movie I want to watch. I may choose three or four and keep going back and forth. I read the back of the box and ask others in the family what they think. I make a decision, but then I might ask people who have seen the movies which one is the best and change my mind again. Sometimes I get so frustrated that I end up watching nothing. I turn the television on and flip from channel to channel for an hour and then go to bed. This is a ridiculous waste of time, and it is another habit I am in the process of breaking. As you can see, I am not perfect in this area either, so if you need to change too, we can change together.

My main point is that even being double-minded in small things, which would not seem to matter very much, can still steal your peace, and it is simply not worth it.

The only way to find out if I will enjoy a movie that I have not seen is to start viewing it. If it does not suit me, I can try another one, but at least I need to do something besides be double-minded.

According to Scripture, it is the little foxes that spoil the vine. In other words, it is not always big things that cause misery; often it is small, almost imperceptible things—things we would not think matter at all.

Some people who lack peace search in all the wrong places for the sources of their problem, but it may simply result from being indecisive, even in the small matters of everyday life. To overcome this, they must practice being decision makers in less-consequential situations, and it will help them gain confidence for larger issues.

CHOOSE WHOM YOU WILL SERVE

Joshua was obviously a man who had his mind made up about what he was going to do, and it didn't matter to him what others did. He said, "And if it seems evil to you to serve the Lord, choose for yourselves this day whom you will serve, whether the gods which your fathers served on the other side of the River, or the gods of the Amorites, in whose land you dwell; but as for me and my house, we will serve the Lord" (Joshua 24:15). We should not wait to see what other people will do before making our own decisions, especially when it comes to serving God.

James talked about believers who cannot make their minds up whether they want Jesus or the world when he wrote: "Come close to God and He will come close to you. [Recognize that you are] sinners, get your soiled hands clean; [realize that you have been disloyal] wavering individuals with divided interests, and purify your hearts [of your spiritual adultery]" (4:8). James referred to people with divided interests as "spiritual adulter[ers]": They choose the world as a friend, therefore making God their enemy.

We cannot serve God and the world. We are in the world, but the Bible instructs not to be like it. We can live in it, but we cannot love it. God must have first place at all times.

Keeping the Lord first requires consistent decisions and a refusal to be double-minded. Just about the time we make a decision to do the right thing, someone will come along and try to convince us to compromise. We have to stand firm on what we believe is right for us.

James referred to those who cannot decide whether they want God or the world as "sinners" and told them to purify their hearts of being double-minded. Satan tried to tempt Jesus with the world and all it had to offer, but Jesus quickly responded by quoting

Scriptures to him. Jesus knew what He wanted, He knew what was really important, and He stood firm on His original decision to do what God had sent Him to do (see Luke 4).

Temptation will come. It is a defining moment in our lives each time we face temptation yet remain firm on what we know is right. The devil's ultimate plan is to destroy us. He may make sin look inviting in the beginning, but in the end, we will be sorry if we fall into his trap.

I repeat, don't be double-minded. Make up your mind to serve the Lord, and don't bow down to the devil or anyone through whom he is trying to work. Be like Joshua: Have a firm attitude toward others who try to move you off of your righteous stand. No one else will stand before God and give an account of your life, only you will (see Romans 14:12), so make your own decisions.

Every decision is a seed you sow, and every seed produces a harvest. *Before* changing your mind and giving in to temptation, ask yourself if you want to reap the harvest of the seed you are being tempted to sow.

The Bible is literally filled with promises of good things to those who follow God's commands. Decide to follow Jesus, and don't ever change your mind.

In Luke 10, we see that Jesus visited two sisters named Mary and Martha. These women had quite different natures. One was very interested in *seeking* Jesus; the other was interested in *impressing* Him.

Martha was busy about much serving. She wanted everything to be clean and in the right place. She became angry with her sister, Mary, because she was sitting at the feet of Jesus, wanting to learn all she could and enjoy Him while He was present.

Martha even complained to Jesus and told Him to tell Mary to get up and help her. Jesus replied by saying, "Martha, Martha, you are anxious and troubled about many things; there is need of only one [thing]. . . . Mary has chosen the good portion [that which is to her advantage]" (Luke 10:41–42).

Mary made a firm choice, and even when Martha became angry with her, she did not change her mind. We must realize that people will often get angry with us if we don't make the choices they want us to make, but we should remain steadfast and follow our own hearts.

Learn to relax and be more like Mary. Martha believed that she had to take care of everything herself. She wanted everything to be perfect. Sometimes we can find ourselves like Martha, tense even when we don't have anything to be tense about. It isn't really our circumstances that make us tense; most of the time it is our own approach to life. In the next chapter we will examine ways to relax and enjoy trusting God's faithfulness to take care of us.

STAY SUPERNATURALLY RELAXED

The longer we know the Lord, the more relaxed we should become when we face situations that try to steal our peace. Previous experience with God is valuable because we learn that somehow He always comes through. Each time we face a new crisis, we can remember that even though He may not have done exactly what we wanted Him to do, He always did something that worked out. Relaxing in the face of trials helps us to maintain our peace with God.

New believers who do not have personal examples on which to build their confidence in God must be more dependent on examples in the Bible of God's faithfulness. The testimonies of other believers can also greatly encourage them.

Remember, Jesus said that we are to come to Him when we have problems, and He will give us rest. The *Amplified Bible* translates His words as: "Come to Me, all you who labor and are heavy-laden and overburdened, and I will cause you to rest [I will ease and relieve and refresh your souls.]" (Matthew 11:28).

That sounds to me like Jesus wants us to live in a relaxed state, not tense, uptight, worried, or anxious about yesterday, today, or tomorrow. We can stop reasoning and trying to figure out what we need to do. And the Lord doesn't want us to be upset with other people who aren't doing what we want them to, either.

Jesus wants us to trust Him and relax. I call this being *supernaturally relaxed*, because in the natural we may have difficulty learning how or finding time to relax. But when God adds His *super* to our *natural*, we end up with *supernatural*. We can have supernatural relaxation!

Jesus was saying, "Come to Me about anything, because I always want to help you with everything." There's nothing too little and nothing too big to take to Him. You can't take too much. You can't have too many requests.

JESUS INTERCEDES FOR US

I believe that in order to stay relaxed, you must understand the present-day ministry of Jesus. Jesus keeps working on your behalf as long as you keep your trust in Him. Even as you are reading this book, you can pray: "Lord, I leave all my situations and circumstances in Your hands. I leave the past behind. I know I can trust You to work all my situations together for my good. Things are going to be different from now on, because I am going to relax and simply enjoy You."

Release your confidence in God through faith-filled words, and through short little prayers throughout your day. Every prayer doesn't have to be long and eloquent. Pray your way through the day.

One of the most blessed present-day ministries of Jesus is that He is interceding for us. The Word says of Jesus: "Therefore He is able also to save to the uttermost (completely, perfectly, finally, and for all time and eternity) those who come to God through Him, since He is always living to make petition to God and intercede with Him and intervene for them" (Hebrews 7:25).

All that Jesus asks of the Father, God answers. So whatever He is praying for me, whatever He is praying for you, we're going to get it! Jesus never stops praying for us. This means that we can relax, because the Word promises that Jesus sits at the right hand of the Father and intercedes for us (see Romans 8:34).

In order to stay supernaturally relaxed, it is important to understand the relationship between the Vine (Jesus) and the branches (us, the believers). John 15:4–5 teaches that Jesus is the Vine, and the Father is the Vinedresser. He cuts away any branch that doesn't bear fruit, but He cleanses and repeatedly prunes every branch that continues to bear fruit to make it even more productive.

I realized a long time ago that pruning is just a fact of life. We are pruned if we do bear fruit and pruned if we don't! According to *Webster's New College Dictionary,* the word *prune* means to cut off or remove living or dead parts, to shape or stimulate growth, to remove or cut out as unnecessary, to reduce, to remove the superfluous or undesirable. In other words, God is going to deal with us because we are as branches that should be bearing fruit, ultimately so the world can pick that fruit and be fed. God wants us to meet people's needs, be a blessing to them, and live for His glory.

The more strength of Jesus' life that we receive through Him, the Vine, the more fruit will grow on us, the branches. But branches don't have to struggle to bear fruit, just as we don't have to labor or be heavily burdened to produce good results in our lives. We don't reach our goals by trying, but by believing. We're supposed to abide in Jesus, and as we just "hang on" the Vine, Jesus will pour His life into us so that we bear fruit.

ABIDE IN CHRIST

All we need is more of Jesus! The more we relax and trust Him, the more we are abiding in Him. I have never seen a peach tree frustrated, upset, and all stressed-out trying to produce peaches. The tree rests in the ground, and the life from the vine flows into the branches and produces fruit. This is God's will for each of us: resting in Jesus and producing good fruit.

Whenever I return home from ministering in conferences, I renew and revitalize myself by abiding in Jesus. I pray, meditate on His Word, and spend time with Him. I say, "Thank You, Lord, for strengthening me. Thank You for refueling me. I need You, Jesus. I can't do anything without You."

I know I must abide in Him if I want to bear good fruit. Abiding replenishes the energy I use in my conferences. For many years I ministered in my conferences, returned home, and went right back to the office or out on another trip without spending the time I needed with the Lord. I always ended up worn-out, depressed, crying, and wanting to get out of ministry because of the pressure.

If we drive our automobiles without filling up the tanks, we ultimately run out of gasoline and break down somewhere on the road and have to be towed in. We can do the same thing as individuals. We will break down mentally, physically, emotionally, and spiritually if we don't stay full of Jesus by abiding in Him.

Most mornings, Dave and I spend from two to three hours with the Lord, praying, reading, meditating, pondering, writing, resting, trusting, and abiding in the Lord. By the time I face my family or work responsibilities, I'm full of good fruit in case anybody has a need. Sometimes people "pick on us," and when they do, we want them to be able to pick good fruit.

If I abide in Jesus, the Vine, I'll always have what I need to give to others. If I don't spend time with the Lord, I will become like the fig tree that was full of leaves but without fruit. The Bible said Jesus was hungry when He saw a fig tree in the distance, and He went to get something to eat from it, but there was no fruit on it. So He cursed it and He said, "Fruit will never grow on you again" (see Matthew 21:19). I remember thinking that it wasn't the fig tree's fault. Then I read that when the fig tree has leaves, it is also supposed to have fruit. I believe He cursed it because it was a phony—it had leaves but no fruit.

I think a lot of people are like fruitless fig trees. They have all the Christian paraphernalia (the leaves), but they don't have the fruit of real faith in their lives. They look like they have the lives of Christians: They have the bumper stickers, the fish on their cars, the big Bibles they carry to work, and they say, "Praise the Lord" on a regular basis. But when a coworker goes to them, hungering for kindness, patience, mercy, or love, they don't have what is needed—there's no fruit (good works or pleasant attitude) because they have not been hanging (abiding) on the Vine. They also live with the curse of not having the fruit of peace in their own lives.

I am afraid not to spend time with God because as a minister of God's Word, I don't do anything fancy when I teach. I know that if I don't have the anointing from abiding in Christ, I'm finished before I ever open my mouth.

Jesus said that if we dwell in Him, He will dwell in us. If we live in Him, He will live in us. He said that we cannot bear fruit without abiding in Him. But if we *live,* which implies daily abiding, in Him we will bear *abundant fruit* (again see John 15:4–5). Whether it is teaching or anything else I do in life, I have learned by experience that I need Him and cannot do anything of real value without Him. Unless the Lord builds the house, we labor in vain that build it (see Psalm 127:1).

To have peace, it is very important that we abide in Christ, and this means to spend time with Him on a consistent basis. In the world we live in today, a little bit of time with God is not enough. God has to be first in our thoughts, in our conversations, in our finances, and in our schedules. Don't try to work God into your schedule; work your schedule around Him. Put Him first, and everything will work properly.

If you put God first in everything, then you will find yourself getting things done supernaturally. He may even send someone to help you whom you were not expecting. I have had two people tell me recently that God moved on the hearts of people they knew to help them with housework or other duties; the helpers said they felt that God placed it on their hearts and wanted to do it without charging any fee.

This same thing happened to me many years ago, when I started my ministry. I had four young children, no money, and not much time to prepare for ministry. God sent a friend who offered to help me two days a week without pay.

I want to say again, if you put God first in everything, then you will find yourself getting things done supernaturally. Putting God first is not about having all the Christian paraphernalia I mentioned that we might refer to as "fig leaves." Don't forget that when Adam and Eve found themselves in trouble, they covered themselves up with fig leaves too. Fig leaves weren't adequate to meet their need to cover themselves, so God provided the sufficient covering for them (see Genesis 3:21).

We are not capable of making ourselves fruit-bearing Christians. Bearing fruit is the work of the Holy Spirit, and God gets the glory. God promises to graft us into Himself so that His life pours through us (see Romans 11:17).

The picture of being grafted in to the vine is an interesting concept because it requires taking a branch that is almost dead and wrapping it tightly to a living vine. This process brings life back into the almost-dead branch. This branch cannot do anything but receive life from the Vine. Like grafted branches, we are simply to relax in God's presence and let His abundant life flow through us.

TRUST YOURSELF TO GOD

There is nothing that we can give to God, except ourselves. We can show appreciation for all He has done for us and praise Him for His goodness.

Trust yourself to God; He wants you! He wants to take care of you and be your everything. Total surrender of your life will bring an awesome peace with God—the peace that passes understanding.

We will keep our peace if we surrender our guilt for past sins to God. God wants us to ask for and receive His free gift of forgiveness, which has always been available to us. I encourage you to form a habit: When you ask God to forgive your sins, follow up by saying, "I receive that forgiveness right now, and I let go of the guilt."

Learn how to receive; see yourself as a branch hanging onto the Vine. All you can do is receive life from that Vine. Confess, "I receive, Lord. I give myself to You, and I receive You as my every-thing in life: my Savior, Lord, Strength, Peace, Righteousness, Joy, Justification, Sanctification, and all other things."

All the branch does is receive what the Vine offers. To *receive* means to act like a receptacle and simply take in what is being offered. To stay supernaturally relaxed, become a receiver and live by grace, and not by works or fleshly effort.

Living by grace is trusting in God's energy, instead of our own work and effort, to do what needs to be done. And look what Christ can do: Hebrews 1:3 says that He upholds and maintains and guides and propels the universe by "His mighty word of power"!

God makes this earth and all of the planets and stars spin per-fectly through space. We don't even know how big the universe is. If He can do that, shouldn't we relax, knowing He can take care of us too? If He can run the entire universe, surely He can manage each of us.

Hebrews 1:3 goes on to say that Jesus "accomplished our cleans-ing of sins and riddance of guilt" by offering Himself, then He *sat down* at the right hand of God. Sitting down is a picture of being relaxed because the work was done.

So, Jesus is relaxed. He's taking care of the universe, but it's not even an effort for Him. Why isn't He running around heaven, wor-ried about our situations? Why isn't He wringing His hands, trying to figure out what to do? Surely there must be a lot of work involved in keeping this whole universe running. Yet He does it and remains perfectly calm. As we learn to live in Him, we, too, can enjoy this supernatural ease and relaxation.

RELAX IN THE KEEPING POWER OF GOD

A lady who works for me says that she doesn't have a "big" testi-mony. She just grew up in the church, loving God. She got married, was filled with the Holy Spirit, then came to work for us. Through our ministry, she was moved by the testimonies of drug addicts and people who have suffered abuse. One day she asked God, "Lord, why don't I have a testimony?"

He said, "You do have a testimony. Your testimony is that I kept you from all of it." God had kept her from the pain that results from being separated from Him. The keeping power of God is a great testimony!

Psalm 91 teaches that He will give His angels charge over us, and they will protect and defend us. This same woman was sitting in a boat one day, reading that very chapter. Her husband was fishing when the boat hit a wave and the lawn chair she was in fell over. She banged her head on the side of the boat at the same time she was reading about God's protection. She said, "Lord, I don't understand this! The Bible says that You'll protect me, and here I've hit my head."

God said to her, "You're not dead, are you?"

It's true that a few things happen in our lives that we don't like, but what has God kept us from that we never even knew Satan had planned against us? I marvel at the fact that we can drive in traffic and stay alive. We need to thank God for His keeping power. We can relax knowing that He is our Keeper. Daily, God protects us and keeps us from the power of the enemy. We are sealed in the Holy Spirit and preserved for the final day of redemption when Jesus will return.

I don't know how I've done what I've done over these past years. I look back at my calendars, and I see how hard I've worked. I read some of my prayer journals and remember some of the things I've gone through with people, and the hurt I've felt. I think, *How did I ever get through that?* But God held me together. He strengthened me. He kept me. And I can see now that I worried about a lot of things I didn't have to worry about because they worked out okay anyway. God has a plan, and He is working His plan. We can trust that and relax. Psalm 145:14 says, "The Lord upholds all those [of His own] who are falling and raises up all those who are bowed down."

This continual care of God is uninterrupted in our lives. There's never a moment when He's not taking care of us. The Bible says that God never sleeps nor slumbers. When you go to sleep at night, He stays up and watches over you. You can relax.

SIMPLY BELIEVE

The Bible tells us that we are to live sanctified lives, but then it turns right around and says God will do the work to sanctify us. We are to simply put our trust in Him, hang on to the Vine, and He does the work through us, as these verses promise: "And may the God of peace Himself sanctify you through and through [separate you from profane things, make you pure and wholly consecrated to God]; and may your spirit and soul and body be preserved sound and complete [and found] blameless at the coming of our Lord Jesus Christ (the Messiah). Faithful is He Who is calling you [to Himself] and utterly trustworthy, and He will also do it [fulfill His call by hallowing and keeping you]" (1 Thessalonians 5:23-24).

The disciples asked Jesus, "What must we do to be working the works of God? What must we do to please God?"

Jesus replied, "This is the work (service) that God asks of you: that you believe in the One Whom He has sent [that you cleave to, trust, rely on, and have faith in His Messenger]" (John 6:29).

Joy and peace are found in believing, according to Romans 15:13. Simple, childlike believing enables us to live with an ease that releases joy and peace. Hebrews 4 teaches us that those who have believed enter the rest of God.

As believers, we are supposed to *believe*. Otherwise we'd be called *achievers*. But we're *believers*, and to be believers we must first learn how to *be* instead of *do*.

Relax; all the good things that God has planned for you will come to you through Him, not through your works. Romans 11:36 confirms, "For from Him and through Him and to Him are all things. [For all things originate with Him and come from Him; all things live through Him, and all things center in and tend to consummate and to end in Him.] To Him be glory forever! Amen (so be it)."

To be at peace with God, we have to learn how to *maintain* peace. Maintaining requires watchfulness and daily attention. As we will continue studying in the next chapter, we must avoid strife with others in order to stay supernaturally relaxed.

AVOID STRIFE TO MAINTAIN PEACE WITH GOD

I've discovered over the years that peace is one of the greatest gifts God has given to us. But Satan works incessantly to steal our peace, so we must be aware of his tactics and be determined to live peaceful lives so we can live powerful lives. Once we have peace with God, we must learn to maintain it in order to enjoy it every day of our lives. Maintaining peace means that we must pursue peace, crave it, and go after it with all of our might.

Peace and power work together. Peace allows the anointing of God's presence to flow through our lives. That grace gives us the power to live the way God wants us to live, and to enjoy what God has provided for us.

I believe that the level of peace we walk in and the level of prosperity we have are directly connected. We can prosper from God's blessings, but if we lose our peace in the process, we may also lose our prosperity too.

The loss of peace opens a door for the devil to rob us. Ephesians 4:26–27 verifies this when it says if we become angry, we should not let the sun go down on our anger. It says we should not give the devil any such foothold in our lives.

There was a time when our ministry was growing so fast that it was actually creating problems. We couldn't hire enough people. We didn't have enough space, and we had difficulty keeping up with the growth. It was important to keep our peace, but I felt that we were running to keep up with God all the time. He was blessing us, but we had to learn how to handle the blessings and stay peaceful.

The loss of peace can come from anything that causes us to feel we are on overload. Problems may make us feel that way, and even success and growth can make us feel overwhelmed sometimes. At that time in our ministry, we suddenly found ourselves needing to deal with things we had never dealt with before, and we had to learn to trust God in an entirely new way.

We wanted to grow and prosper, but we strongly felt that God had instructed us to maintain our peace in order to do so. God works in an atmosphere of peace, not in turmoil and strife. I believe that God opens the door for many people to be blessed, but they quickly lose the blessing because they allow their emotions to rule when they should be diligent to walk in peace.

One of the ways we maintain peace with God is by maintaining peace with the people in our lives. Our new growth meant we had to make a lot of new decisions, and Dave and I had to work at staying out of strife because we did not always agree.

Avoiding strife with people is such an important aspect of peace that I have devoted an entire section of this book, which you will read later, to teach the various ways God has taught me to maintain peace with others as unto the Lord. But because the way we treat other people is important to God, I also want to make clear how maintaining peace in our relationships with others helps us to be at peace with God.

God does not like it if I mistreat someone. It grieves His Holy Spirit, and I feel a sudden loss of peace. I remember one night when I could not sleep. I tossed and turned until five o'clock, at which time I finally asked, "Lord, what is wrong with me? Why can't I sleep?"

He instantly showed me a situation from the previous day when I was quite impatient and rude to someone. I never apologized; I justified my actions and went on my way. I had grieved the Holy Spirit, and the loss of peace was keeping me awake. As soon as I repented of my sin, my peace returned and I went to sleep. And the next day, I also apologized to the person as soon as I could.

As servants of the Lord, we must not have strife, because where there is strife, there is neither power to enjoy life nor prosperity in any area, including our relationships. Peace and prosperity are two components of the abundant life that God wants us to have. We cannot represent Him properly if we are in strife.

The relationship between Abram (later Abraham) and Lot illustrates the importance of maintaining peace in our relationships with others. Genesis 12 records the covenant of peace that God made with Abraham and his heirs. Abraham became extremely rich and powerful because God blessed him. God chose him to be the man through whom He would bless all the nations on the face of the earth.

I find it interesting that in the very next chapter, Genesis 13, strife came between the herdsmen of Lot and Abraham's cattle (see v. 7). Strife is the exact opposite of peace. God gave Abraham peace, and Satan went immediately to stir up strife. God wanted to bless Abraham, and Satan wanted to steal his blessing.

Sometimes God's abundance can cause problems that lead to strife. He had blessed Abraham and Lot with so many possessions and cattle that the land could not nourish and support them. They had to regroup.

The Bible says that Abraham went to Lot and said, "Let there be no strife, I beg of you, between you and me, or between your herdsmen and my herdsmen" (Genesis 13:8). He told Lot that they were going to have to separate, so Lot should choose the land he wanted, and Abraham would take what was left.

Abraham took a humble position to avoid strife, knowing that if he did what was right, God would always bless him. But Lot, who would have had nothing if Abraham hadn't given it to him, chose the best part: the Jordan Valley. Abraham didn't say a thing; he just took the leftovers. He knew God would bless him if he stayed in peace. People who walk in peace in order to honor God cannot lose in life.

But then God took Abraham up on a hill and said, "Now, you look to the north, to the south, to the east, and the west—and everything you see, I'll give to you" (see vv. 14–15). What a great deal! Abraham gave up one valley, and God gave him everything he could see.

HUMILITY BRINGS PEACE

God honored Abraham's humility and blessed him abundantly with fruitful land. I believe that God's got a good plan for all of us, but prideful attitudes can prevent us from having all that God wants us to have. A bad attitude is one of the most important things on which we can work with God to overcome.

The Bible says that strife and contention come only by pride. You cannot have strife if you don't have pride. Pride was Lucifer's sin, and it is so deceptive that proud people don't know that they are proud. When people are deceived by pride, they blame others for everything that goes wrong and fail to see their own faults.

Romans 12:16–17 says,

Live in harmony with one another; do not be haughty (snobbish, high-minded, exclusive), but readily adjust yourself to [people, things] and give yourselves to humble tasks. Never overestimate yourself or be wise in your own conceits. Repay no one evil for evil, but take thought for what is honest and proper and noble [aiming to be above reproach] in the sight of everyone.

Some people are basically impossible to get along with, but I love Romans 12:18, which says, "*If possible, as far as it depends on you,* live at peace with everyone" (italics mine). We can't do their part, but we *must* do our part of maintaining peace with others.

I challenge you to be a maker and a maintainer of peace today and every day of your life. Go the extra mile to keep peace—even if it means apologizing to somebody when you really don't think you're wrong. I'm not suggesting that you let everybody take advantage of you. But I am suggesting that you live life with humility so you can enjoy peace and the blessings that result from it.

The Bible says there are times that we will look like sheep being led to the slaughter. But right in the midst of all these things, we are more than conquerors. If two people are arguing, the one who is proud, stubborn, and refuses to apologize is the loser, not the winner. The one who looks like a sheep on his way to disaster but humbles himself and says, "Look, I don't want any trouble. If I was wrong, I'm sorry. Please forgive me" is the winner. He took the position that Jesus would have taken if He were there, dealing with that same situation.

Humility is *hard* on our flesh. But the Bible tells us to walk in the Spirit, not in the flesh. We need to learn how to follow the leading of the Holy Spirit. We also need to recognize when we are not following the ways of the Lord.

People use the phrase, "Well, I got in the flesh," but we need to learn how to get out of it just as quickly as we got in. We mustn't get selfish and stay that way for long periods of time. The Bible says not to let the sun go down on our anger (see Ephesians 4:26). God knew there would be times when we would get angry, but as soon as we know we're angry, we can keep that emotion from controlling us. We can come back to a place of peace before the day is over. It requires some humility and a decision.

We can be Peacemakers and Peace Maintainers. To do so, we will have to treat people nicely who haven't been so nice to us. We can have abundant lives, but we will have to do what the Bible says in order to have it. God's promises of a good life are for "whosoever will"; not just whosoever will receive the promises, but whosoever will *obey* what He tells them to do. Then the promises will be enacted in their lives.

That's why it is so important to know what the Word of God says, and let God work it out in our lives through our obedience to Him. It is hard to say we are sorry, but we can do all things through Christ. He will give us the grace to be Peacemakers.

One morning, Dave corrected me about something when I wasn't feeling good. My first thought was, *Oh my, not this morning!* I was in Africa, preaching. I was already fighting jet lag, my back was hurting, my eyes were extremely dry, I was tired, and in general I did not feel good when my husband decided to correct me.

Why is it that when somebody corrects us, the first thing we do is get mad? That's what I did. Now, I had gained a little bit of control over my emotions, so I didn't *show* my anger. But inside, I was not happy.

Naturally, the first thing we want to do when people correct us is start telling them everything that's wrong with them. Dave was describing a certain situation where he felt I hadn't shown him respect. My response was, "Well, there are many times when you don't show *me* respect."

He said, "We aren't talking about me. We're talking about you." Talk about a flesh burner! Whoa! Lord, have mercy!

Now, I've learned a few things after twenty-five years in ministry. I was getting ready to preach that morning, and I knew better than to get into the pulpit with strife in my heart! Strife steals our peace and shuts down the anointing. So, I started praying for two things.

I said, "God, help me keep my mouth shut." That's the first thing to pray for if you don't want war. Never overestimate your own ability to keep quiet just because you want to. You have to *pray* for help in this area.

Then I said, "God, if he's right . . . give me the grace to receive it." I've learned that just because we don't *think* somebody's right, that doesn't mean they're not.

It is interesting how human beings have problems with being corrected. That same spirit of pride that causes us to mistreat people will also prevent us from receiving correction.

The Bible says, "Only a fool hates correction" (see Proverbs 15:5). If you correct a wise man, he becomes wiser. If you correct a fool, he gets angry and won't even consider receiving it.

Why is it so devastating when somebody tells us we're not doing something right or tells us, "I need you to change this"? I believe that our insecurity can cause our pride to rise in defense and say, "Nobody's going tell me anything. I'm right, and everybody else is wrong." If we don't learn to recognize this Peace Stealer, we will go around the same stupid mountain, again and again, dealing with the same problems.

PRAYER BRINGS PEACE

Well, it turned out that God showed me Dave was right. I made my first round of apologies, but I really wasn't sincere. I was still a little bit mad, because though I agreed with God that Dave was right, I still didn't like the way he told me. I didn't like his attitude or his timing. I was willing to say that I was wrong, but I wanted also to talk about what Dave had done wrong. He wouldn't talk about that.

I could *feel* my flesh just screaming. I had to pray, "God, give me grace. Give me the grace to forgive. Help me talk to Dave. I don't want to talk to him. God, help me talk to him." When we get mad, a wall goes up. We say silently, "You hurt me, and I am not letting you back into my life to do it again." I know this is exactly the way we all are. Then we just become polite. We talk only if we absolutely have to and use very few words. We answer questions with a simple yes or no, but we offer no further conversation. We avoid the person who hurt us as much as possible.

Dave knew I was hurting, but he also knew I was really trying to do what was right. Even when we are trying to do right, our flesh can still hurt. God's Word teaches us we are to die to self. That means we say yes to God and His will and no to our flesh that wants to rebel. Dave reached out and patted me on the arm or leg to show love and understanding while I was trying to get over the correction he gave me.

We were traveling with many people on the plane that day, but I didn't want to talk to anybody. They were all asking, "Why are you so quiet?"

I said, "I'm just having a quiet day." But the truth was I was hurting too bad to talk. My emotions were whacko, and I really wanted to just be left alone. The entire day was a struggle for me not to cry or scream. It was very difficult for me to be civil to people, but I knew that God was dealing with me and correcting me. I knew I needed to submit to His dealings if I was going to make progress and overcome in the area of being disrespectful.

Sometimes, even after we choose to do what is right, we may hurt for a while. It is the pain that is doing the good work in us. It is actually changing us and making us better.

I have learned that if we don't listen to God when He tries to correct us, then He will bring pressure from some other direction to get our attention. I am sure God had been dealing with me for a long time about my disrespectful attitude toward Dave and some of the wrong things I said to him, but I was not listening to God. So he led Dave to correct me.

I had a bad habit, and God knew that He needed to help me get free if I was going to do all He had for me to do in the ministry. The Lord wanted to bless my life, but my attitude was hindering Him.

I kept praying for God to give me grace to submit to His dealing and no longer be angry with Dave. I wanted to do right and knew that grace is the power of the Holy Spirit to help us do what we can't. After some time went by, I felt much better and knew God had done a work in me that would help me enjoy more peace in my life.

If you want to be a maker and maintainer of peace when some-body hurts you, you better not think that you can do it just by decision or self-will. Start praying, because emotions are strong, and they are a controlling force in our lives. Pride gets all tangled up in our emotions and causes strife and eventually lots of broken relationships.

Strife causes stress that can even lead to sickness and disease. God did not create us to live in the war zone all the time. We are supposed to have peace, and when something happens to disturb our peace, we have to work to get it back.

We've seen that the Word says to live in harmony with others, and be ready to adapt and adjust ourselves to people. We want them to adapt to us, but God puts the responsibility on *each one* of us to give ourselves to humble tasks.

When Dave corrected me, it didn't really take me all that long to get my attitude right again. Well, perhaps it was a couple of days (though it seemed like a month), but forty-eight hours was a big improvement over the way I used to stay offended for weeks. Isn't it amazing how time goes so slowly when we're upset about something?

Finally, I knew that I had the grace to give a sincere apology. So, I said to my husband, "Look, I'm really sorry. If I've ever spoken disrespectfully, please forgive me. I don't want to do that, but you know my mouth gets me into trouble sometimes." Everything was fine after that. Peace returned!

God has dealt with me since then about my mouth. Most of us say things that hurt and wound other people. I probably will have to endure correction in this area again, but I really do want to be all that God wants me to be. My desire to please God motivates me to go through whatever I need to in order to be in His perfect will.

PEACE RELEASES ANOINTING

I encourage you always to pursue peace. You won't have peace with God until you have peace with the people He has placed in your life. It is important to understand that in order to have peace with God, you must work through whatever issues are causing strife in your life and quickly bring closure to them. Don't pretend everything is okay when you are eaten up inside with strife.

God knows everything that goes on behind closed doors, including the doors to our hearts. If our relationships aren't right, our lives won't be right. And if our private lives are not right, our public lives are not right. Whatever we do in private affects our public lives and ministries.

Pride will absolutely ruin us. But the mighty God who dwells inside of us gives us the power to humble ourselves and say, "I'm sorry," even if we don't feel like it.

If you need to come to a new level of peace in your life, make a decision to become a maker and maintainer of peace. The Word says, "Blessed (enjoying enviable happiness, spiritually prosperous—with life-joy and satisfaction in God's favor . . . regardless of their outward conditions) are the makers and maintainers of peace, for they shall be called the sons of God!" (Matthew 5:9).

It's one thing to be a *child of God,* but to be called a *son* or a *daughter of God* implies a level of maturity: someone who can handle blessing, responsibility, and authority that children cannot manage.

The blessing of peace keeps the anointing and power of God flowing through our lives so that, like Abraham, we can bless other people on God's behalf. God gives gifts to people, and He wants to fill those gifts with His anointed presence to bring blessing. It might be a gift to preach and teach God's Word, to sing, to lead, to encourage, or to administrate.

There are certain character qualities that God will bless (anoint with power) and certain qualities that He won't. Exodus 29 gives a detailed description of where the priest was to put the anointing oil. It was to be on the utensils, the altar, the priest's garments, and the turban on his head, but he was not to put anointing oil upon the flesh. God will not anoint our fleshly actions or our fleshly behavior.

We have to learn to surrender our wills to God and let the Holy Spirit lead us if we want to maintain peace and carry its anointing power in our lives. But first and foremost, I encourage you to pursue peace through prayer today, and be determined to keep the strife out of your life. Without peace you won't have the power to enjoy life. Pursue peace with God, with yourself, and with your fellow man.

If you lack peace, pray something like this: "Father, I pray for peace with You. I don't understand everything that is going on in my life. It's not going the way I want it, but I am deciding to trust You. Help me to have peaceful relationships, and give me the power (the anointing of Your grace) to be a maker and a maintainer of peace with others, in the name of Jesus. Amen."

In the next part of this book, I will explain seven ways that I found to have peace with myself before I could focus on keeping peace with others. Through wisdom from God's Word, you can learn to have peace and enjoy your life every day, wherever you are. So next, let's look at how slowing down will help you to keep peace with yourself.

Part 2

BE AT PEACE
WITH YOURSELF

Now the mind of the flesh [which is sense and reason without the Holy Spirit] is death [death that comprises all the miseries arising from sin, both here and hereafter]. But the mind of the [Holy] Spirit is life and [soul] peace [both now and forever].

—The apostle Paul, *Romans 8:6*

STOP RUSHING

Much of the world is in a hurry, always rushing, yet very few people even know where they are going in life. If we want to be at peace with ourselves and enjoy life, we must stop rushing all the time.

People rush to get to yet another event that has no real meaning for them, or that they really don't even want to attend. *Hurry* is the pace of the twenty-first century; rushing has become a disease of epidemic proportions. We hurry so much, we finally come to the place where we cannot slow down.

I can remember the days when I worked so hard and hurried so much that even if I took a vacation, it was almost over by the time I geared down enough to rest. Hurry was definitely one of the Peace Stealers in my life and still can be, if I do not stay alert to its pressure.

Life is too precious to rush through it. I find at times that a day has gone by in a blur; at the conclusion of it I know I was very busy all day yet cannot really remember enjoying much, if any, of it. I have committed to learn to do things in God's rhythm, not the world's pace.

Jesus was never in a hurry when He was here on earth, and God is absolutely not in a hurry now. Ecclesiastes 3:1 states, "TO EVERYTHING there is a season, and a time for every matter or purpose under heaven." We should let each thing in our lives have its season and realize we can enjoy that season without rushing into the next one.

It is permissible to enjoy our morning coffee or tea without feeling we must hurry to get to the next thing. We can get dressed calmly without rushing. We can leave the house in a timely fashion, without frantically running out the door already behind schedule. Rushing is a bad habit, but we can break bad habits and form good ones to replace them.

The way we get a day started is important. Often how we start is how the entire day goes. I have found if I allow the "hurry-up" spirit to grab me early in the day, everything within me gets into high gear, and I never seem to slow down or really relax the rest of the day. Hurry creates pressure that in turn creates stress.

Stress is the root cause of many illnesses and is therefore something each one of us desperately needs to resolve. God did not create us to hurry, rush, live under pressure and stress day after day. Jesus said, "My peace I leave with you." He wants us to have peace.

Pace is very important in life. Our pace not only affects us but others around us. I don't like to be around people who are always in a rush; they are usually short-tempered and impatient. They certainly don't minister peace. They make me feel as if I also need to hurry, which I am desperately trying to avoid.

I have noticed in fine-dining restaurants that the hostess who seats people walks very slowly while leading customers to their tables. The waiters or waitresses don't rush the table for orders; they give you plenty of time to think. I am sure this is because they want the customers to enjoy their experience, and they know that will not be possible if they are rushed.

When following one of the hostesses who is exuding peace simply by the way she walks me to the table, often I am behind her thinking, *Get going, you're moving too slow.* Then I am reminded (I am sure by the Holy Spirit) that I don't need to be in a hurry to enjoy the nice meal I am about to pay for.

Our pace of living affects the quality of our lives. When we eat too fast, we don't properly digest our food; when we rush through life, we don't properly digest it either. God has given life to us as a gift, and what a pitiful shame to do nothing but rush through each day and never, as they say, "stop to smell the roses." Each thing we do in life has a sweet fragrance, and we should learn to take it into ourselves and enjoy the aroma.

RUSHING BEGINS IN THE MIND

Rushing begins in the mind, just as all actions do. *I have to hurry* is a thought pattern we should avoid. When other people say to us, "Hurry up!" we can learn to resist following their suggestion or demand. It unsettles us and makes us feel rushed when thoughts constantly fly through our minds, one following upon another (especially thoughts that go in many different directions).

Those of us who have a bad habit of rushing need to decide that we don't have to do this. We can do only one thing at a time! When we hurry, we make more mistakes and often forget things that end up costing us more time than we would have used had we maintained a godly pace.

Did you know that you can think things on purpose? You can choose what you think about, and by doing so you help assure what your actions will be. Yes, you can purposefully think thoughts such as *I don't have to hurry. I have time to do whatever I need to do.* Speaking such affirmations out loud is also helpful.

Positive statements help give direction for future actions. Get up in the morning, and as soon as you feel rushed, say, "I am glad I don't have to hurry. I have all the time I need. I will do things today at a pace that enables me to enjoy each task."

This may sound strange, but the Bible teaches us to speak of the nonexistent things that God has foretold and promised as if they already exist (see Romans 4:17). God created the world with words, our words also hold creative power; words affect our futures. Take a step of faith, and try saying what you want, not just what you have at the current time, and I believe you will enjoy positive results.

If we feel hurried, we usually say, "I am so sick and tired of hurrying all the time! That is all I ever do: hurry, hurry, hurry." Statements like those may be facts describing the way things are, but circumstances don't have to stay that way. I repeat, *say what you want, not what you have.*

Peace of mind must precede peace in our lives. This verse promises perfect peace to those who keep their minds on God: "You will guard him and keep him in perfect and constant peace whose mind [both its inclination and its character] is stayed on You, because he commits himself to You, leans on You, and hopes confidently in You" (Isaiah 26:3).

Thinking too much about everything we have to do sets the wheels in motion for rushing. We often feel overwhelmed when we think of all the future will require of us. This type of thinking is called *anxiety.* As we discussed earlier, when we spend today trying to figure out tomorrow, we struggle simply because God gives us grace, which is His strength and power, one day at a time. When we try to live tomorrow today, even if only in our minds, we feel pressured and begin to lose peace.

We will never enjoy the peaceful and fruitful lives that God intends for us unless we learn to think right. I repeat what I have said on many occasions: *Where the mind goes, the man follows.*

LEARN TO LIVE WITH MARGIN

Living without margin is one of the main reasons we feel we need to hurry. To live with margin means to leave room on either side of planned events or appointments to take care of unexpected things that come up. We seem to plan our days in an unrealistic way, as if everything will go exactly according to our plans and desires, which it never does. One unplanned phone call or traffic jam can change our entire timetable. One set of misplaced car keys can upset a whole day's scheduling.

I was feeling tremendously rushed every day at the office. I raced in and flew through my many appointments, and I am sure that I made all the people I met with feel as if I could hardly wait to get rid of them. I was always behind schedule and never got finished. At the end of every day, I was frustrated and went home feeling totally drained. It was so bad that I actually got to the point where I literally despised even going to the office.

Then I learned about the principle of adding margin to my life, and I feel like a new person. I told my secretary that I wanted her to find out how much time each person who needed to meet with me felt he would require, and then just add ten to fifteen minutes to each appointment. This margin would cover any unexpected things that came up during the meeting, and if we didn't use the margin, it would be an extra blessing.

Now, one of our managers might be scheduled to meet with me for one hour, but when we finish in forty minutes, it is glorious! I almost always get finished with my day's schedule and usually have some time to spare. Adding margin has been one of the biggest blessings in my life. I was always the type of person who never wanted to waste one moment, therefore, I planned everything to the second so I had no downtime.

If Dave and I needed to be on a flight leaving at ten o'clock, I wanted to arrive at 9:30 or 9:45, rush through the ticket counter, run down the hall, and hurry to get on the plane. Dave refused to do this because he is not a person who is willing to hurry. He has one pace—it is called *Peaceful*. He insisted we arrive at the airport no less than one hour early; this caused many arguments between us literally for years. I must say, though, that he was right, and I was wrong.

Having breathing room between planned events of the day is healthy, and it is actually mandatory if one is intending to enjoy his or her life.

One of the worst things a person can become is a busy man or woman. I have noticed upon meeting people and asking how they are that most respond, "Busy," and many say, "Tired." Surely life is meant to be more. If our testimony of life is "I'm busy and tired," that is very sad indeed.

Margin is another word for *wisdom*. It makes absolutely no sense to live without it, and nothing truly succeeds without it. We know from experience that we always encounter things we did not plan for, so why not plan for the unplanned, which is what margin is?

KNOW YOUR LIMITS

We are not all alike, nor do we all have the same tolerance level. Some people, by virtue of their temperaments or even natural stamina, can do more than others. Know yourself, and don't be ashamed to admit you have limits. Don't try to keep up with some other busy person you know—just be yourself.

I can accomplish a lot; I thrive on activity. Some of the people who work with me comment often that they don't know how I do all that I do. God has given me a lot of natural drive, and I am very passionate about what I am called to do; but I have had to face the fact that I have my limits, and so does everyone else.

I spent years pushing past my limits and eventually became ill and very discouraged, thinking, *If this is all life is, I would rather go to heaven.* After pushing myself beyond reason and becoming very ill three different times, I knew I needed to change.

I finally admitted I had limits and saw that it was not wrong to have them. I had to face the fact that I was not able to do everything I or other people wanted me to do. I had to make choices just like everyone else. I had to be willing to say no to people who wanted to hear yes, and even to things I really wanted to do.

High achievers often feel it is a personal failure to say, "I can't do any more than I am doing." That is, of course, wrong thinking, and Satan uses condemnation to destroy people. Many "driven" people are just insecure people who are getting their worth and value from their accomplishments in life.

I heard a story about a woman who worked in a shipyard, and her job was cleaning the ships. She believed that her job had value because she was doing it, not that her value was based on the job she did. This gave her wonderful freedom to enjoy herself, her job, and all of life. Many people would feel belittled by her job, but not her—she knew *she* had value. Our attitudes about ourselves really do affect all of our lives.

Learning that my worth and value are rooted in God through Christ has been life-changing. Quite often, people strive to have prestigious jobs so they feel important; this causes a lot of heartache in life. I know because I experienced it. I once was seeking promotion and success, but for all the wrong reasons. We could all learn a lesson from this woman's story. *You make what you do important;* you are not important because you do it.

I believe that some people don't have peace with themselves because they actually don't approve of themselves, and they overcommit while trying to find worth. They stay busy trying to accomplish something that will make them feel important and valuable. When we come to terms of peace with ourselves, we don't have to live to impress people; we are free to follow the Holy Spirit, who always leads us into peace and balanced living.

"I can do all things through Christ" (Philippians 4:13 KJV) doesn't mean what some people try to make it mean. We can do *what we are called to do,* but we cannot do everything *we would like to do,* nor everything everyone else would like us to do. We have limits! God Himself has placed these limits on us. Only He has no limits. He gives us the energy and grace to do what He wants us to do. Jesus said He came that we might have and enjoy life, and I don't believe that is possible as long as we are rushing.

God gives us all gifts and talents, but they are not all the same. The Giver of the gifts is the same, but the gifts differ. He hands them out according to His will and for His overall purpose in life. God makes sure that everything in life is taken care of.

Sometimes Dave and I notice people doing jobs like washing

windows on high-rise buildings or walking on construction beams high in the air, and we marvel that God calls someone to do every task that needs to be done. We would not want to do what these people seem to enjoy doing, but then they probably would not want to do what we do either. It has been helpful to me to realize that God gives us all talents and limits. We can do well and with peace only what God has assigned to us. Being overcommitted in order to feel good about ourselves is not wisdom and will never minister peace.

According to James Dobson, overcommitment is the number-one marriage killer. I have discovered that Satan wants us to be either uncommitted or overcommitted. His entire goal is to keep us out of balance, one way or the other. First Peter 5:8 says, "Be well balanced . . . for that enemy of yours, the devil, roams around like a lion roaring . . . seeking someone to . . . devour." Satan cannot devour just anyone; he has to find someone who is out of balance.

The world applauds our being overcommitted, but heaven doesn't. A busy person with too much to do is usually considered a success by the world's standards, but not by God's. How can we be successful if we fail at relationships (which are usually what suffer the most in the life of a busy person)? Most extremely busy people don't even take the time to really know themselves, let alone anyone else.

What is the point in parenting children if they are all going to be strangers to you? Why be married if you never have anything left of yourself to share with your marriage partner? I can remember coming home so tired each night that I could not even think, let alone have meaningful conversation. I thought I was doing my duty, being responsible—but now I realize I was being deceived, and the deception was aimed at destroying the life Jesus desired for me to have.

Don't give your family and friends the scraps you have left over while you give the world your best. The world will let you down in the end. It will take everything you have and disappear when you are in need. I don't mean to sound cynical, but even Scripture verifies my comment. Solomon wrote, "So I hated life, because what is done under the sun was grievous to me; for all is vanity and a striving after the wind and a feeding on it. And I hated all my labor in which I had toiled under the sun, seeing that I must leave it to the man who will succeed me" (Ecclesiastes 2:17–18).

The writer of Ecclesiastes was a "busy" man, one who tried everything that could be tried and did everything there was to do. Yet, at the end of his experience, he was unfulfilled and bitter.

How many people have given all of themselves to something that never gave anything back? A great example of this is what motivational teachers refer to as "climbing the ladder to success only to find that it was leaning against the wrong building." It's true, I've never heard of any person who has said on his or her deathbed, "Gee, I really wish I had spent more time at the office."

I recently talked with a woman in ministry whom I have known for many years. I saw her at one of my conferences and noticed right away that she seemed unhappy and totally worn-out. The joy, zeal, and enthusiasm she had previously were no longer there. I invited her to come early the next day and speak with me.

When I asked her if she was all right, she told me that she had a serious case of burnout. She said, "For the first time, I am not enjoying everyday life. I have worked so hard and given myself to meet everyone's needs without requiring anything for myself. Now I am bordering on being bitter and fighting the temptation to quit and give up."

This woman needed balance; she needed to review all of her commitments and see which ones were really producing the fruit she was called to produce. Not everything that seems good is actually God's will for an individual. In fact, *good* is often the enemy of the *best*. We can easily lose our focus and get sidetracked. We are busy all the time, we work hard, but we don't get the things accomplished that minister fulfillment to us as individuals.

I believe when we are in the will of God and giving ourselves to what He has called us to do, we will sense satisfaction and fulfillment. We will get tired, but it will be a tired we recover from, not one that never goes away. When we are flowing in God's will, our schedules always leave time for good relationships.

Great relationships are one of the most precious treasures in life, but we must feed them regularly by putting time into them. If you find you have no time to develop and maintain strong, intimate relationships with God, with yourself, and with your family and friends, then you are absolutely too busy.

We all need to take a serious inventory of what we are doing with our time, get out the pruning shears, and as the Spirit of God leads, cut things out of our lives until we no longer have to rush. *Then* we will be able to live with peace and joy.

Realizing that we have limits and cannot do everything, and then making choices to do what is most important, will definitely increase our level of peace. Peace equals power; without it, we live weak, frustrated lives. Remember, we should strive to let the peace of God rule in our lives as an umpire. If we have peace, we can keep doing what we are doing, but if we do not have peace, we know we need to make a change. If you hear yourself complaining all the time, it is an indication that you need to make some adjustments. If you are doing what God wants you to do, you should not be complaining about it.

Take Charge of Your Schedule

I remember murmuring about my schedule to the Lord, complaining how terribly busy I always was. He responded in my heart by saying, "You make your schedule. If you don't like it, change it. I never told you that you had to do all the things you are doing." He put the responsibility right back on me.

If we are honest, we really are the only ones who can do anything about the busyness of our lives. We complain frequently about being overworked and too involved, but we never do anything about it. We expect everyone to feel sorry for us because we are under pressure that we place on ourselves. We say we would love to have just one free evening at home with nothing to do. Yet when, by some miracle of God, we find ourselves alone for the evening, we are so tense from all our other hurrying that we cannot sit still and enjoy it.

One evening at about 5:15 PM, when I was home alone working on this book, our electricity suddenly went out. We were without power for three hours, and I was absolutely amazed at how I kept looking for something I could do. I eventually decided I would go to my aunt's house because she did have power, so I could find something to do there. I got in my car, started it, headed down the driveway, pushed the button to open our electric gate, and realized we had no electricity, therefore the gate would not open. There was a way to open it manually, but I didn't know how.

I finally thought, *Well, I guess God has trapped me in this house with absolutely nothing to do but look out the window, and He probably has a lesson in it for me.* Perhaps the lesson is found in Psalm 46:10: "Be still, and know that I am God" (KJV)!

Two days later we had a bad storm, actually one of the worst I can remember, and hundreds of thousands of homes—including ours—in St. Louis were without power for over twenty-four hours. I settled in more quickly the second time but found it amusing to watch how not only I, but also others in our neighborhood responded to having nothing to do. One of our sons, who had shared that day how tired he was from a recent trip and needed to rest that evening, got in his car and went to the office because the power was on there. I think it is safe to say that most of us are addicted to activity.

Make your own schedule. Don't allow circumstances and demands from other people to make it for you. Simplify life. Do what you really need to do, but don't be afraid to say no to things that take your time yet produce few positive results.

I recently spoke with a young woman who had a husband, small children, and a part-time job. She shared how she felt so pressured by all of life, and how she committed to things, then resented doing them. She was even beginning to resent the people who were asking her to do them. Her attitude was becoming bitter, and she was confused.

I strongly encouraged her to be realistic about what she could sanely accomplish and remain peaceful. I suggested that she simplify her life as much as possible. In other words, I encouraged her to be in charge of her own schedule.

BE HONEST WITH YOURSELF

What is stress? Stress is too much to do in too little time. A fight with someone you love. A boss who is never pleased. Car trouble. Too little money and too many bills. Another red light when you are already late. The Internet not working when you desperately need it.

Actually, situations themselves do not cause stress; it is our re-action to the situation that is the real problem. For example, we blame the red light for being there at the wrong time when, in real-ity, we should have left home sooner, leaving some margin in our schedule. Only the truth makes us free. As long as we are making excuses for the stress in our lives rather than taking responsibility, we will never experience change.

I spent years trying to get rid of everything that bothered me and found out it was impossible. I wanted all of the people around me to change so they would never upset me; I also discovered that is not going to happen. Out of desperation to enjoy peace in my life, I became willing to change my approach to life. One of the things I had to do was slow down!

In 2 Timothy 4:5, Paul gave Timothy instructions about his life and ministry, saying, "As for you, be calm and cool and steady, accept and suffer unflinchingly every hardship, do the work of an evangelist, fully perform all the duties of your ministry." Paul then said, "I am . . . about to be sacrificed [my life is about to be poured out as a drink offering]" (v. 6). Paul knew his time on earth was almost up, and he was giving Timothy instructions that he might not get another opportunity to give.

If we were dying and wanted to impart last words to those we were training, I believe we would choose things we felt were very important. Paul said, "Be calm"; in other words, "Don't let things upset you. Live your life at a pace that enables you to enjoy it. Even when difficulties arise, accept them, and keep doing what God has called you to do."

Calm is the picture I get of Jesus when I think of Him and His earthly ministry. (We will talk more about the fruit of living a calm life in a later chapter.) I don't ever picture Jesus rushing from one thing to the next, being impatient with people who were not moving as fast as He wanted them to. Jesus lived in a manner that allowed Him to be discerning about what was going on around Him. He knew of danger before it approached and was able to avoid things that Satan had planned for His destruction. We need this kind of spiritual sensitivity in our own lives. We will not have it if we don't slow down.

CAREFULLY CHOOSE
WHAT YOU NEED TO BE INVOLVED IN

We cannot be involved in everything and remain calm, cool, and steady. My own definition of hurry is this: *Hurry is our flesh trying to do more than the Spirit is leading us to do.* If God is leading us to do something, surely we should be able to do it and remain peaceful. He is the Author and Finisher of our faith, according to Hebrews 12:2, but He is not obligated to finish anything He did not begin. Often we begin projects in the flesh, and when we feel overwhelmed, we start praying for God to do something. We should learn to pray *before* we make plans, not afterwards.

Don't engage in everything that is going on around you. Choose carefully what activities you need to participate in. I often refer to it as "choosing your battles carefully." There are many things I could get involved in at my office that I have learned to just stay out of and let some other qualified person handle. Previously, I wanted to be part of everything, especially things that pertained to some problem at the ministry. I learned the hard way that I simply cannot be involved in everything; too much is going on for me to do that. I pick my battles now, and it has greatly increased my level of peace.

Moses was trying to be involved in too much, and in a moment of intense frustration, he told God the burden was too heavy for him. The Lord told him to choose seventy other qualified men, whom He would anoint to give them authority, then let them help with the burden of trying to lead millions of people through the wilderness (see Numbers 11).

If we don't learn to delegate work and authority, we will always feel overwhelmed. Please notice I said, work *and* authority. Don't ever give someone responsibility without the authority that goes with it. I found myself at times trying to give someone else a job to do while still wanting to be in control of it. By doing this, I was not relieved of the burden I had. My actions said to the other person, "I don't really trust you," which destroyed that person's confidence and affected the outcome of his work.

In Exodus 18, we see another situation in which Moses was overworked, only this time Moses' father-in-law, Jethro, saw all that Moses was doing for the people and told him it was too much. There are times in our lives when someone else will recognize what we can't see. We should be open to hearing that it is time to delegate some of our workload to another qualified individual.

Jethro told Moses that if he did not make a change, he would wear out both himself and the Israelites. Even people get worn-out when we don't let them help us, if God has put them in our lives for that purpose. They will feel stifled, unfulfilled, and frustrated. I believe we frequently lose people because we will not permit them to do what God has assigned them. If you have the idea that you are the only one who can do what needs to be done, you need to seriously consider what I am saying. Don't let pride destroy you—ask for help!

Exodus 18 talks about leaders who could oversee thousands, hundreds, fifties, and tens of people. Not everyone is qualified to lead the same number. If you are anointed to lead thousands and won't let others lead the tens, fifties, and hundreds, you will burn out, lose your peace, and not enjoy your work or your life.

Moses was wise enough to heed what his father-in-law said. He began to judge only the hard cases among the people while allowing other qualified people to judge the easier ones. He actually preserved his ministry by asking for help. We often have the mistaken idea that if we let others help us, we will be losing something, when actually the exact opposite is true.

I firmly believe that God provides for whatever He assigns to us. He will make sure we have all the people we need to help us, but it is not their fault if we won't rely on them.

If you find yourself trying to do something and you don't have the help you need, you might need to ask yourself if you are doing the right thing. Why would God ask you to do something, then sit by and watch you be frustrated and miserable because the burden is too much? God meets all of our needs, including the people we need to work alongside us. This passage of Scripture gives an example of this act of wisdom.

So the Twelve [apostles] convened the multitude of the disciples and said, It is not seemly or desirable or right that we should have to give up or neglect [preaching] the Word of God in order to attend to serving at tables and superintending the distribution of food. Therefore select out from among yourselves, brethren, seven men of good and attested character and repute, full of the [Holy] Spirit and wisdom, whom we may assign to look after this business and duty. But we will continue to devote ourselves steadfastly to prayer and the ministry of the Word. (Acts 6:2–4)

Had the apostles not recognized their need for help, their priorities would have remained out of line and their true assignment unfulfilled. They would have ended up frustrated, just like the people they were trying to serve. They could have lost their peace, and therefore, their power. It is very possible that the loss of peace was what triggered their decision to ask for help. This is a very good example for us to follow.

A mother can delegate some of the household chores to her children. True, they may not do the job as perfectly as she would, but they will relieve some pressure and also learn, as time goes by, to do chores with more excellence. No matter what station we are in, we can always delegate some of our responsibilities to others at the right time, therefore making it possible to do what we are assigned to do in life with peace and enjoyment. When you start to feel frustrated and begin losing your peace, ask yourself what you are doing that you could delegate to someone else.

I heard a man say that his wife desperately needed more time, so she "bought" some by hiring household help to do some of the chores. I thought this was a good way to look at it. We all feel occasionally that we are out of time—that there is never enough. "Buy" some time by either hiring someone to help or assigning chores to available people.

Once again, I want to stress that whoever you assign to jobs probably won't do the job *exactly* the way you would. Look for a good outcome, and don't be so concerned about the methods they use. We may all get to the same place by taking a different route, but the important thing is that we arrive. One person may prefer dusting the house before vacuuming the floors, while another may want to vacuum first and dust later. I can't see that it makes any difference as long as both jobs get done. We should be humble enough to admit that *our way* of doing things is not the *only way.*

When we have to consistently hurry, we have not managed our lives well. We have shoved too many things into too little space, or we are trying to do more than our share and not allowing others to help us.

Once you learn to slow down, you will have time to evaluate your real priorities in life. The first place I suggest you begin is in self-acceptance. In the next chapter we will observe how deep peace begins when you learn to love who God made you to be.

ACCEPT YOURSELF

Many, perhaps even most people, are not at peace with themselves, and they may not even be aware of it. Our enemy, Satan, begins to work early in our lives, poisoning our thinking and attitudes toward ourselves. He knows we are not a threat or danger to him if we have no confidence.

Our goal is not to be self-confident but to have confidence in who we are in Christ. We should know the value of being children of God and the position it gives us. As children of God, we can pray boldly in faith, knowing that God hears and answers our prayers. We can look forward to the inheritance that is ours by virtue of our personal relationship with Jesus. We can enjoy righteousness, peace, joy, good health, prosperity, and success in all we lay our hands to do, intimacy with God through Jesus, and many other wonderful benefits.

We can develop godly character and be used mightily by God to lead others to Christ and help hurting people. Yes, our lives can be absolutely amazingly wonderful through Jesus; however, Satan is the deceiver, and as such, he seeks continually to steal what Jesus died to provide for us.

If you are not at peace with yourself, you won't enjoy your life. You are one person you never get away from, not even for one second. You are everywhere you go, therefore, if you don't like and accept yourself, you cannot possibly be anything other than miserable. Also, if we don't accept ourselves, we will find it hard, if not impossible, to accept others.

Our faults stand between us and self-acceptance. We think that if we could only behave better, we could like ourselves. We are proud of our strengths, natural gifts, and talents, but we despise and are embarrassed by our weaknesses. We rejoice in our successes and feel depressed about our failures. We struggle and strive for perfection, but somehow it always eludes us. Our pursuit is in vain.

Andrew Murray said in his book *Consecrated to God* that we are "not perfected, yet perfect."

PERFECT IN CHRIST

God's Word states that if we are willing to share His sufferings, we shall also share His glory (see Romans 8:17). We have a command (or perhaps it is a promise) in Matthew 5:48: "Be perfect, therefore, as your heavenly Father is perfect" (NIV).

In the past, I had always received that verse as a harsh command, yet it could be God's promise to us that because He is perfect and is working in us, we can also look forward to sharing in His perfection. I think the *Amplified Bible* makes the verse easier to understand: "You, therefore, must be perfect [growing into complete maturity of godliness in mind and character, having reached the proper height of virtue and integrity], as your heavenly Father is perfect."

The apostle Paul said that although he had not already been made perfect, he pressed on toward the goal. He then said that those of us who are imperfect should be thus minded, to let go of what was behind (mistakes) and press on. In essence, he was saying that in God's eyes, by faith in Jesus Christ, he was perfect, yet he was not totally perfected (see Philippians 3:12–15).

Was there ever a time when Jesus was not perfect? The answer must be no; we know that Jesus was and is always perfect, the spotless, sinless Lamb of God who was found worthy to take away our sins. Hebrews 7:28 confirms His perfection, saying, "For the Law sets up men in their weakness [frail, sinful, dying human beings] as high priests, but the word of [God's] oath, which [was spoken later] after the institution of the Law, [chooses and appoints as priest One Whose appointment is complete and permanent], a Son Who has been made perfect forever."

This Scripture tells us plainly that Jesus was made perfect forever, yet Hebrews 5:8–9 says that although He was a Son, He *learned* obedience through His sufferings and thereby *became* perfectly equipped to be the Author of our salvation. This makes it clear that He was perfect, yet was also being perfected. At each moment of His life, He was totally perfect, and yet He needed to be perfected through suffering in order to become our Savior.

Perfection is a state God's grace places us into through our faith in Jesus Christ, and He works in and through us in degrees of glory. I saw my babies and my grandchildren as perfect. I even said many times as I looked at them, "You are perfect." On the other hand, they had faults; they needed to mature, grow, and change.

We must learn to see ourselves in Christ, not in ourselves. Corrie ten Boom taught that if you look at the world, you will be oppressed, if you look at yourself, you will be depressed, but if you look at Jesus, you will be at rest. How true it is that if we look at ourselves—at what we are in our own abilities—we cannot be anything except depressed and totally discouraged. But when we look to Christ, "the author and perfecter of our faith," we can enter His rest and believe that He is continually working in us (Hebrews 12:2 NIV).

According to Andrew Murray, there are degrees of perfection: perfect, more perfect, and most perfect. There is perfect and waiting to be perfected. This is simply another way of saying that God has made us to be perfect, and we are growing into it. It is like a child saying, "My mother gave me her wedding dress to use when I get married, and I am growing into it year by year. It is still my dress, even though it does not fit me yet."

We always say, "Nobody is perfect." What we mean is that nobody manifests perfect behavior, and that is a correct statement. Our behavior, however, is quite different from our identities. The Bible says that faith in Jesus makes us righteous, but in our experience, we don't always do the right thing.

Well, if we are righteous, why don't we always do right? Simply because we are still growing into people who do what is right. We do less and less wrong, and more and more right, the longer we serve God. Consider this verse: "For our sake He made Christ [virtually] to be sin Who knew no sin, so that in and through Him we might become [endued with, viewed as being in, and examples of] the righteousness of God [what we ought to be, approved and acceptable and in right relationship with Him, by His goodness]" (2 Corinthians 5:21).

I have said for years, "My *who* is completely different than my *do*." In other words, who I am *in Christ* is one thing, and what I do *in myself* is a completely different thing altogether. We are to *become* examples of righteousness.

When we are born again, we receive new identities; God makes us His children, just as when my children were born, they became Meyers. They will never be more or less Meyers than they were on those days. In one moment of time, each became forever and completely a Meyer. Did they always act like a Meyer? Did they always act the way we would have liked our children who represent us to act? Of course not, but they were nonetheless Meyers.

Religion frequently teaches us to *do things right* (follow rules and regulations) to prove *we are right* with God. True Bible Christianity teaches the opposite: we cannot *do right* until God has *made us right* with Him, which He does at our new birth.

Second Corinthians 5:17 says, "Therefore, if anyone is in Christ, he is a new creation; the old has gone, the new has come!" (NIV). We suddenly become new creatures. I like to say we are new spiritual clay. We have in us the stuff we need in order to learn how to act the way God wants us to act.

It is vital for us to understand these things if we are to ever accept ourselves. We must believe that even though we are not where we need to be, neither are we where we used to be. We are, this very moment, perfect in God's eyes and on our way to perfection.

SELF-ACCEPTANCE IS A FOUNDATION FOR PEACE

We have no foundation of peace if we don't have peace with God and ourselves. Peace with God should take us to the foundational principle of having peace with ourselves. If God loves us unconditionally, then we can love ourselves unconditionally. If He accepts us, we should be able to accept ourselves. Peace within ourselves, which is self-acceptance, is based on God's *having made us* perfect and righteous in Christ; it is not based on our own works and behavior.

In His Word, God refers to us (His believers) as being "holy." Romans 12:1 says to offer our bodies a living sacrifice, "holy" and acceptable unto God. First Corinthians 3:17 explains that God's temple is "holy," and we (believers) are His temple. Ephesians 3:5 speaks of God's "holy apostles (consecrated messengers) and prophets." These Scriptures, and others like them, clearly show that God views us as holy, perfect, and righteous. We either accept it or we reject it, and the choice we make greatly affects how we view ourselves.

We are the house of God; we are His home. He has come to live in us; we are His new base of operation, so to speak. He works through us (His born-again children) to draw the world unto Himself.

He wants peace in His house! Have you ever screamed to your children, "I want some peace in this house"? I have, and chances are you have too. Hear God gently saying that to you right now, and come to terms of peace with who you are.

Accept yourself right where you are, and let God help you get to where you want to be. He loves and accepts you each step of the way. He is changing you from glory to glory (see 2 Corinthians

3:18). Get into agreement with God, and you will see new power in your life unlike anything you have experienced before.

Being at peace with yourself in light of who God is transforming you to become will give you a firm foundation upon which to build a good life. Remember, Satan wants you weak and powerless; God wants you to be strong and powerful, ready to enjoy life, so He can use you for His purposes on earth. But we cannot grow spiritually and become perfected for His use until we are at peace with ourselves.

ARE YOUR FAULTS DISTRACTING YOU?

To make spiritual progress, we need to keep our eyes on Jesus instead of ourselves. Hebrews 12:2 teaches us to look away from all that will distract us from Jesus, who leads us and is the Source of our incentive to have faith, and who will bring our faith to maturity and perfection.

When we keep our eyes (our thoughts) on everything that is wrong with us, it prevents us from paying attention to the Lord. We need to see everything that is right with Him and believe He is working to reproduce it in us rather than taking a continual inventory of all of our faults. We should not have our eyes on other people, comparing ourselves with them; we should have our eyes on Jesus. He, not other people, is our example to follow. We will eventually stand before God, not people, and give an account of our lives.

And get your eyes off yourself; don't meditate on everything you think you do right, or everything you think you do wrong. Focus on who God says you are.

The Holy Spirit will convict you in areas where you need it, and when He does, your response should not be to feel condemnation. It should be appreciation that God cares enough about you to send His Spirit daily to help you stay on the narrow path that leads to life.

When I learned to respond to God's correction (conviction) with appreciation instead of condemnation, it closed a door to Satan that I had allowed to remain open all of my life. We cannot grow without conviction of our sins, yet if we always respond with condemnation, that also prevents our growth. God intends that conviction of sin lift us up and out of wrong behavior, but condemnation presses us down and holds us prisoner to the sin. We can never get beyond something we stay condemned about.

Verbalize Your Acceptance of Yourself

Many people have a bad habit of saying negative, downgrading things about themselves. This is dangerous and wrong. Words are containers of power; they carry either creative or destructive influence. Proverbs 18:21 states that the power of life and death are in the tongue, and those who indulge it will eat the fruit of it for life or death. In other words, I can speak death or life to others, my circumstances, and myself.

Previously in my life, I had a bad habit of saying ungodly, negative things about myself. What was in my heart came out of my mouth, just as Matthew 12:34 confirms, and I saw that truth operating in my life. I had a bad attitude about myself; I didn't like myself, so I said things that were proof of what was in my heart.

I frequently ask in conferences where I am teaching, "How many of you regularly say negative, downgrading things about your own self out of your own mouth?" Most in the audience raise their hands.

Negative self-talk is a big problem that we need to seriously address. If you don't understand the tremendous power of words, please obtain and read my book entitled *Me and My Big Mouth*.

As I gained revelation from God's Word, I began to see how devastating this bad habit of speaking against myself was, and I slowly began to replace those bad things I said with good things. It was initially a step of faith, because I felt foolish standing around by myself, saying good things about myself. I started doing it when alone because I certainly did not have the boldness to say anything complimentary about myself in front of anybody. Instead of saying, "I am so stupid" when I made mistakes, I changed my response to "I made a mistake, but God loves me unconditionally, and He is changing me." Instead of saying, "I never do anything right," I said, "I am the righteousness of God in Christ, and He is working in me."

I am not suggesting that we form a habit of telling people how wonderful we think we are—that would be prideful and unacceptable behavior. But we should say good things rather than bad things when the occasion arises.

For example, if someone asks you what your gifts, talents, and abilities are, don't say, "I don't have any. I'm really not very smart." Say, "God has gifted me to do many things," and then describe the things you are good at.

Perhaps you are good at encouraging people; that is a gift from God. Or you may love simply to help people, and that is one of the greatest gifts God gives. I don't know what I would do in life if I did not have people who just help with whatever needs to be done. You may not have gifts that are "showy," but that does not make them any less important.

Ask God to forgive you for all the times you have said negative things about yourself, your life, and your future. Make a decision to start speaking in positive terms to everything in your life, including yourself.

Say out loud several times a day, "I accept myself. God has created me with His very own hand, and I am not a mistake. I have a glorious future, and I intend to go forward and greet each day with peace and joy."

For years, I wished I were just a little thinner, that my voice were not so deep, that I didn't talk so much, that I were not so straightforward in my approach to people, and so on. I have since discovered that many of the things I didn't want were the very qualities I needed in order to do what God has called me to do.

How can we ever have peace within ourselves if we always want to be something we're not? How can we have peace if we are mad at ourselves because we are what we are, or under condemnation because we are not perfected in behavior?

I recently read a statement by Watchman Nee that blessed me; he said that "we shall forever be what we are." He did not mean that God isn't changing us in behavior as we grow in Him, but he did mean that God has given each of us a specific temperament, and we shall always be, at the root, those persons God made us to be.

God gave me my bold voice and personality. I can learn not to be harsh and rude, but I will always be bold and aggressive. I am a preacher and teacher of God's Word. I am a mouth in the body of Christ, so to speak. God uses my mouth. I will always talk a lot. I can learn not to enter into idle talk, which we will discuss later, or say things that hurt people; but I will never be a quiet, soft-spoken person.

You will always be you, so accept the basic you and let God be God in your life. Stop wrestling with yourself, focus on your strengths, and enter into peace.

FOCUS ON YOUR UNIQUE STRENGTHS

Part of self-acceptance is realizing that you are unique in yourself and will never be exactly like someone else. God wants variation, not boring sameness. Actually, if we look around, we see that God is extremely creative. We enjoy different flowers, trees, birds, weather. It seems that a lot of what God has created has many varieties, even people.

Don't struggle to be a carbon copy of someone you admire. You are unique, and there is something you can do that nobody else in the entire world can do exactly the way you can. God had to teach me the all-important lesson of not comparing myself with others and competing with them or their abilities. He had to teach me to "be free to be me" before He could use me the way He had planned.

I taught home Bible studies for five years, and then for one year, God sort of sat me on a shelf and I did nothing. During that year I decided I needed to settle down and live a "normal" life. I decided I needed to be a "normal woman." I had always thought my hopes and ambitions were out of the ordinary, but Satan was tormenting me with thoughts that I was really weird and something was wrong with me.

I kept my house clean and neat but had no real interest in decorating to the degree that many of my friends did. They went to craft classes and had home-decorating parties on a regular basis. I could hardly sew a button on my husband's shirt, while one of my friends made clothes for her entire family. I felt destiny calling me while they were totally content doing things that really bored me. What they were doing was important also, it just was not what I was called to do.

I began to think that I just needed to straighten up and be what a woman "ought to be." I wasn't sure exactly what that was, so I tried to pattern myself after other women I knew. One friend was really sweet in nature, so I tried to speak softly and be sweet like her. Another had a garden and canned vegetables, so I tried that. I also took sewing lessons and attempted to make some clothes for my family. I was miserable, to say the least. I had forced myself into a mold that God had never designed for me.

All of these carnal ideas were birthed out of deep-rooted insecurities left over from my abusive past. I was insecure in who I was, I felt deeply flawed, and I had a shame-based nature, so I kept trying to reshape myself into what seemed acceptable to the world.

Woman preachers were not exactly at the top of the list of what the world applauded, especially in 1976 when I began, and even more so in the denomination we were part of. I am sure these fleshly efforts of mine grieved the Lord, yet He allowed me to go through the process of comparing, competing, and being miserable until I finally realized I was not *weird*, I was *unique*. Something unique has value because it is one of a kind, whereas something just like many others is not as valuable.

I was comparing myself to wonderful women who were operating in their natural, God-given abilities. They were happy because they were doing exactly what God had assigned to them. I was unhappy because I also was trying to do what God had assigned to them to do. God patiently forms each of us in our mother's wombs with His very own hand. When you consider your strengths, remember this verse:

> For you created my inmost being;
>   you knit me together in my mother's womb.

I praise you because I am fearfully and wonderfully made;
    your works are wonderful, I know that full well.
My frame was not hidden from you
    when I was made in the secret place.
When I was woven together in the depths of the earth,
    your eyes saw my unformed body.
All the days ordained for me
    were written in your book
before one of them came to be. (Psalm 139:13–16 NIV)

We are not accidents, not something that just got thrown to-gether with no forethought. Each of us is here on purpose, chosen to live in this particular time period on purpose. Fighting yourself is like fighting God, because you are His handiwork, predestined to good works (see Ephesians 2:10).

When Paul was converted, he certainly had heard about the great apostle Peter. I am sure Peter was someone everyone looked up to because of the great way in which God used him and the strong gifts he expressed. Peter was a leader among leaders. One would think that Paul would have sought out Peter for approval and friendship, yet we see just the opposite. Paul went away into Arabia and remained there for three years first, then he finally went to Jerusalem to become acquainted with Peter. Then, after a period of fourteen more years, during which he ministered where God led him, he went to Jerusalem again to meet with Peter and some of the other apostles (see Galatians 1:17–2:12).

Paul had confidence in his call and did not feel the need to com-pare himself with Peter or anyone else. We see evidence of this fact in other Scriptures: In Galatians 1:10, Paul stated that if he had been trying to be popular with people, he would not have become an apostle of the Lord. Why? Because following people rather than God can get us on the wrong paths for our lives. God does not want copies—He wants originals. Paul was an original, not a copy of Peter or the others, and that is how God wants it.

In the beginning of my ministry, I tried to get into several different groups of well-known preachers. I wanted their approval, and I wanted to compare what I was doing with what they were doing to see if I needed to change anything. Although I made improvement the year I spent "doing nothing" (except struggling to be what I thought was a regular woman), I still had insecurities and would have become a carbon copy of someone else if I had had the opportunity to do so.

I was quite frustrated when God would not allow me to have friends in ministry at that time, but I didn't understand that He was training me personally and did not want any interference in those early days of preparation for my calling.

Insecure people are not good at saying no! They are not good at being different; they usually bend in the direction everyone is going, rather than following their hearts wholly. When God was ready to promote our ministry to a more visible platform, one of the things I often heard was, "You are a breath of fresh air! You're unique, not like everyone else out there." That does not mean all the others were not wonderful and needed, it simply means we need variety.

Paul's message was the same as Peter's, yet with a different emphasis, and that is the way it should be in order for people to mature spiritually. We often fear being different; we are bored with sameness, yet somehow we feel safe with it.

Comparing ourselves with others and trying to be like them will definitely steal our peace; it is one of the most frustrating things we can go through. Beware of comparing any aspect of your natural or spiritual life with anyone else's—it will produce only turmoil.

Spiritual Comparisons

I remember hearing one preacher talk of how often he saw Jesus. I had never seen Jesus, so I wondered what was wrong with me. Another person I knew prayed four hours every morning. I could not find enough to pray about to keep praying for four hours and always ended up bored and sleepy, so I wondered what was wrong with me. I had no gift to remember large portions of Scripture like someone I knew, who memorized all the Psalms and Proverbs as well as other entire books of the Bible, so I wondered what was wrong with me. I finally realized that nothing was necessarily wrong with me because I could not do what they could. The fact was, I was preaching all over the world, and none of them were doing that.

Whatever we cannot do, there are many other things we can. Whatever someone else can do, there are also things they cannot. Don't play the devil's game any longer. Don't compare yourself with anyone in any way, especially not spiritually. We can see other people's good examples, but they must never become our standard. Even if we learn from them how to do something, we still will not do it exactly the same way.

Dave taught me how to play golf, and he taught me according to how he swung the golf club, but I don't swing mine the way he does and never will. We see this same example over and over. I hold the steering wheel of the car differently from the way he does, we apply the brakes differently, when I iron a shirt I start with the collar, my friend starts with the sleeve. What is the difference how we iron the shirt as long as it gets ironed properly?

I know people who say they have never felt the presence of God, and it really frustrated them when they heard others say things like "Did you feel God in this place tonight?" Some have great emotional experiences when they are born again or receive the baptism of the Holy Spirit, while others take it completely by faith and feel absolutely nothing, although they do see the fruit in their lives later.

At some time or another, I think we all fall into the trap of wondering why we are not like others we know or why we don't have the same experiences they do, but it *is a trap*—and a dangerous one. We are caught in a snare set by Satan when we enter into spiritual competition and comparison and become dissatisfied with what God is giving to us.

We should trust that God will do the best thing for each of us and let Him choose what that is. If we trust God in this way, we can lay aside our fears and insecurities about ourselves. How we respond to God in different areas can be the result of many different things, such as our natural temperaments, past teachings, and levels of natural boldness. For example, Thomas was a doubter and God loved Him, but He also corrected him for having little faith. Seeing and feeling are great, but Jesus said, "Blessed are those who believe and have not seen" (see John 20:29).

I am sure we would all like to see into the spiritual realm and have an abundance of supernatural experiences, but being frustrated if we don't only steals our peace and certainly does not produce visions of Jesus. I have had some "experiences" with the Lord, but I have also gone for many years without anything but faith.

I went through all the frustration, all the wondering what was wrong with me, wondering if I had committed some sin and God could not get through to me, wondering, reasoning, anxiety, unrest, no peace. . . . Then I found the answer: *Don't compare your spiritual life with that of anyone you know or anyone you read about.* Be yourself. You are unique, and God has a plan just for you.

COMPARING CIRCUMSTANCES

Comparing your circumstances with those of other people will steal your peace and cause confusion about God's unique plan for you. Remember, the devil wants to devour the blessings that God has set for you. The Word says to "withstand him; be firm in faith [against his onset—rooted, established, strong, immovable, and determined], knowing that the same (identical) sufferings are appointed to your brotherhood (the whole body of Christians) throughout the world" (1 Peter 5:9).

This Scripture shows us that we are to resist the devil quickly, stand firm against him at the onset of his attack, and know that everyone is going through difficulties in life. When we are in tough times, it seems Satan taunts us with thoughts that no one has it as bad as we do, but that is not true. There is someone in much worse circumstances than ours, no matter how difficult your or my situation may seem.

Realizing this builds gratitude and thankfulness, rather than self-pity, in our hearts. We should not be glad that others are suffering, but it does help us not to think we are the only ones waiting for a breakthrough from God. No matter how long we may have been waiting for God to do something we have prayed about, someone else has waited longer. No matter how sick, or poor, or lonely, or frightened any one of us may be, someone, somewhere is in worse condition.

God never promised us a life without trials; in fact, He promised us the opposite. He said there would be trials but that we should not fear them. "For He [God] Himself has said, I will not in any way fail you nor give you up nor leave you without support. [I will] not, [I will] not, [I will] not in any degree leave you helpless nor forsake nor let [you] down (relax My hold on you)! [Assuredly not!]" (Hebrews 13:5).

The presence of trials and tribulations does not mean that God has forgotten us or that He does not love us. We sometimes look at someone who seems to be having a wonderful life while we are suffering and ask, "God, why don't You love me the way You do that person?" We are tempted to think the same old question: *What is wrong with me?*

No matter what Satan uses, his purpose is the same: He wants us to think something is desperately wrong with us, and that we should have someone else's life or be like someone else. He wants to keep us from self-acceptance and the freedom to be who we are and *enjoy our lives.*

Don't despise your life and wish for another just because you are going through trials. If you had someone else's life, your trials might well be worse than the ones you have now. Besides, whatever you are going through right now, remember, *this too shall pass!*

Look beyond where you are, see with the eyes of faith, and believe God for even the impossible. The Bible says that Abraham had no reason at all to hope, but he hoped on in faith that God's promise to Him would be fulfilled (see Romans 4:18). A hopeful mind and attitude ministers peace and joy, while fear and discouragement steal both.

Don't concentrate on your problems; keep your mind on Jesus and His good plan for your life. As you read God's promises in the Word, adapt the Word as a personal letter to yourself. For example, paraphrasing Isaiah 26:3 as a personal letter to you, God is saying, "I will guard you and keep you in perfect and constant peace as you keep your mind on Me, because you commit yourself to Me, lean on Me, and hope confidently in Me."

Where the mind goes, the man follows. If we let our minds dwell on negative things (our problems instead of God's answers), our problems seem to multiply. The more we think about a problem, even a little one, the larger it seems to be.

I can honestly say now that I like myself. I admit it took a long time to get from where I was to where I am, but I really had nothing better to do than press on in God, and neither do you. For much of my life, I literally hated myself, and I know now that type of attitude is insulting to God, who carefully made us.

It costs nothing to be positive and believe that God can change you and your life. Jump-start your blessings by saying you love your life, and be thankful in all things, no matter what the circumstances may be, knowing this is God's will for you.

Each time you are tempted (which you will be) to compare yourself, or any aspect of your life, with anyone else, resist Satan at his onset. Don't even entertain thoughts of comparison to others. You are an individual, you are unique, and you have a right to enjoy your life, which must include enjoying your unique self.

Embrace your life. Wrap your arms around yourself right now as an act of faith and say out loud, "I accept myself, and I love myself in a balanced way. I'm not selfish, but I do affirm myself as a child of God, and I do believe He has created me and has a purpose for my life."

ACCEPTING YOUR UNIQUENESS OPENS THE DOOR TO BLESSINGS

I mentioned earlier that God had put me "on a shelf" for a one-year interval during my ministry, at which time I decided I had a wild imagination and was not really called to ministry at all. I tried to be what I thought the world expected me to be as a woman, wife, and mother. I felt during that year that God was doing absolutely nothing in my life; I saw no progress in my ministry, so I concluded that it was over when actually it was only about to begin.

During that year of comparing, competing, and finally coming to the realization that even if I was less than perfect, I still had to be me, God was actually doing one of the greatest works in me He has ever done. He was setting me free to be me! This had to take place before God could promote me into the next level of my ministry. Right at the end of that year of trials, our family began going to a new church in town, and a short while later, I found myself teaching a weekly Bible study that was eventually attended by over four hundred people.

I became an associate pastor at that church, taught Bible college three times a week, and learned a great deal that prepared me for the next challenge of my ministry, which included the media ministry that I am currently enjoying. Our daily television program is available to 2.5 billion people, we are on 350 radio stations, and I've had the privilege of writing nearly 60 books, as well as other very fruitful outreaches.

Our television program is aired around the world in 21 different languages, and we are adding new ones all the time. We air in the nation of India in 11 languages and recently had the great privilege of doing a major conference in Hyderabad. In 4 days, we ministered to 850,000 people with 250,000 decisions for Jesus Christ. Wow! What a privilege to be part of something like that.

None of this would be happening today if I had not stopped comparing myself with others and competing with them. It is vital for your future that you take this seriously and ask God to reveal any areas of comparison in your life.

If God has a plan for you and me, He certainly won't bring it to pass as long as we are trying to be other people. God will never give us grace to be people other than ourselves. Without grace, life is filled with struggle, it is not a life we enjoy; but with His grace (power of the Holy Spirit), we can enter the rest (peace) of the Lord and experience joy unspeakable and full of glory.

When I was trapped in self-rejection, comparing and competing with many of the people God had placed in my life, He led me to an article that was life-changing for me. I want to share excerpts from it with you, and I pray it blesses you as it did me.

The following article about "the consciousness of sin, and longing for holiness" was a letter Hudson Taylor, missionary to China in the 1800s, wrote to his sister and was later reprinted; it is entitled "The Exchanged Life." Hudson Taylor wrote:

Every day, almost every hour, the consciousness of sin oppressed me. I knew that if only I could abide in Christ all would be well, but I could not. I began the day with prayer, determined not to take my mind off of Him for a moment; but pressure of duties, sometimes very trying, constant interruptions apt to be so wearing, often caused me to forget Him. . . . Each day brought its register of sin and failure, of lack of power. To will was indeed present with me, but how to perform I found not. . . .

The last month or more has been, perhaps, the happiest period of my life; and I long to tell you a little of what the

Lord has done for my soul. I do not know how far I may be able to make myself intelligible about it, for there is nothing new or strange or wonderful—and yet, all is new! In a word: "Whereas I was blind, now I see. . . ."

I felt the ingratitude, the danger, the sin of not living nearer to God. I prayed, agonized, fasted, strove, made resolutions, read the Word more diligently, sought for more time for retirement and meditation to be alone with God—but all was without avail. Every day, almost every hour, the consciousness of sin oppressed me. . . . I hated myself; I hated my sin; and yet I gained no strength against it.

I felt I was a child of God: His Spirit in my heart would cry, in spite of all, "Abba, Father," but to rise to my privileges as a child [of God], I was utterly powerless.

I thought that holiness was to be gradually attained by diligent use of the means of grace. I felt that there was nothing I so much desired in this world, nothing I so much needed. But the more I pursued and strove after holiness, the more it eluded my grasp, till hope itself almost died out. . . . I knew I was powerless. I told the Lord so and asked Him to give me help and strength. . . .

When my agony of soul was at its height, a sentence in a letter from dear [John] McCarthy [in Hangchow, China] was used to remove the scales from my eyes, and the Spirit of God revealed the truth of our oneness with Jesus as I had never seen it before. McCarthy, who had been much exercised by the same sense of failure, but saw the light before I did, wrote (I quote from memory) "But how to get faith strengthened? Not by striving after faith, but by resting on the Faithful One."

As I read I saw it all! "If we believe not, He [remains] abideth faithful." I looked unto Jesus and saw (and when I saw, oh, how joy flowed) that He had said, "I will never leave you."

"Ah, *there* is rest!" I thought. "I have striven in vain to rest in Him. I'll strive no more. For has He not promised to abide with *me*—never to leave me, never to fail me?" And . . . He never will!

Joy will flow in our lives when we get our eyes off of ourselves and onto Jesus—off of what is wrong with us, and onto what is right with Him. Finally, when we realize that we are one with Him, we can live the "exchanged life" rather than a frustrating one.

Jesus took our old lives and has given us new ones. His life is in us, and He has given us His peace (see John 14:27). His joy is ours. He was made poor so that we might be made rich; He took our sin and gave us His righteousness; He took our sickness and diseases and the pain of our punishment and gave us His strength. Yes, He took everything bad and has given us lives to enjoy along with the peace that passes understanding.

Remember, Jesus said, "I came that [you] may have and enjoy life, and have it in abundance (to the full, till it overflows)." So enjoy the strengths that God has given to you, and focus on the life He wants you to enjoy. In the next chapter I will share with you how to avoid the paralysis of self-analysis and find peace by keeping your priorities in focus.

KEEP YOUR PRIORITIES IN ORDER

I believe that one of the reasons people lose their peace and fail to have the things they want is because they get their priorities out of line. There are so many choices to which people can give their time and attention. Without clear priorities, people can become paralyzed with indecision; I call this *paralysis of analysis*.

Some of the choices we have are bad options and are easy to recognize as something to avoid, but many of our options are good. Yet even good things can get our priorities all messed up. What is a top priority for somebody else could be a problem for us. So we have to be careful that we don't just do what everybody else is doing. We need to do what God is leading us individually to do.

When setting our priorities, it's important to understand that Jesus is the holding power of all that is good in our lives. Colossians 1:17 says, "And He Himself existed before all things, and in Him all things consist (cohere, are held together)." That is why He should always be our first priority. Jesus holds everything together.

A couple can't have a good marriage if Jesus isn't holding it together. In fact, people won't have good personal relationships with *anybody* if Jesus is not leading and influencing individuals to love each other. Finances are a mess without Jesus. Our thoughts are clouded and confused without Jesus. Our emotions are out of control without Him.

Colossians 1:18 continues: "He also is the Head of [His] body, the church; seeing He is the Beginning, the Firstborn from among the dead, *so that He alone in everything and in every respect might occupy the chief place [stand first and be preeminent]*" (italics mine). Jesus is the head of the church body; therefore, He alone, in every respect, should occupy the chief place, stand first and be preeminent, in each of our lives.

That means if Jesus is not first place in our lives, then we need to rearrange our priorities. Matthew 6:33 says that if we seek the kingdom of God and His righteousness, that all other things will be added to our lives. The *Amplified Bible* translation of this verse says we are to "seek His way of doing and being right."

Seeking the kingdom means finding out how God wants things done. Finding out how He wants us to treat people. Finding out how He wants us to act in situations and circumstances. Finding out what He wants us to do with our money. Finding out what kind of an attitude we should have. Even finding out what kind of entertainment Jesus approves of for us.

Our lives will not be blessed if we keep God in a little Sunday-morning box and let Him have our priority attention for only forty-five minutes, once a week during a church service. As long as we are here in this world, we will have to resist becoming like the world—and it is a daily battle. *The church is full of worldly, carnal, fleshly believers, and that is why we are not affecting the world the way we should be.*

If Christians were putting Jesus first in everything, then the world would be in a better condition. There are, of course, sincere, God-fearing, dedicated believers in every church and in society, but not nearly as many as there should be. Each of us should remember the importance of walking in the Spirit, not in the flesh. The world is watching us, we are Christ's representatives; God is making His appeal to the world through us (see 2 Corinthians 5:20).

ESTABLISH GRACE AS YOUR PRIORITY

Our first priority of life should not be to earn a living or get an education. In fact, First Corinthians 8:1 says that "knowledge causes people to be puffed up," but love "edifies." This tells us that focusing on our love-walk is a more important priority than learning a career skill. (I am not saying that God is against higher education, but wouldn't it be an awesome world if everyone were required to spend four concentrated years of education to learn how to walk in love?)

Often we don't think about what our priorities are, but we still have them. Our priorities are whatever is first in our thoughts and in how we plan our time. Having real peace in our lives requires making God first above all other things that demand our attention.

If you put God first in your finances, first in your time, first in your conversation, first in your thoughts, first in your decisions, your life will be a success. I am living evidence of this truth. Before I learned to put God first, I was living in the worst messes that anybody could have. I had a bad attitude and couldn't think two positive thoughts in a row. I didn't like anybody, and nobody liked me. The abuse in my childhood had left me full of bitterness, resentment, and unforgiveness.

Even when I became a believer, I still thought I could achieve approval only through good works. I didn't understand the simple fact that Jesus loved me, and God's grace just didn't make any sense to me. But eventually I learned that God's grace is better than our works.

Works breed reasoning and anxiety that will eventually strangle our peace. Grace and works are two totally different entities, which cannot partnership together. If grace has anything to do with works, then it's no longer grace, and if works have anything to do with grace, then they're no longer works. Romans 11:6 explains, "But if it is by grace (His unmerited favor and graciousness), it is no longer conditioned on works or anything men have done. Otherwise, grace would no longer be grace [it would be meaningless]." Even after putting God first, I had to learn to let grace (God's power) bring about the fruit of my ministry.

I had no peace when I tried to accomplish through works what was in my heart to do. As you will read shortly, I couldn't even enjoy a relaxing bubble bath as long as I thought works would help me find my answers. It was several years ago that God brought this vivid lesson to my attention.

I had already seen tremendous growth in our ministry through national radio and TV. My secretary at that time, who was also our office manager, and her husband, who was our bookkeeper, lived in an apartment in the lower level of our home. They had been with us for several years and took care of our house and teenage son whenever we traveled.

Consequently, we talked a lot about business in our house. God had been trying to teach me that I needed to delegate work and stay out of some things if I wanted to have peace in my life. He had been showing me I should let Dave handle some of the things that frustrated me, and that I didn't even have to know about them. I could just go on about my business.

But one night, I knew Dave was going to discuss some business matters with that couple, and I wanted to hear them too. Even though God had instructed me to let Dave handle many of the things that were stealing my peace, I still wanted to get in on *everything*. So this particular night, I put aside some things I really needed to do in order to sit in on their meeting. They just kept talking about other things, and it seemed to me that they weren't going to discuss business issues after all, so I finally said something about getting started.

Dave said, "Well, we're just not ready yet. Why don't you go ahead and take your bath?" So, reluctantly, I went upstairs and ran the bathwater and got into the tub, but as soon as I did, I heard everyone talking downstairs and realized they were starting their business meeting. There I was, a grown woman, nearly fifty years old at the time, and I wanted to hear what they were saying so badly that I got out of the bathtub and tried to listen to their conversation through the grate in the floor!

When that didn't work, I went to open the bathroom door so I could listen from the stairway, when suddenly the Holy Spirit made me realize how stupid I looked. I remember His saying to me, "Why don't you just get in the bathtub, Joyce, and mind your own business?"

I tell all this to help you realize that I know firsthand how difficult it is to let go of works and to trust God's grace to carry us where we want to go. I know how difficult it is to delegate jobs to other people and then trust that those jobs will be done properly without any involvement from us.

If we cannot let the grace of God work for us in small areas, we will never learn to let it work for us in the big ones. I was so nosey, I could not even stay in the bathtub when I thought Dave was discussing business and I wasn't going to know what was going on. That being the case, how could I ever advance to trusting God to take care of larger matters?

God wants you to understand that you have two choices: You can enjoy your life while He takes care of what needs to be done for you, or you can labor and struggle in vain through your own works. He is willing to build your life or allow you to do it, but His grace and your works are not both going to bring results that you want. If you choose His grace, you will have to lay aside the works of your flesh you are planning to do.

God wants us always to be in a position of trusting Him. Worry is the work of our flesh and is unscriptural. Worry, reasoning, and frustration are internal types of work that do not please God. To worry is to torment yourself with disturbing thoughts, and is a clear indicator that God is not first in your life.

God's Grace Is Sufficient for Today

God will give you all the grace you need for today, and He will also give you grace for tomorrow, but as I've said, tomorrow's grace won't show up until tomorrow. The grace of God is just like manna was to the Israelites; every morning the manna came down out of the sky and was enough for that day. Whenever someone tried to store up provision for the next day, it rotted. It's the same way with grace. We are to learn to live our lives one day at a time.

When we have to stand in faith and believe God for a breakthrough in an area, we want to know immediately when the answer will come. God's answer is that it will come—one day at a time. And worrying or trying to make it happen will not help it come any faster.

The Lord's Prayer will help you stay in peace while you are waiting for a breakthrough. In Matthew 6:11, Jesus taught us to pray, saying, "Give us this day our daily bread." God wants us to pray *every day* for whatever provision we need for that day. Jesus also said to "stop being perpetually uneasy (anxious and worried)" about our lives (v. 25).

I realized I was frustrated as soon as I got up in the mornings. I was always in such a hurry, no matter what I was doing, I had my mind on the next thing I needed to do. As I was brushing my teeth one morning, I discovered I was hurrying because I was thinking about making the bed, and God told me, "Slow down. Brush your teeth."

God continued to show me how misplaced priorities were robbing me of the peace and enjoyment in my life. I'd rush to make my bed, but because I never kept my mind on what I was doing, I was already anxious about the next thing I needed to do. As I started making the bed, I thought, *I better lay out some meat to thaw for dinner.* So I'd leave the bed half made and rush downstairs to get meat out of the freezer, but on the way there I'd see a pile of dirty clothes and think, *I better put those clothes in the washer and get the laundry started.* Just as I put soap in the washer, the phone would ring, so I ran back upstairs to the kitchen to answer the phone.

While I talked on the phone, I realized that I needed to load the dishwasher, so I put a few dishes in the dishwasher as I talked. But then whoever was on the phone said, "Would you like to go to town with me?" and I'd think, *Well, I do need to get some stamps to mail some letters,* so I'd hurry to get dressed to go to town.

I'd carry on like that all day, never finishing what I started. By the time Dave came home, everything was in shambles and he asked casually, "So, what did you do all day?"

That offended me and I threw a fit, saying, "What do you mean, what did I *do* all day? I've been running around here like a maniac trying to work!"

Now, that is not the way to enjoy your life. That is anxiety! And anxiety is work that never accomplishes anything.

Peace begins with our keeping priorities straight moment by moment. It is a challenge to thoroughly enjoy every moment that God gives us. But when we learn to do this, we will enjoy our days. When we learn to enjoy our days, we will find that we are enjoying our lives.

We can learn to *enjoy* making the bed, doing laundry, and washing the dishes. We can enjoy getting meals for our families, going to the grocery store, and taking time to talk with friends. If we don't enjoy every phase of our day, we will miss the life that God intended for us to enjoy.

Life cannot just be filled with things that are fun to do. But we can enjoy the more mundane things that we *need* to accomplish by staying filled with the Holy Spirit. Ephesians 5:18 says, "Ever be filled and stimulated with the [Holy] Spirit." We can do this by singing spiritual songs while we work, and by keeping an attitude of praise in our hearts and talking to the Lord as we work. We stay filled with the Holy Spirit by giving thanks to God as we go about our daily tasks (see vv. 19–20).

If you have never hummed a little tune as you worked, you will be surprised at how quickly this simple act lifts your spirit. The Lord designed us, so He alone knows what it takes for us to enjoy our lives and be free from anxiety. Keeping a melody in our hearts and an attitude of praise toward God will keep Him in first place on our list of priorities.

I challenge you to examine your life and ask yourself: How much of my life am I wasting on anxiety? You won't have peace if you waste too much of it. Time is something that we can never get back. Learn to enjoy all of your day. Have fun even while doing strenuous chores. And don't waste time worrying or being frustrated about circumstances that you can't change.

GIVE GOD THE BEST PART OF YOUR DAY

I've trained myself now to start each day by giving God the first-fruits of my time. I've realized that I'm not going to get through the day peacefully if I don't spend time with God.

So, each morning, I get coffee, and usually while still in my pajamas, I just spend as much time with God as I need to in order to feel I can behave properly and walk in the fruit of the Spirit throughout the day.

When I first started doing this, I used the time to murmur to God about all my trials in life, so one morning the Holy Spirit spoke to me and said, "Now, Joyce, are you going to fellowship with Me this morning, or with your problem?"

I learned to use the best part of my day to give God the best part of my heart. Giving God the first moments of the morning helps keep my priorities straight for the rest of the day. In fact, I've written a little book that will help you get in the habit of beginning your day with God, called *Starting Your Day Right*. Each short devotion encourages you to meditate on God's Word during this time and reminds you to ask Him to help you rely on His grace your whole day.

Don't use this gift of time with God to meditate on your problems. Don't spend that time worrying about all the things that you want God to do for you that He's not done yet, or trying to figure out ways you can get Him to do them. During this time with God, set your heart as the psalmist did, who wrote, "But I trusted in, relied on, and was confident in You, O Lord; I said, You are my God. *My times are in Your hands*" (Psalm 31:14–15, italics mine).

The Bible says to "lean on, trust in, and be confident in the Lord with all your heart and mind and do not rely on your own insight or understanding. In all your ways know, recognize, and acknowledge Him, and He will direct and make straight and plain your paths. Be not wise in your own eyes" (Proverbs 3:5–7).

What's the sense in our saying that we trust God, then spending our day trying to figure out how and when our problems will be solved? God wants to hear us say, "Lord, I don't know how You're going to do this. I don't care how You do it. However You do it, I know it's going to be right. I can't do it anyway, so I'm not going to frustrate myself trying to figure out how I can do it, God. I trust all my circumstances to You. *My times are in Your hands.* Trusting You is my first priority in life."

STAY IN PERFECT PEACE

God wants us to enjoy perfect peace, and we cannot do that unless we give Him our worries. "Therefore humble yourselves [demote, lower yourselves in your own estimation] under the mighty hand of God, *that in due time* He may exalt you, casting the whole of your care [all your anxieties, all your worries, all your concerns, once and for all] on Him, for He cares for you affectionately and cares about you watchfully" (1 Peter 5:6–7).

The way you humble yourself under the mighty hand of God is to refuse to try to figure everything out. Reasoning and worry are works of our flesh. Remember, as I said at the beginning of this chapter, peace will come by grace, but not by works.

Ezekiel 20:40 says that we should bring the Lord our firstfruits, the choicest selections of all our offerings. To stay in perfect peace, we should give God the best of our time and our goods. We must be honest with ourselves about what our priorities really are and start making changes to keep God in first place.

Being too busy is not an acceptable excuse for not keeping focused on what is truly important. Everyone sets his or her own schedule. We need to establish boundaries, and we need to learn to say no when people ask us to do something that leads us away from peace (I will talk more about saying no in the next chapter).

Be honest with yourself as you examine how you spend your time. Don't give God your leftovers; don't give Him the part of your day when you're worn-out and you can't think straight or hardly keep your eyes open. Give God the firstfruits of your attention. Give Him the best part of your day. That's where your real priorities will be found.

God needs to be your priority in *everything* you do. From getting dressed to setting your schedule, you can ask God for wisdom to make choices that will glorify Him. You can intermingle your time with God into everything you do to such a degree that you can pray without ceasing (as I suggested earlier, pray your way through the day). As you become aware of His presence, it will not be possible to compartmentalize God or separate secular activities from sacred ones. Even ordinary events will become sacred because He is involved in them.

You can just talk to God as you go about your day, asking Him to direct you in the choices you are making and to empower you for the jobs you need to get done. As you acknowledge that God is always with you, you will keep Him first in everything you set out to do, and He will show you a direct path that will lead you to peace. You will experience pleasure, knowing you are partnering with God in all you do.

Following the moment-by-moment leading of the Holy Spirit will cause you to enjoy every day of your life. The Spirit of God is creative; His mercies are new every morning, so if you follow the leadership of the Holy Spirit, He will keep your priorities straight. He will make sure your time with Him is right, and that your family time is right, and that you are fulfilling the work He has for you to do.

God will also energize you by grace to do whatever He leads you to do. If your priorities get out of order, you will labor in vain and tire quickly. In the next chapter we will look at how making healthy choices will help avoid stress, exhaustion, and upset so you can learn to enjoy your quiet times with God.

PROTECT YOUR HEALTH

No matter what people own in life or what their positions are, if their health is not good, they will not enjoy anything. Good health is one of the greatest treasures we have; it is a gift from God. The psalmist wrote, "Bless (affectionately, gratefully praise) the Lord, O my soul, and forget not [one of] all His benefits—Who forgives [every one of] all your iniquities, Who heals [each one of] all your diseases" (Psalm 103:2–3).

The apostle John wrote, "Beloved, I would that you prosper and be in health, even as I know your soul prospers" (see 3 John 1:2). We should do all we possibly can to protect our health, both physically and emotionally. It is sad to see people in our society regularly abuse their bodies and then wonder why they get sick.

I have discovered that it is much harder for me to remain peaceful under any kind of opposition if I also have the added stress of not feeling well. If I am really tired, it is more difficult for me to get along with people or display the fruit of the Spirit.

I have had long periods of time in my life of not feeling well, and I have heard the doctors say over and over, "You are under stress." Their diagnosis always frustrated me because I did not know how to live any way other than under stress. I thought I had no choice except to do all the things I was doing, even though I often admitted, "I can't do all this. It is too much."

Stress-related illnesses are rampant. I asked Dr. Don Colbert, a nutrition expert whom I greatly respect, to share how stress affects our health and nerves. He wrote, "Approximately 75–90% of all visits to primary-care physicians are for stress-related disorders. Chronic stress has actually been linked to most of the leading causes of death, including heart disease, cancer, lung ailments, accidents, cirrhosis, and suicide."

Dr. Colbert agrees that individuals must learn to protect themselves against stress, saying,

Few people realize that the fast-paced lives they are living, the increasing demands on their schedules, and the way that they cope or react to stress or stressful situations are all in their control. Yes, we all have a choice to continue this hectic schedule; we can choose to react by becoming more and more frustrated, or we can learn to limit the demands on our everyday lives and react in love rather than frustration.

The following excerpt from Dr. Colbert is a report he shared with me of how the Canadian physician Hans Selye accidentally discovered the effects of stress on the physical body.

Selye's vision was not to discover the effects of stress but to discover the next new female sex hormone. He had made an extract from ovaries and injected the extract solution into rats. However, Selye was not very skillful with his injection techniques. He always dropped the rats and spent much of the morning chasing the rodents around the room, using a broom to get them out from behind a desk or a sink. At the end of a few months, Selye discovered that the rats had developed enlarged adrenal glands, shrunken immune tissues, and peptic ulcers.

Selye, however, thought this was due to the ovarian extract that he was injecting into the rats. So, he tested another group, and he injected them with only saline solution. Due to his poor coordination, however, he also dropped these rats, chased them around his lab, and also got the broom after them. At the end of the experiment, the control rats had also developed the enlarged adrenal glands, the shrunken immune tissues, and the peptic ulcers. Selye then figured out that the cause *was not what he was injecting,* but *the tremendous stress he was putting the rats under* while trying to inject them. He had literally stressed the little creatures out. Dr. Selye determined that when stress is maintained long enough, the body undergoes three distinct stages: (1) the alarm stage, (2) the resistance stage, and (3) the exhaustion stage.

The alarm stage is the fight-or-flight emergency system that God created in our bodies for survival. The brain sends a signal to the pituitary gland to release a hormone that activates the adrenal glands. Adrenaline then sends the body into high alert. The brain becomes focused, the eyesight sharpens, and muscles clench as the body prepares for fighting or fleeing. This amazing alarm system has enabled multitudes of people to survive vicious attacks from animals, auto accidents, and other traumas. The body's hormonal system returns to normal when the perceived attack is over.

However, this alarm reaction is being activated hundreds of times a day in many Christians due to deadlines at work, financial pressures, arguments with a spouse or children, traffic jams, as well as all the common stresses of modern life. In other words, frustration, anger, guilt, grief, anxiety, fear, as well as most other emotions, will also set off this alarm system, which can then lead to a heart attack or stroke.

Dr. Selye's second stage of stress is called the resistance stage. When someone is undergoing a chronic stress such as having a child on drugs or alcohol or in jail, long-standing marital problems, a chronic illness, long-term unemployment, or some other situation over which he feels he has lost control over an extended period of time, [this] generally leads to the resistance stage of stress. This is another emergency system that God has placed within us so that we may survive periods of famine, disease, and pestilence. During this stage, our cortisol and adrenaline levels become elevated. Cortisol is very similar to the medication *cortisone*, which doctors give to treat asthma, arthritis, chronic obstructive pulmonary disease, as well as numerous other illnesses. However, release of cortisol can lead to elevation of blood sugar, which can eventually lead to diabetes and weight gain, especially in the abdominal area. Over time, it can result in bone loss, which can lead to osteopenia and osteoporosis. Elevated cortisol also leads to hypertension, memory loss, sleep deprivation, and a compromised immune system.

The resistance stage is similar to having the accelerator of your car stuck to the floorboard. Your system is all geared up and is unable to gear down, even at night. Individuals in this resistance stage generally have insomnia, or they wake up at two or three in the morning and find it very difficult to fall back to sleep. After patients have been living in the resistance stage for months or years, they will eventually enter into stage 3 of stress, which is the exhaustion stage.

People have entered the exhaustion stage when they feel burned-out. Examples of this stage are individuals with chronic fatigue, fibromyalgia, most autoimmune diseases including lupus, rheumatoid arthritis, MS, and usually cancer. In other words, these people have had the accelerator pressed to the floor for so long that eventually they run out of gas, and the powerful, robust bodies that God has given them, which He designed for health, begin to degenerate and die. The body is more prone to bacterial and viral infections, allergies, candida, environmental illness, inflammation of joints, and severe fatigue.*

It is obvious from this report that stress destroys the body's immune defense system. Once the immune system breaks down, it can be a difficult and lengthy process to restore it back to full health.

---

*Reprinted with permission. For more of Dr. Colbert's advice on better health, please visit his website at www.drcolbert.com.

To restore the immune system, people have to do what they should have done to begin with: Get lots of good rest; eat good-quality food, not junk food with no nutritional value; maintain peaceful lifestyles; and live balanced lives, which include worship, work, rest, and play. And people need to exercise as their systems permit them.

But we shouldn't wait until we are forced into doing the right thing. Let's act voluntarily and keep our health. The symptoms of stress are real, and though we can take medicine to mask or allevi-ate them, the root cause of many illnesses that we have is simply a stressful lifestyle. Unless we deal with the lifestyle, we will always have a new symptom pop up in some new way. The world will not change, so we must.

Dr. Colbert instructs people who are suffering from stress to avoid overcommitment and learn to be satisfied in order to circum-vent overspending. He writes,

> The majority of our stress comes from the demands everyday life places on us and our choosing to walk the frustration-walk instead of the love-walk: by trying to enforce unenforce-able rules. By simply walking the love-walk instead of the frustration-walk, one will be able to pull the roots of stress out of his or her life.

Stress depletes our bodies, our immune systems become weak, and sickness and depression can set in. Some stress is actually good for us; you might say it exercises various organs in the body. God designed our bodies to handle a certain amount of stress; it is only when we continually push ourselves beyond reasonable limits that we break down under the strain. It is when we get out of balance that we open a door for sickness in our lives. Excessive stress over a long period of time eventually causes our organs to just plain wear out.

Each time we say, "I am exhausted," we should realize that we are exhausting something in our bodies also. We recover from normal stress through proper rest; however, we can cause irreversible damage when we don't get needed rest.

We live in stressful times, but by following Jesus' advice and casting our cares on Him, we can live stress-free in a stressful world. If we will exalt Jesus, lift Him up, and put Him first by following the leadership of His Spirit, we will not end up exhausted.

Is Jesus exalted, or are you exhausted? To exalt someone is to put him above other things, to make him first. To be exhausted is to be completely worn-out, having no energy and being susceptible to sickness.

There is a popular worship song entitled "He Is Exalted." I was trying to sing this song once during a time when I was extremely tired, and I got my words mixed up and sang to the Lord, "You are exhausted."

He stopped me and said, "No, Joyce, I am exalted. You are the one who is exhausted."

Remember, God will always energize us to do *what He leads us to do*. It is only when we go beyond His will to follow our own will or other people's that we are likely to get exhausted. Second Corinthians 2:14 says that God always "leads us in triumph." It is not His will for us to live defeated, weak lives; He wants us to be more than conquerors. His will for us is strength, not weakness and sickness.

ARE YOU SUFFERING FROM EXHAUSTION?

Are you excessively tired all the time, and even after sleeping, do you wake up feeling tired all over again? Do you go to doctors, but they cannot find anything wrong with you? You may be experiencing some of the symptoms of exhaustion, or what I call burnout. Long periods of overexertion and stress can cause constant fatigue, headaches, sleeplessness, gastrointestinal problems, tenseness, a feeling of being tied in knots, and an inability to relax.

Some other signals of burnout are crying, being easily angered, negativity, irritability, depression, cynicism (scornful, mocking of the virtues of others), and bitterness toward others' blessings and even their good health.

Burnout causes us to be out of control, and when this happens, we are no longer producing good fruit in our daily lives. Burnout steals our joy, making peace impossible to find. When our bodies are not at peace, everything seems to be in turmoil.

God established the law of resting on the Sabbath to prevent burnout in our lives (see Mark 2:27). The law of the Sabbath simply says we can work six days, but by the seventh, we need to rest and spend time worshiping God. Even God rested after six days of work. He, of course, never gets tired but gave us this example so we would follow the pattern. In Exodus 23:10–12, we find that even the land had to rest after six years, and the Israelites were not to sow in it the seventh year. During this rest, everything recovered and prepared for future production.

Everything rested on the Sabbath: people, servants, and domestic animals. These were days of complete relaxation for the mind, emotions, and body. In Leviticus 26, we see that much turmoil and trouble come due to ignoring God's ordinances.

Today in America, almost every business is open seven days a week. Some of them are even open twenty-four hours a day, seven days a week. I have heard that after the pilgrims landed on Plymouth Rock and began to establish America, a drummer walked through the streets, signaling everyone to go to church on the Sabbath. After church, they rested the entire day. Sabbath-breakers were actually arrested!

People say we are free from the law of the Old Testament and that keeping the Sabbath was part of that old system. That's good, because people who broke the Sabbath then were stoned. Thankfully, we are not to be legalistic about it, but we do need to honor the spirit of the Sabbath principle. Jesus said the Sabbath was designed for man, which simply implies that we must rest at least one out of seven days. When we make ourselves available 24/7, we are in danger of burnout.

People today are quick to argue that they cannot afford to take a day off, but I say that they cannot afford not to do it. We often hear, "I am too busy to do that. I would never get everything done if I did that." My answer is, "Then you are too busy, and something needs to change in your life."

When we are too busy to obey God's ordinances, we will pay the price. Remember, the Bible says we reap only what we sow. If we sow continual stress with no rest to offset it, we will reap the results in our bodies, emotions, and minds.

If someone says, "Well, my boss insists that I work seven days a week," then I would say to get a new job. I learned from the story of Epaphroditus, who was working with Paul in the ministry and became so sick from overwork that he almost died, that even if I am overworking "for Jesus" (in my way of thinking), I will still pay the price for abusing my body.

Regular time set apart for God is one of the quickest ways to restore a tired mind and body. Jesus invited us to rest when He called for those "who labor and are heavy-laden and overburdened." He promised to ease and relieve and refresh our souls. He even offered "recreation and blessed quiet" for our souls (Matthew 11:28–30). Just lay your burdens on Jesus, spend time with Him, rest in His presence, and you will experience a glorious restoration. God delights in restoring all things.

DON'T WAIT UNTIL IT IS TOO LATE

The question is not *Do you have stress?* Everyone has stress. The question is *Are you managing your stress?* Use wisdom, which is really sanctified common sense. Realize you cannot spend something you don't have. Spending what one does not have is what causes financial stress and ultimately financial collapse. Spending energy we don't have has the exact same effect except it's on our physical health, rather than the financial realm.

Our bodies warn us when they are running low on energy. We should respect them. I can remember conferences in which I conducted five sessions consisting of three hours each, and instead of going home to rest like I needed to, I went to the shopping mall.

Of course, I felt extremely tired, but I would not go home. My head hurt, my feet hurt, I was grouchy and often felt discouraged, but I would not rest. I was not respecting my body; I was not listening to the warning signals it was giving me. I have since learned better. If I am out doing anything and I start to feel I am running out of energy, I don't wait until I am completely depleted. I go home while I still have some strength. I have learned the dangers of total exhaustion and have a reverential fear of abusing my body.

I ignored warnings in the past and paid the price. I am encouraging you not to wait until it is too late, and you have lost your health. Begin right now to respect your body, and treasure the health God has given you. I am grateful to be able to say that God has restored me, and I feel good most of the time. I also must say that I will probably have to be extra careful for the rest of my life. Once we push our bodies past where God intended them to go, we have weaknesses that will show up quickly with the slightest provocation.

Faith and prayer work. God will restore. He is the God of restoration, but we must also realize that we cannot continually ignore warnings. God is merciful, but He is also just. He put natural safety alarms in our bodies to indicate when we need rest, and He teaches us what to do when those alarms sound. He means what He says: We are the dwelling places of the Holy Spirit, and we should not do anything to hurt God's temple (see 1 Corinthians 3:17, 6:19).

FREQUENT UPSET DAMAGES YOUR HEALTH

I spent many years getting upset frequently. There were probably very few days when I did not get aggravated about something, and often I did so several times each day. As I studied God's Word and gained wisdom, I began to realize that this required a lot of energy. I was tired most of the time and didn't have any energy to spare, so I knew I had to calm down. Jesus told His disciples, as recorded in John 14:27, that they were to stop allowing themselves to be "agitated and disturbed." He told them, in essence, to relax.

I don't know how much energy is required to get really upset and then to try to calm down, but I am sure it is a lot. It takes energy to resist getting frustrated, but not nearly as much as going through the entire cycle.

Eventually I learned to resist becoming upset as soon as I felt distressed. I learned to talk to myself and actually calm myself down by doing so. I asked God for help each time I started to feel that I was losing my peace. I was learning to "hold" my peace, just as Moses told the Israelites to do. He reassured them, "The LORD shall fight for you, and ye shall hold your peace" (Exodus 14:14 KJV). Frequently losing our tempers or having fits is damaging to our health.

What we often do to our bodies reminds me of a rubber band: When you stretch it too far, it breaks, and you have to tie it into a knot for continued use. Let this occur several times, and eventually all you have is knots. Like a rubber band, we can be stretched only so far, and then we ultimately break under the strain.

All the upset stretches us beyond our limits, and ultimately we break, so we tie a knot and keep going, then another and another until we go to the doctor and say, "I feel as if I am tied in knots and cannot relax." We don't know how accurate the statement really is.

Psalm 39:4–6 says, in essence, it is useless to be in turmoil, and how true that statement is. It does no good at all. The only one fulfilled when we get upset is the devil. He sets us up to get us frustrated anyway, so of course, he is delighted. He is the thief who only comes to kill, steal, and destroy. He wants to kill us, steal our health, and destroy our bodies and minds. We should do as Jesus did and say, "Get thee behind me, Satan. You are an offense, and you are in my way."

We might look at our bodies and energy levels as a bank account. We have enough for our lifetime. But if we spend it all early, we will feel depleted in our later years. I hate to see young people abusing their bodies through eating junk food excessively, never resting, and even perhaps using damaging chemical substances. I have tried to speak to a few, but I always get the same response. "Oh man, I feel great, got all kinds of energy." They don't understand that if they overspend today, they will do without later on in life.

LEARN TO SAY NO

One of the reasons I previously found myself stressed-out, burned-out, and sick was from not knowing how to say no. We all want to please people, but we might kill ourselves trying to do so.

I wanted to take every ministry opportunity that came my way, but it just was not possible. We must all learn to let God's Spirit, and not other people's desires, lead us. Frequently people tell me that God has showed them that I am supposed to come to their churches or conferences and be their speaker. There was a time when that would pressure me because I thought, *If I say no, then I am, in reality, saying they didn't hear from God.*

Other people cannot hear from God for us. We are individuals and have the right to hear from God ourselves. I started realizing that no matter what they thought they had heard, I could not do the engagement with peace and confidence if I had not heard it myself. Remember, God has no obligation to help me finish something He did not tell me to do.

Dr. Colbert teaches that many people are unable to say no

because they have passive personalities. He explains that most people fall into one of three personality categories: passive, aggressive, or assertive. He wrote the following scenario to show a typical situation for a passive person:

> If you are passive, you usually have problems expressing your thoughts and feelings and find it difficult to stand up for yourself. Other people, especially the aggressive type, tend to walk all over you; they are able to manipulate and even make decisions for you. Passive individuals usually feel guilty and like they have to apologize. They usually have poor self-esteem and maintain poor eye contact or look away and down to the floor when you talk with them.
>
> I have found so many Christians who are passive, and much of the stress that they are under is directly related to their passivity. You see, when someone is passive, other people's problems become his problems.
>
> For example, a passive person will not be able to say no when people ask him to do something. An aggressive person at work may ask a passive fellow employee to stay later to help him finish his work because he has an important appointment. The passive individual is unable to say no, so he stays overtime, doing the other person's work. This may create problems with his spouse, since he comes home late from work, and this trend continues because the aggressive person will continue to put more and more on the back of the passive person, and the passive person allows it. Many times this is because the passive person has a good heart and good motives, and he lets the fear of rejection control his life. Instead he should assert his feelings and ideas and risk not being accepted.*

Are you saying yes with your mouth while your heart is screaming no? If so, you will eventually be stressed-out, burned-out, and

*Reprinted with permission.

possibly sick. We just cannot go on like that forever without ultimately breaking down under the strain. Be true to your own heart.

Don't be afraid to say no. Don't fear the rejection of others. No matter how many people you please, there will always be someone who will not be pleased. Face it now, and get it over with.

Learn that you can enjoy your life even if everyone does not think you are wonderful. Don't be addicted to approval from people; if God approves, that is all that really matters.

Don't try so hard to keep other people happy that it costs you your joy, peace, and health. None of the people who put pressure on you will stand before God and give an account of your life; only you will do that. Be prepared to be able to say to Him, "I followed my heart to the best of my ability."

Being committed is very good, but being overcommitted is very dangerous. As I said earlier, know your limits and don't hesitate to say no if you know that you need to. Tell people when you don't have peace about being involved in a certain activity or project. They should respect your rights and want you to have peace in your life. If they don't, then it is clear they are not thinking of what is good for you.

Remember that people can be very selfish. It is good to be a blessing, to do things for others and serve them, but not to the point that we get sick trying to keep everyone we know happy. I am not saying that we should never do anything we don't want to do. There are always times when we will serve others sacrificially, but we must not let their desires control us and push us into exhaustion and high levels of stress.

God has assigned a life span to each of us, and although we don't know exactly how long we have on earth, we should certainly desire to live out the fullness of our years. We want to burn on, not burn out. We should live with passion and zeal, not with exhaustion; we should be good examples to others.

Learn to say no when you need to—it will help you stay healthy!

BEND BEFORE YOU BREAK

People with aggressive personalities have their own sets of stress inducers that can work havoc in their health. Dr. Colbert writes:

People with aggressive behavior generally dominate, intimidate, and bully others, and they are very confrontational. They tend to view their own needs as priority, and they stop at nothing to get what they want. Most of us have encountered aggressive drivers who cut us off in traffic or shake their fists at us.

God desires for Christians to be neither passive nor aggressive, but *assertive*. Assertiveness allows people to communicate confidently, boldly, and clearly their thoughts, feelings, and desires. But unless they were raised in loving, stable home environments where they received encouragement, freedom to express themselves, and discipline with love, support, and acceptance, most Christians never learn assertiveness.

Many Christians grew up in dysfunctional families. Instead of being programmed for success, they were programmed for failure. They heard they were no good, that they would never amount to anything, that they were losers. Some children responded passively to this environment; some became angry and aggressive.*

While we can see the danger of being too passive, we can also see that being inflexible and aggressive will not lead to healthy situations. Learning to be adaptable, considering the welfare of those around us, is one way we can keep peace.

Don't expect the world to adapt to you; be ready to bend before you break. When you start to feel stressed because things aren't going your way, and you sense peace ebbing away, quickly see what you can change to relieve the pressure. Most often you will need to

*Reprinted with permission.

simplify, simplify, simplify. The more simple your life, the more peace you will enjoy.

Keep in mind that being assertive is the healthy goal you are working toward. Assertiveness is like leather: It is tough to tear apart and will show only a small indention under the impact of a hammer, while aggressiveness is like brittle sandstone that easily crumbles if it is struck with a hard blow. Likewise an aggressive person's temper easily breaks or snaps under pressure, but an assertive person is able to stay flexible and in one piece.

We can see from pondering this comparison why Satan's plans can thrive in the life of an aggressive person. He intends to break us by applying force and pressure. However, he will not succeed if in the process we are willing to bend and remain flexible. His plans cause the stiff-necked or stubborn individuals to crumble easily, so they fall apart.

I used to be one of those aggressive people, but I realized long ago that it was not worth it. A little humility can preserve a lot of health. The Word warns us: "Be not like the horse or the mule, which lack understanding, which must have their mouths held firm with bit and bridle, or else they will not come with you" (Psalm 32:9).

The Word tells us to resist the devil, but if we resist the wrong things in life, we sacrifice precious energy. Stop trying to change things you cannot change. Let God be God! Adapt when you need to, and the reward will be worth it.

Flexibility will cause you to look young when others appear older than they actually are, you will have energy while others are tired, and you will still be bearing fruit in old age, long after others have retired.

People break when they try to do something about something they cannot do anything about. They burn out when they are trying to get something that only God can give or trying to make something go away that only God can remove. Resisting everything in life that we don't want creates a pressure inside of us that does a lot of damage to our health.

We all have things happen that we didn't plan for. We may get dressed in the morning, and we find a spot on our clothing. We didn't plan for that and don't have time for it. We can be frustrated and upset while we change clothes, we can go out with the spot on the clothes, or we can choose peacefully to change clothes since we have a situation we cannot do anything about. Think about it. What is the point in getting upset about something that will not change as a result of our being upset?

I remember a time, while conducting a conference, when we sent some luggage home early in one of our ministry trucks, thinking we no longer needed it. When we arrived at the airport, we discovered we did not have our tickets. To our dismay, we remembered they were in the luggage we sent home. We shared our story with the ticket agent, who said he could do nothing about it; the only possible solution was for us to repurchase tickets.

I felt upset building within me, then remembered my own messages and simply had a little talk with myself. I said, "Joyce, this is something you cannot do anything about; getting upset won't change it. So buy the tickets, and go home."

These types of situations occur regularly in all of our lives. Preserve your health by no longer trying to do something about something you cannot do anything about! Learning to stay calm in potentially upsetting situations is a great victory. Stability in all kinds of circumstances indicates great spiritual maturity.

PEACE BRINGS RESTORATION

One of the stress inducers we face daily in our society is noise. We live in a noisy society. In order to enjoy a peaceful atmosphere, we must create one. Outer peace develops inner peace. Find a place where you can go that is quiet, a place where you will not be interrupted, and learn to enjoy simply being quiet for periods of time. I have a certain chair in my living room where I sit and recover.

The chair is a white recliner that faces a window to our yard, which is filled with trees. In the spring and summer, I can watch the birds, rabbits, and squirrels. There was a time when I would have considered that boring, but not any longer—now I love it.

When I return from a conference now, I go home, take a hot bath, and then sit in that chair. Sometimes I sit there for several hours. I may read a little, pray, or just look out the patio door window, but the point is I am *sitting still and enjoying the quiet*. I have discovered that quiet helps me recover.

Being still has a soothing effect on us. Peace produces more peace. If we find peaceful places and remain in them for a while, we will begin to feel calmness engulf our souls. We cannot live noisy lives continually and expect to feel peaceful.

Some people have to have some noise in their atmospheres all the time. They always have music, or the television or radio, playing. They want someone with them all the time so they can talk. Each of these things done in balance is good, but we also need complete quiet and what I call *alone time*.

Jesus made sure He had seasons of peace and alone time. He ministered to the people, but He slipped away regularly from the crowds to be alone and pray. "But so much the more the news spread abroad concerning Him, and great crowds kept coming together to hear [Him] and to be healed by Him of their infirmities. But He Himself withdrew [in retirement] to the wilderness (desert) and prayed" (Luke 5:15–16). Surely if Jesus needed this type of lifestyle, we do also.

In Luke 9, we read of one occasion when Jesus took Peter, James, and John with Him to a mountain to pray, and they saw His face transfigured (changed). Verse 29 says, "And as He was praying, the appearance of His countenance became altered (different), and His raiment became dazzling white [flashing with the brilliance of lightning]."

When we get alone and take time for prayer, we will also be changed: Our weaknesses will turn into strengths. Our countenances will reflect the peace of being in God's presence. Isaiah 40:31 confirms, "But those who wait for the Lord [who expect, look for, and hope in Him] shall change and renew their strength and power; they shall lift their wings and mount up [close to God] as eagles [mount up to the sun]; they shall run and not be weary, they shall walk and not faint or become tired."

Waiting on God quietly does more to restore our bodies, minds, and emotions than anything else. We need it regularly. Insist on having it; don't let anyone take it from you. Work your schedule around God; don't try to work Him into your schedule.

You may have tried everything to feel better, but I encourage you to take my suggestion and try regular doses of quiet. I believe you will see restoration and increased peace. Remember, outer peace helps develop inner peace. Rest in God's presence, and you will take His peace with you when you go back to normal activity.

If you have peace, you can minister peace to others. Jesus was able to speak peace to the storm only because He had peace within Him. I believe He had peace within because He regularly found time to rest simply in quiet and spend time with His heavenly Father.

I hope that you can see how important it is to relieve yourself of emotional stress in order to hold your peace. In the next chapter we will look at how balancing your spending habits is both a practical and powerful way to maintain the peace you have found so far.

AVOID FINANCIAL PRESSURE

According to a survey our ministry conducted, the number-one problem most people face is financial pressure. Being in debt and not having enough money creates terrible stress on people, and it definitely steals our peace. Financial pressure is also one of the major causes of problems in marriages and is the culprit behind many divorces and even suicides.

We realize that people can find themselves in unfortunate circumstances that they could not control, but usually people create financial pressure through a lack of wisdom. When you have more money going out than coming in, it will eventually cause major problems.

The first step in people's receiving help is to face truth about how they reached their current condition. Most people who are pressured by debt feel sorry for themselves, believing they are not at fault, thinking that they are not responsible for the debts they have.

If we are feeling financial pressure, we must ask, "Were my circumstances really beyond my control, or could things have been different if I had made better choices?"

Of course, we cannot blame our debts on someone else, and repentance is the first step to recovery. Spending more money than we have is a sin, just like any other excess in our lives, and it requires God's forgiveness.

Only truth sets us free. You may have heard the statement "The truth hurts," which is true, but staying in bondage hurts even worse. If we have managed our finances poorly, made unwise choices, or acted out of emotion, we should simply admit it to ourselves and to God, ask His forgiveness, and begin immediately reversing the situation through the power of right choices.

If your finances are causing you to lose peace, ask God for a plan, get professional help if you need it, and be willing to wait on obtaining things you desire. Making bad choices is what gets us in trouble, and making right choices is what will get us out of trouble. However, making one right choice will not undo the negative result that years of bad choices have caused.

Prepare to remain steadfast. Patience will be vital to work yourself out of financial stress, but it will be worth it in the end. Anyone can be financially blessed and stable if he or she really wants to be.

Every person can prosper. Every person can have financial security, but that man or woman must follow God's guidelines. To simplify it, we can say that His guidelines are to tithe and give offerings and use wisdom in spending. God will always provide what we need if we are givers. He may not always provide everything we would like to have.

God definitely wants to bless, radically and outrageously, all of His children. The Word says that the Lord takes pleasure in the prosperity of His servant (see Psalm 35:27).

God wants us to prosper, but not out of proportion to our spiritual growth. If people are immature or carnal, which means they live according to fleshly desires, they don't really need an abundance of money and things because they will probably use them only in selfish ways. Possessions can actually take us away from God rather than bring us closer to Him, unless we understand they are tools to use as a blessing in a hurting world. God will release more and more to us as we grow spiritually. Ask God for what you want and desire, but also ask Him not to give you any more than He knows you can handle.

CREDIT CARDS

Almost everyone uses credit cards. We use them for convenience. We pay with credit cards and then weekly write checks out of our account to cover the charges. We put the checks in an envelope until the bill comes. It is easy to charge things, but it is also easy to lose track of the total being charged.

I highly recommend that you either follow our example or keep a running total of items charged so you know at all times the state of your finances. Losing track of what is going on is probably one of the major causes for financial pressure.

Using credit cards responsibly is not a problem, but when people charge things they don't have the money to pay for, it is a problem. Many people don't know how to delay gratification. We are accustomed to instant everything: We want what we want *now!*

Are you spending tomorrow's prosperity today? You are if you are charging merchandise that you don't currently have the money to pay for. If you spend tomorrow's paycheck today, what will you do when tomorrow comes? You will have to use credit cards again, and the cycle will never end.

The amount of credit-card debt in the world is unbelievable. The pressure that the media put on people to acquire new products is amazing. We are merchandise-crazy in our society; the quest to have the newest items is out of control. People will work two jobs and ignore their families, sometimes losing them in the process, just to have bigger houses or newer model cars.

Are things really that important? Do you have drawers and closets full of things you went in debt to have that you really don't even enjoy now? Are you making payments on things that have already worn out or that you have lost track of? The world says, "Buy now, pay later," but that is not what wisdom says. Wisdom says, "Do now what you will be satisfied with later." We cannot be satisfied paying for something for months and even years after we no longer are using it. The desire for instant gratification is stealing many people's financial peace.

We know from Scripture that God wants His children to be abundantly blessed, and He provides the following plan for it to happen:

> Will a man rob or defraud God? Yet you rob and defraud Me. But you say, In what way do we rob or defraud You? [You have withheld your] tithes and offerings. You are cursed with the curse, for you are robbing Me, even this whole nation. . . . Bring all the tithes (the whole tenth of your income) into the storehouse, that there may be food in My house, and prove Me now by it, says the Lord of hosts, if I will not open the windows of heaven for you and pour you out a blessing, that there shall not be room enough to receive it. (Malachi 3:8–10)

If we do what God tells us to do, He will never fail to do what He promises to do. His way works. Millions will testify to miraculous breakthroughs in their finances as a result of tithing (giving 10 percent).

As I mentioned at the beginning of this chapter, being willing to tithe and give other offerings as God leads is the first step to overcoming the pressure of debt. Many say, "I cannot afford to do that. After all, I am in debt!" I say, "You cannot afford not to do it. If you don't, you will stay in debt."

One way to remember the simple principle of financial gain is that tithing brings increase, while credit cards bring decrease to your financial peace. Most of us, at some time or other in our lives, experience firsthand the pressure of credit-card debt. Some people are wearing their tithe right now, or they are driving it, or they have used it up on a vacation they did not even enjoy or on other equally unwise things. Give to God what belongs to God, and He will always make sure you have your other needs met.

Early in our marriage, I begged Dave for a credit card. We didn't have much money, and I wanted to buy things. He really did not want to get one but finally relented.

We began with caution, but like most people, we ended up using the card for things we really did not need but simply wanted. Soon we had a huge balance and were making minimum payments, which never reduced the principal amount we owed. We were paying interest on things we had already used up and certainly could have done without.

Again, wisdom is to do now what will bring satisfaction and contentment later, while impulse is to do now what will later bring regret and even despair. Instant gratification—getting something we really want immediately—feels good, but later on, when we are paying and paying, we usually are not satisfied.

Dave was wise enough to refuse to live like that, so we cut up the card and kept making payments until we paid off the balance. We did without credit cards for years because we had proven we were not able to handle them. We did eventually get them again, but only after we had developed enough self-control to use them only for convenience in paying for things while in the store. Then we went right home and deducted the money from our checking account.

One of our managers has shared openly that he and his wife did the same thing as Dave and I, and millions of others, had done. When they decided to get out of debt, they paid for eight years on credit cards, while not using them, in order to pay them totally off.

When people are making payments on houses, one or two cars, school loans, furniture, perhaps other loans, and two or three credit cards, how could they possibly be anything other than stressed to the maximum degree? Very few individuals make enough to handle that kind of payment pressure.

No matter how much money someone makes, that is not the proper way to manage it. We have known of people who became bitter at their employers, thinking they were not paid enough to do their jobs, when in reality they were simply living beyond their means. Don't blame the results of a bad decision on someone else—only the truth will make you free.

Be very careful about making any kind of purchase on time payments, and when you do, be sure you look seriously at how long you will be making the payment and how much interest you will pay over the months or years involved. Ask yourself if you believe it will be worth it to you later on, as well as right now. Remember that emotions subside. We can all do things in excitement and be very sorry later on in life.

Through the convenience of the financial aids on the Internet, you can find a site that will give you an amortization schedule that will calculate how long it will take you to pay off a current debt. For example, if you have $20,000 of credit-card debt, which you are paying at $300 per month with an interest rate of 12.99 percent, it will take you 10 years to pay it off! And you will pay over $15,000 in interest charges! If you pay $500 per month, it will take you nearly 5 years to pay off the loan, but you will still pay over $6,000 in interest.

Obviously, the gratification that you may feel when purchasing items on credit will not be so tempting if you calculate the amount of interest and the amount of time it will take you to pay off your debt.

FILING BANKRUPTCY

If debt has overwhelmed you, you may have filed bankruptcy—or perhaps you are thinking about making that decision now. I don't mean any of what I am about to say to condemn anyone, but I do wish to make it plain how filing bankruptcy affects your credit rating later in life and sometimes follows you all of your life.

First, let me say there may be legitimate reasons to file bankruptcy. When I was eighteen years old, I was married to a man who would not work, committed adultery, stole things, wrote bad checks, and eventually ended up in prison. When we were divorced, I suddenly found that I was responsible legally to pay all of his debts. At that time I felt I had no choice, it seemed impossible and unfair for me to pay for his debt, so I decided to file bankruptcy. Had I known God as I do now and been aware of His Word and delivering power, I might have made a different choice.

It took a few years to overcome my bad credit rating. Bankruptcy should never be our first choice; we should do everything we possibly can to pay our debts. First Timothy 3 teaches us that Christians should have a good reputation with the world so no one has a reason to judge them. Not paying our bills does not help our reputation.

Today, filing bankruptcy is far too easy and becomes an answer for far too many people. It certainly should not be the solution for poor financial management. When people live excessively, they will eventually need to suffer to bring things back into balance. Bankruptcy may relieve current pressure, but it creates another type of pressure for years to come.

We find many people in financial trouble today; actually, the number is quite astounding. It is usually a result of poor management and choices. Some people have since learned wisdom and are making better choices, but they still find they are paying the price for past mistakes. God forgives us, but creditors are not quite as forgiving as God is. They want their money!

Even though God is forgiving, He expects us to pay for what we have taken from others. The Word says, "The wicked borrow and pay not again [for they may be unable], but the [uncompromisingly] righteous deal kindly and give [for they are able]. For such as are blessed of God shall [in the end] inherit the earth" (Psalm 37:21–22).

I believe God wants people to pay their debts, and He helps people, quite often through miracles, when they begin doing what is right. It is encouraging to hear of testimonies about how God has miraculously gotten someone completely out of debt. It is good to believe for a miracle, but at the same time, we need to do what we can.

As a matter of fact, I believe people don't receive miracles if they have not been sowing seeds of obedience to God. I tell people all the time, "If you do what you can do, God will do what you cannot do." Don't be the type of person who believes God for a miracle in his finances but who is not willing to do what he can do to help the process.

If you have poor credit and a lot of debt, you might have to work extra hard for a few years and show diligence in paying off your bills. Most companies will work with people having financial difficulty if the people are willing to do something. Even if you can pay only ten dollars per month on a loan balance, do what you can. Remember that God blesses diligence, but He does not bless laziness and excuses.

Don't take the easy way out (bankruptcy) just because you might be able to legally. Do all you possibly can in order not to have a bad financial reputation.

If you have already ruined your credit rating, I do believe you can overcome it, but you will need to be patient and persistent. If you are making financial decisions right now and still can avoid making bad choices, I pray this book will help you really think about what you are doing and the long-term effects of your choices.

Remember, what we sow today, we reap tomorrow, and tomorrow always comes. Too often people want instant gratification, and they don't think about tomorrow, but I repeat: *Tomorrow always comes.*

RESOURCES FOR FINANCIAL PROSPERITY

God gives resources to all of us. He is not a respecter of persons; He does not play favorites. God gives all of us time, energy, gifts, talents, and finances. If we make right choices with what we have, it will always multiply. If we make wrong choices, we deplete our resources and end up with nothing.

Let's take energy as an example. Most young people feel good, they have lots of energy and can go and go like the Energizer bunny. As I mentioned in the previous chapter, often they don't take care of themselves; they actually abuse their bodies and later on in life find themselves sick and facing serious health issues.

Time is another good example. We all have the exact same amount, yet some people accomplish a lot while others do nothing. Some people constantly say they have no time, yet they have as much as anyone else. Very often in my life, I have used my day to work on a book or teaching for an upcoming conference, while other people I knew played all day. A concert pianist spent a lot of time practicing while other children were playing. A person who wins a gold medal at the Olympics in figure skating practiced while others played.

Those who accomplished their objectives made a choice that brought an unusual reward. They were not just "lucky" or blessed more than others; they worked hard, and they used their time to accomplish their goals in life.

I am certainly not saying that we don't need to play at times, and I realize there have been times in my life when I was a workaholic, but God did say to work six days and rest one. Our world is way out of balance when people want to play more than work, and they too often seek entertainment.

People often ask me how I accomplish what I do, and the answer is *I work*. I don't feel that I am out of balance; I make sure I have fun and get rest, but I am also a hard worker. I am using my time to leave a legacy for the world in books, tapes, television, and radio programs. I want my being here to matter. I don't want just to pass through the world and take up space for eighty or ninety years, then die and have nobody remember I was here. I want people to be reading my books several hundred years from now, unless Jesus returns.

Time is a resource, and most people waste a lot of theirs. I heard myself say one day that I felt I "spent" a lot of my time getting dressed, putting on makeup, fixing my hair, getting my nails done, and so forth. God spoke to my heart and said, "That is right, you 'spend' time, so make sure it is worth it."

Any area of our lives can get out of balance. I strongly believe we should look as nice as possible, and to do so we must spend some time on personal grooming. Some people don't put in any time on their appearances, and others spend too much. All we really need in any area is balance.

Another resource is gifts and talents. Everyone can do things; they have abilities and should be using them. If we don't use something, we often lose it; or if it lies dormant, it doesn't do us or anyone else any good.

What am I doing with what God has given me? This should be one of the questions we regularly ask ourselves. If we are not satisfied with the answer, we need to make changes.

There are many things I cannot do; for example, I cannot sing well enough to do anything other than make a joyful noise, but I can talk. I have a gift of communication, and God is using it since I offered all my abilities and myself to Him. Everyone should stop moaning about what he or she cannot do, and start doing what he or she can do. If you use your resources, God will be pleased, and He will multiply what you have.

Matthew 25:15–29 teaches us about resources a master gave his servants. The Bible refers to these resources as "talents." In this passage of Scripture, the talents were money that the servants were to use properly until the master's return, at which time he would require an accounting. As you read the story, you will find that one took what he had been given and increased it five times. Another servant took his and increased it two times. Another did nothing with his, except hide it in fear that the master would be upset if he lost it.

When the master returned, he was very pleased with the two who had multiplied what he had given them, but he rebuked the one who did nothing. The master called him "wicked and lazy and idle" (v. 26) and took from him what he had and gave it to the one who had multiplied most.

This is God's way. He gives to all people what they can handle and waits to see what they do with it. Those who do nothing always become losers in life, and those who work hard, investing their resources and multiplying, always become winners. The master told the two who invested and had a good return he would put them in charge of more and allow them to share in their master's joy.

I believe people are happier and experience more joy and peace in life when they are using their resources. We all have a built-in knowledge that it is right to make progress and wrong to sit idle and watch life pass us by.

Usually people who do nothing are jealous of those who prosper. Don't be jealous of what someone has if you are not willing to do what he or she did to get it.

God expects us to manage what He gives us and to use it wisely so it will increase. We are not blessed in any way when we waste our resources, and we always pay the price for waste. One of our resources is the ability to work. In fact, the Bible instructs us to work!

> For while we were yet with you, we gave you this rule and charge: If anyone will not work, neither let him eat. Indeed, we hear that some among you are disorderly [that they are passing their lives in idleness, neglectful of duty], being busy with other people's affairs instead of their own and doing no work. Now we charge and exhort such persons [as ministers in Him exhorting those] in the Lord Jesus Christ (the Messiah) that they work in quietness and earn their own food and other necessities. (2 Thessalonians 3:10–12)

This, of course, does not apply to those who are too old or ill to work. God provides for them in other ways, but those of us who can work, He expects to do so. God worked and then rested from His labors, and we should follow His example. Deuteronomy 28:11–12 declares that God will bless the work of our hands; He doesn't bless our laziness.

DISCIPLINE AND SELF-CONTROL

Relieving financial pressure will require discipline and self-control. The Bible teaches in many places the importance of discipline. If we don't discipline ourselves, our circumstances will eventually do it for us. God's Word tells us to be temperate, which means to be marked by moderation, to hold ourselves within limits (to compromise between two extremes or find the middle ground).

Clearly, we are to maintain balance. It is wrong to overspend, but it is also wrong to underspend. You may be at a point where you need to stop spending for a while, or perhaps you need to take some of your money and go do something with it. God gives us money not to hoard, but to enjoy. Wisdom saves some, spends some, and gives some.

My husband is a very good financial manager, and that is his motto: "Save some, spend some, and give some within your borders, and you will always be blessed!"

Don't let emotions rule you—discipline them. Don't let them take charge or lead your decisions. As I stated previously, emotions rise, but they also subside. Emotions can rally you to begin a thing, but they won't be there for the finish. You may experience excitement about making a purchase but feel depression when it is time to make the payment. Emotions are fickle—they change regularly. To depend on them is a foolish choice.

Part of discipline is always to know the state of your finances. Balance your checkbook regularly; if you do not, you may think you have more money than you do and write checks that will be returned, marked "insufficient funds." When that happens, the bank usually charges at least a ten- or fifteen-dollar fee for handling. This costs you more money and only adds to the problem.

It is amazing to me how many people write checks they don't have the money to cover. In our ministry, people have sometimes given offerings and purchased products with bad checks or credit cards that have already reached their approved limits.

This should not occur with anybody, but definitely not among Christians. We are the light of the world; we are supposedly setting an example for others to follow. We are to be excellent and show forth integrity. Obviously, writing bad checks does not help accomplish any of our biblical goals.

I realize we can all make mistakes. I have had a check returned a couple of times in my life. But it was because I just added wrong or forgot to deduct a check, not that I wasn't paying any attention to my finances.

Too many people spend money without knowing how much they have. I dealt with one person who seemed to have no ability to look ahead. If she had three hundred dollars in her account, she thought she could spend it. She forgot that she still had not paid her electric bill that month.

Look ahead at what bills are going to be due, and consider when your next paycheck will be, before spending money just because it is in your bank account. Never run your account to zero, because there will always be something that you did not expect. Put aside money for emergencies, and you will enjoy a lot more peace.

COMMON SENSE

Managing our finances is not really that difficult if we learn to follow some commonsense principles.

1. Tithe and give offerings regularly.
2. Don't spend more money than you have coming in.

3. Always know the state of your finances.
4. Always plan for emergencies.
5. Don't waste money.
6. Don't spend tomorrow's prosperity today.
7. Let emotions subside before you decide to make a purchase.
8. Use tremendous wisdom with credit cards.
9. Practice delayed gratification; resist impulse purchases.
10. Always follow the guideline of "Save some, spend some, and give some within your means."

SAVE SOME

Always save a portion of whatever income you earn, no matter how small it may be—make a commitment and stick to it. One gentleman shared that his father had taught him always to give 10 percent of everything he earned and to save 10 percent. He had been practicing his father's advice all of his life, and at the age of thirty-seven he already had a sizeable amount of money and no debt. His house and car were both paid for, and at a very early age he was able to work out of his home as a consultant, making his own hours, with no financial pressure at all.

Even saving 1 percent would be better than nothing. It would be a place to begin, and you could increase from there. Do something, lest you do nothing! Without some cash saved, you will never be able to buy things without paying interest. Save for things you eventually want to buy, save for retirement, save for emergencies. *Save—save—save.* Have several accounts at one time that you are putting some money into for future needs. Save all year for Christmas, for example, and when that time comes, you will be prepared.

When Dave was a young boy, he hid money in his socks. He paid cash for his first car, which was preowned, but he later paid cash for a new car when he was about twenty-two. That is amazing, but anyone can do it if he is willing to start saving and be diligent at it. Although Dave no longer hides money in his socks, he calls his various accounts his "stash" or his "socks." Everyone in our family has learned a lot about finances just by watching Dave. He is a very patient man and can wait on things he wants. He saves and does things at the right time.

As a result of his administrative gifts, we have been able to pay cash for everything at the ministry. We have been in ministry since 1976 and in our own ministry since 1985. Since incorporating, we have made payments on only one piece of equipment (a five-hundred-dollar copy machine). We even paid cash for the building we now occupy. That sounds almost impossible in today's economy, but it can be done.

Dave simply won't buy things for which he cannot pay. He had to do without some things in the beginning while saving, but once he gained momentum and had money saved, it put him, instead of the debt collector, in charge.

We could have borrowed money and built our ministry headquarters in one year, but we took five years to build it because we wanted to move in debt-free. Patience is always worth it in the end! I am certainly not judging anyone who cannot pay cash for everything he or she does, but I am sharing that it is possible through saving regularly.

SPEND SOME

I already mentioned the fact that some people actually need to spend some of their money. Maybe it's time you did something special for yourself; it ministers to your weary emotions to do so, and that is not wrong at all. I realize this may excite you, but make sure you are one who actually *needs* to spend. And I am referring to spending out of what you have saved. Don't spend what you need for other things, and whatever you do, don't go spend what you don't have.

The ones who actually *need* to spend are people who have a tendency to be excessive in saving. They hoard things, save everything for the future, and spend nothing for now. Most of the time, people hoard out of fear or greed. I noticed that when I began saving money, I accumulated a certain amount and thought it was awesome, and the more I saved, the more I wanted to save and became unwilling to spend any of it. I wanted a big balance in my account. I then noticed that when I refused to spend any, God stopped supplying. He wants us to enjoy what He gives as well as save for the future.

If I spent some as He directed, He then replenished it and gave more besides. It is like the principle of pruning bushes. Without pruning (cutting back), they can keep getting bigger and bigger, but they also become a problem. If we prune them, they grow right back, but in better shape and condition than before.

Some people won't spend anything on themselves because they don't feel they are worthy of anything. Some are martyrs; they want to be able to say that they never do anything for themselves, hoping it will invoke pity. Some people are just plain stingy, and they hoard everything because it makes them feel secure and powerful to own things. Whatever the reason, it is wrong to be out of balance. A balanced person saves some, spends some, and gives some.

If you are working your way out of debt, and as a result you are never able to spend anything on yourself, I believe God will do special things for you through other people. When you are doing your part, God always does His part. Ask Him to bless you supernaturally, but refuse to go deeper in debt.

GIVE SOME

Giving is actually one of the wisest choices anyone ever makes. The Bible says to give and it shall be given to you, and "good measure, pressed down, shaken together, and running over" will men give back to you (Luke 6:38). Giving is wisdom, because it actually causes increase. Learning to give is one of the greatest things that ever happened to me, and many others will testify to the same thing. I heard one woman, who has a very wonderful life, recently say, "My life is a result of giving." That is a statement we should ponder.

Are you a giver? If not, you should start today. God requires the first 10 percent of all of our increase (as we saw in Malachi 3). We are to give it to the "storehouse," the place or places where we are spiritually fed (see Exodus 34:26). In addition to that, He leads us to give other offerings at various times and on special occasions.

When you give, do it with a great attitude. Don't ever give as an obligation, but realize it is a privilege. Second Corinthians 9 gives us a lot of wonderful insight about the principles of giving. It says we should not give "reluctantly or sorrowfully or under compulsion, for God loves . . . a cheerful . . . giver, [whose heart is in his giving]" (v.7). The attitude with which we give is very important to God. We are to give to bless. God blesses us so we can be a blessing.

Many people find it difficult to give, especially when they are not accustomed to doing it. The basic nature of the flesh is to be selfish; we want to own things, not give them away. But when people receive Jesus Christ as Savior, their nature changes; they receive the nature of God. This nature comes as a seed on the inside of their spirits, and they are to water that seed with God's Word. As they do so, they begin to want to do what God would do. God is a giver; those who serve Him must be givers also.

Dave grew up in a church whose minister taught the blessing of tithing; therefore, we have been tithing since we got married. We have always seen God meet our needs. In thirty-six years of marriage, Dave has been without a job only about two days, if my memory serves me correctly. We had some tight years, but we always paid bills on time and never did without the necessities of life.

In 1976, when God touched my life and called us into ministry, we began giving more than ever. We wanted to go beyond our tithe. We endured times of testing, but we have never been sorry concerning the decision we made. We have continued to increase our giving over the years and have seen God be faithful to increase us as well.

I believe givers receive a harvest back in any area where they have need. Thank God He provides financially, but that is not the only area of provision. He gives us grace. "And God is able to make all grace abound to you, so that in all things at all times, having all that you need, you will abound in every good work" (2 Corinthians 9:8 NIV). We see from this Scripture that God gives grace in abundance so we have *all* our needs met.

FROM POVERTY TO PROSPERITY

If you have been making right choices and are enjoying prosperity, keep doing what you are doing. Don't ever backslide in the principles of wisdom you have learned.

If you find yourself in debt or in need, get started now doing what is right. If you don't, you will still be in the same situation next year, and the year after, and so on. Pay the price to have financial freedom and security. No matter how big of a mess you are in—*if you consistently do what you can do, God will do what you cannot do.* Remember the simple formula: save some, spend some, and give some within your means, and you will soon find your situation changing. Not having to worry about money will greatly increase your peace.

KEEP YOUR THOUGHTS ABOVE LIFE'S STORMS

Although people cannot see our thoughts, they can see the results of them. What is in our minds and hearts is what comes out through the words of our mouths. If we have troubled minds, we will not live peaceful, serene lives. We will not minister peace to others, because we cannot give to others what we do not have within ourselves.

Jesus said we are to be makers and maintainers of peace. Paul said to work for what makes for peace, unity, harmony, and agreement with others. It is very important to make peace a priority, but it begins inside of us.

As I said earlier, Jesus was able to quiet the storm outside because He maintained peace within Himself. Jesus did not have His mind on the storm even though it was raging against Him. While the disciples were frantic and fearful, Jesus slept. He had peace in the midst of the calamity and was able to actually calm it. He had peace; therefore He could speak peace to the circumstances.

Isaiah said if we keep our minds on the Lord, He will *give* us perfect and constant peace (see Isaiah 26:3). God's Word has a great deal to say about our minds and how we think. Proverbs 23:7 teaches us that as a man thinks, so will he become. I say it another way: Where the mind goes, the man follows. Thoughts precede actions!

CAN WE CONTROL OUR THOUGHTS?

We cannot control the thoughts that come to us, but we can control what we continue to think about. For many years of my life, I simply did what most people do: I thought about whatever came into my mind. I did not know I had a choice. The Bible teaches us that the mind is the area Satan tries to control. He offers thoughts for us to entertain on a regular basis; we can either keep them or cast them down and replace them with God's thoughts.

God's written Word is a record of His thoughts toward us and about the way we are to live. The Bible literally covers every area of life. If we order our thoughts and conversation according to God's Word, we will be amazed at how enjoyable and prosperous life will be. But first we must believe that we can choose our own thoughts and that we don't have to meditate on whatever happens to fall into our minds.

Second Corinthians 10:4–5 are important Scriptures for Christians to understand: "The weapons we fight with are not the weapons of the world. On the contrary, they have divine power to demolish strongholds. We demolish arguments and every pretension that sets itself up against the knowledge of God, and we take captive every thought to make it obedient to Christ" (NIV).

This passage of the Word explains that we have spiritual weapons with which we can demolish any argument that "sets itself up against the knowledge of God," and that we have been given divine power to "demolish strongholds" and "take captive every thought and make it obedient" to the knowledge of Christ. These verses teach us that Satan tries to build strongholds in our minds so he can dominate areas of our lives through wrong thinking.

Satan is a liar, and if we believe his lies, he has successfully deceived us in one or more areas. For example, Satan told me for years that I would never have a good life because I had been abused in my childhood. I did not know any different, so I believed what I thought. As I became a student of God's Word, I learned that even though my past had been unpleasant, God had a great future planned for me. I learned it was not too late for me, as Satan had been telling me for years.

God's Word renews our minds; it teaches us a new way of thinking. We can begin to think the way God thinks instead of the way the devil would like us to think. Instead of looking at a nice home and thinking, *I could never own a home like that,* we can think (and say), *God will bless me with a lovely home. He meets all my needs.*

Instead of thinking we will get cancer because three relatives in our family died of it, we can think, *The blood of Jesus protects me, His name is a hiding place for me, God's healing power is working in my body right now, making right anything that is wrong.*

Instead of thinking we absolutely cannot forgive someone who has hurt us, we can think like this: *I am hurting, and what has been done to me is wrong, but I trust God to vindicate me. I can forgive through the power of the Holy Spirit. I will pray for the one who hurt me, I will bless him, and God will give me double blessings for my former trouble.*

Think about what you think about. If you start to feel depressed, discouraged, or angry, stop and examine your thoughts. You will find that you have been thinking thoughts that are producing the negative emotions you are experiencing. We can make ourselves miserable or happy by what we choose to think about.

When writing about the effect stress has on our health, Dr. Colbert included the following review on the importance of keeping our thoughts in line with God's Word:

Perhaps the greatest stresses that one encounters are the [unexpected] storms of life. It may be a personal injury or illness of a family member, friend, or oneself, a marital separation or divorce, the death of a relative or close friend, being fired at work, a lawsuit, finding out your daughter is pregnant out of wedlock or has had an abortion, or that your child is on drugs. These are the storms of life that seem to occur at the most inopportune times. Most of us want these problems to go away, and when they don't, they leave us even more frustrated and stressed than before, and our minds constantly seem to dwell on the problem, with no answer in sight.

When confronted with a problem like this, the first thing we need to do is realize that in this world we will have tribulation—we have been promised that. Jesus said, "I have overcome the world" (John 16:33). And "many are the afflictions of the righteous, but the LORD delivereth him out of them all" (Psalm 34:19 KJV).

So, in other words, we should be able to accept problems as an inevitable part of our lives and see them as potential teachers rather than analyzing, meditating on, and struggling over them.

I once heard a preacher use the term "renting too much space in our minds out to problems." The preacher talked about a man who had bought an apartment complex and rented out 90 percent of the apartments to drug addicts, prostitutes, and gang members, and 10 percent of the complex to law-abiding citizens who actually paid their rent. Well, after a few months, the 90 percent had run off the other 10 percent. Then the drug addicts, prostitutes, and gang members took up the whole complex, and no one was paying rent.

A similar thing happens in our minds when we start pondering, mulling over, and worrying about problems over which we have no control. We end up renting too much space in our minds to these problems, and they eventually take over most of our thoughts. In other words, we dwell on the problem, not the answer. We forget the second part of the Scripture in Psalm 34:19: "Many are the afflictions of the righteous: *but the LORD delivereth him out of them all*" (KJV, italics mine).

Instead of renting so much space to our problems, we have got to learn how to turn the channel of our minds from the worry channel to the praise-and-worship channel, the joy channel, the appreciation channel, the love channel, or the laughter channel, and start focusing on the things that are good in our lives. When we focus too much on a problem, it only makes the problem stronger. Then fretting actually becomes a habit, and the habit becomes very difficult to break.

The average person has about fifty thousand thoughts a day, and for many, these thoughts are mainly pessimistic and negative. When you are confronted with a negative thought, you have the option of either ignoring it or inviting it in and analyzing it, meditating on it, and allowing it to rent more space in your mind.

When you do the latter, you begin to speak out the problem with your mouth, and it becomes a word. You ponder it more, and it becomes an action. You then analyze and meditate on it more, and it becomes a habit, and unfortunately for the majority of Christians, most of their problems are simply negative thoughts that have become habits.

When confronted with a problem that you have no control over, ask God what He wants you to learn from it. Try to find out what He is trying to teach you by permitting the situation to remain longer than you would like.

Do you need to be more patient, more forgiving, more loving? When you allow your problems to be your teacher rather than your punishment, you will begin to learn from them and develop godly character.

Therefore, when one of the storms of life comes on you, how will you react? Will you learn to ignore little, insignificant problems and not rent space in your mind to them? Will you instead change to the appreciation, joy, love, peace, and praise-and-worship channels? When a massive storm, like a hurricane, enters your life, will you allow your thoughts to actually bring you closer to the Lord? Can you practice love, forgiveness, patience, and all the fruits of the Spirit?

Many times, the storms of life actually show us what is really inside our hearts, and unfortunately most Christians fail the test; they react in the flesh, with anger, self-pity, hostility, unforgiveness, fear, or bitterness. I tell patients to practice the love walk during the little trials of life: Practice patience and kindness, instead of being envious or rude. Through intense practice we will be ready for the storms of life; and when they do hit, we will be able to turn the channel in our minds to the love, peace, joy, forgiveness—to all the fruits of the Spirit channel. And thus, we will weather the storm of life and see the storm as a teacher that makes us even wiser.*

We know the fruit of the Spirit dwells in us, but as Dr. Colbert's article illustrates, we never really know how developed it is until it is squeezed. Trials squeeze our fruit and reveal our level of spiritual maturity. We learn more about ourselves during trials than at any other time in life.

We must remember that God is not the author of our problems, but He will use them to help us once we have them. God is good, and He gets good out of everything if we trust Him to do so. Romans 8:28 teaches us that all things work together for good to those who love God and are called according to His purpose. All things may not *feel* good, seem good, or even be good, but God can cause them to work out for good! What the enemy intends for our harm, God means for good (see Genesis 50:20).

FIGHT THE GOOD FIGHT OF FAITH

Keeping our thoughts pure and in the will of God will be a lifetime battle. We must "fight the good fight of the faith," according to First Timothy 6:12. The mind is the battlefield on which we fight. Satan wages war in the realm of our thoughts because he knows that if he can control our thoughts, he can control us and our destinies.

Study again the following verses in the *Amplified Bible*, and ask God to help you really understand the depth of their meaning: "For the weapons of our warfare are not physical [weapons of flesh

*Reprinted with permission.

and blood], but they are mighty before God for the overthrow and destruction of strongholds, [inasmuch as we] refute arguments *and* theories *and* reasonings and every proud and lofty thing that sets itself up against the [true] knowledge of God; and we lead every thought and purpose away captive into the obedience of Christ (the Messiah, the Anointed One)" (2 Corinthians 10:4–5).

Paul said we are to lead every thought captive unto the obedience of Jesus Christ. That means we take authority over wrong thoughts and bring them in subjection to God's will. His will is His Word, so we must think according to His Word to be in obedience to Him. The devil likes to argue with us, tempt us to live in the mental realm of what reasoning dictates to us. He injects proud and lofty thoughts in our minds. He suggests that we are better than other people, saying they are wrong and we are right. He puts judgmental thoughts in our minds. We must cast down these demonically induced thoughts and replace them with humble thoughts of love and concern for others.

Since we are thinking most of the time, we will find the renewing of the mind quite a battle, especially in the beginning of our journey with God. When I initially started learning these principles, I felt all I did all day was cast down thoughts and watch them come right back.

I finally cried out to God, telling Him that I didn't know how to just *not think* about something. He replied that the answer was very simple; I was to form the habit of filling my mind with good things so bad things could find no room.

I was once an extremely negative person, but God has taught me and brought me about-face so that now I am very positive and really have an aversion to being around negative people. Negative thinkers are not the type of people with whom I want to work or fellowship. Romans 12:21 shares one of the most powerful principles in God's Word; it says that we overcome evil with good! It works in every situation.

Being good to people who have treated you badly is the way to win them and break the power of Satan. It is the open door to the radical blessings of God in our lives. Thinking good thoughts is the way to overcome the habit of thinking bad ones. Yes, good always overcomes evil.

God is stronger than the enemy: "You, dear children, are from God and have overcome them, because the one who is in you is greater than the one who is in the world" (1 John 4:4 NIV). This makes reference to the fact that God and everything He represents is greater than the devil and anything he represents. God is good, the devil is evil; therefore, good always overcomes evil.

If we walk in the Spirit, we will not fulfill the lusts of the flesh (see Galatians 5:16). We don't have to spend our lives fighting with sin, temptation, wrong thoughts, lusts of the flesh. We can choose the right thing, and the wrong thing will find no place to exist in us.

There will be times of fighting the good fight of faith, but as in any other war, if we win enough battles, we will eventually win the entire war.

LITTLE BY LITTLE

We overcome the devastations of our past ways of life little by little. We make a big mistake if we look at everything that is wrong in our lives due to many years of bad choices and expect to eradicate the results overnight.

God delivers us from our enemies little by little (see Deuteronomy 7:22). Expecting anything else only sets us up for discouragement. If you discover, as a result of reading this book, that you really have some problems with your thinking processes and need some big changes in your life, don't even think it will all happen overnight or even quickly.

Having your mind totally renewed is a process that can take years. Be thrilled about your progress, and don't be discouraged about what still needs to be done. Be excited about how far you have come, not depressed about how far you still have to go. Even realizing you have a problem is progress.

We have thoughts in literally thousands of different areas, and God deals with them one at a time. The Holy Spirit worked with me for a long time, helping me learn to think better thoughts about myself. Then we worked together on how I viewed other people, my past, my future, the world, my work, and so on. In the beginning of my journey with God, I felt defeated most of the time because I kept thinking about how far I had to go. No matter how much progress I made, I was overwhelmed by what still needed to be done.

Satan wanted to make sure I did not feel at all victorious, but eventually I realized I needed to be careful how I thought about my thoughts. I could think, *I will never change. I'll never be positive enough to overcome all the junk in my mind.* Or I could think, *I may still have problems in many areas of my thinking, but I have made progress, and I will continue making progress. Even if it takes the rest of my life, I will keep pressing forward and will enjoy new victories daily.*

At first, thinking in this new way was awkward, it was work, it required effort. Eventually, being positive was natural, and being negative felt all wrong. Thinking wrong thoughts actually makes me uncomfortable now; I feel a burden on my spirit when I do. Just think how someone would feel who was perhaps twenty-five years old and had never worn shoes in her entire life—when suddenly someone put shoes on her. She would definitely be uncomfortable. When God places this halter on our minds, it is uncomfortable at first; but it is the discipline that leads us into the good plan He has for us. He wants to transform our thinking, as this verse shows:

Do not be conformed to this world (this age), [fashioned after and adapted to its external, superficial customs], but be transformed (changed) by the [entire] renewal of your mind [by its new ideals and its new attitude], so that you may prove [for yourselves] what is the good and acceptable and perfect will of God, even the thing which is good and acceptable and perfect [in His sight for you]. (Romans 12:2)

When our minds are completely renewed, we will prove for ourselves what is the good and perfect will of God. We must think in agreement with God in order to manifest His glory.

Don't be in a hurry! I know from experience that it does not do any good. It only serves to make us feel defeated all the time. Our own wrong expectation sets us up for feelings of failure. I was a very impatient individual most of my life and finally realized that God would move in His timing, no matter how big of a hurry I was in.

I saw the problem in me once I began studying God's Word. I wanted immediate change, and when I didn't get it, I felt discouraged, frustrated, and defeated. But 1 Peter 5:10 states, "After you have suffered a little while, the God of all grace . . . will Himself complete and make you what you ought to be."

Why does He allow us to suffer? I believe the suffering begins when we realize we have a problem and that we cannot change ourselves—only God can. As we wait on Him, trusting Him for deliverance, we will see victory. The waiting tests our faith to see if it is genuine. Everyone goes through the same process, so we may as well settle down and enjoy the journey. If you struggle with keeping your thoughts above life's storms, I encourage you to read my book titled *Battlefield of the Mind*. It will help you learn to renew your mind and stand firmly on God's promises for your life.

We can be transformed from people who worry all the time to people who enjoy peace of mind on a regular basis, but we will have to fight the good fight of faith and not give up if everything does not change as quickly as we would like.

FORGET YOUR PAST

Thinking about the past, especially the bad, does not do any good. We can learn from mistakes we have made, but beyond that, the best thing we can do is repent of our mistakes and forget them.

God is greater than any mistake you or I have made in the past, and we have all made plenty of them. Everyone has some skeletons in his closet that he would rather not expose. God Himself encourages us to forget the past and move on: "Do not [earnestly] remember the former things; neither consider the things of old. Behold, I am doing a new thing! Now it springs forth; do you not perceive and know it and will you not give heed to it? I will even make a way in the wilderness and rivers in the desert" (Isaiah 43:18–19).

God is always doing something new. When we mentally stay in the past, we miss our right now, and our future. We must make an effort not to spend time on things that are useless. We talked about worry and how it does no good, so why engage in it? Dwelling on the past is another excellent example of spending time doing something that does no good. We can apologize to people if we have hurt them, we can ask God to forgive us, but we cannot undo what has been done, so moving on is the only real solution. As I said, we can learn from our mistakes, which is actually very valuable.

Through not using wisdom, you may have ruined a relationship, lost a job, made bad financial choices, or gotten involved in something that did not succeed. Whatever the case might be, take the lesson you learned with you and move on—there is nothing else to do. We learn from the Word of God and from life's experiences (see Proverbs 3:13).

God is merciful and does not hold our sins against us. Hebrews 4:15 states that He is a High Priest who understands our weaknesses and infirmities. That knowledge always comforts me, as I am sure it does you. God is not angry with you if you messed up.

The apostle Paul stated in Philippians 3:12–13 that one thing he definitely attempted to do was let go of what was behind and press on to the things that lay ahead. If he had to do this, perhaps we should not feel so bad when the same thing happens to us. Paul was a great apostle—he received about two-thirds of the New Testament by direct revelation from God—and yet he made mistakes and had to move past them. I am sure he did not permit himself to dwell on the past. We cannot get beyond anything we refuse to let go of mentally.

The Word confirms that not pressing on will rob us of the futures God has planned for us. Hebrews 11 talks of those who pressed on by faith, and verse 15 says, "If they had been thinking with [homesick] remembrance of that country from which they were emigrants, they would have found constant opportunity to return to it." Peter is a great example of a man who made a terrible mistake and had to let it go. God had called and anointed Peter to do something great. He had been one of Jesus' twelve disciples and was actually one of the three with whom Jesus frequently spent special time. Yet, at Jesus' crucifixion (His greatest agony, the hour of His need), Peter disappointed Him by denying that he knew Him. Peter was afraid; it was just that simple.

On resurrection morning, when Mary found the tomb empty, the angel she saw told her to go tell the disciples *and Peter* that Jesus had risen from the dead (see Mark 16:7). It has always really blessed me that the angel mentioned Peter by name. The others were lumped into a group called "disciples," but Peter was singled out. Why? Peter probably felt as if he no longer even had the right to be part of the group; surely his grief was intense.

I am sure Peter felt he had destroyed his chance to serve God, that he had made a fool of himself and failed miserably. Peter had gone out and wept bitterly after he realized what he had done, and that was his time of repentance. Since he had repented, Jesus had already forgiven him, but then He let Peter know that he did not have to live in his mistake. Jesus included Peter in His plans for the future.

If you have made mistakes and find yourself still stuck in the past, I strongly urge you to make a decision to let go. Stop thinking about the past, stop talking about it, and press on.

I also encourage you not to dwell excessively on past victories. Don't turn your past miracles and mighty feats into memorials that you admire; it may prevent you from doing even greater things in the future.

Matthew 6:3 teaches us not to let our right hand know what our left hand is doing concerning good works. I believe this statement partially means not to dwell on the good things we have done. Give God the glory, thank Him for letting you be involved, and then move to the next thing He has for you.

I led a women's ministry in St. Louis for about seven years. We built a weekly congregation with four hundred to five hundred women in attendance. We had wonderful times, learned and grew together, saw mighty works in women's lives, but the time came when it needed to be over. God had directed Dave and me to take our ministry to a larger part of the world. In order to do so, we had to let go of what was behind. It was hard to do and even harder for many of those in attendance. After all, I was moving on to something new, but some felt as if I was abandoning them. For years after we disbanded those weekly meetings, people kept talking to me about "the good ole days" when we had the women's ministry.

I was excited about the future, but they were hanging on to the past. Eventually many of those women were no longer involved in my life and ministry. When God moves, we must move with Him, or we will get left behind.

One of the women actually apologized to me on her deathbed, saying she had been angry with me for over ten years because she felt I had abandoned the women who depended on me. Of course, she realized she was wrong, but she had needlessly suffered emotionally for many years because she was hanging on to the "good ole past."

Had I allowed the emotions of my friends to dictate my decision, I would not be seeing the good fruit I see today worldwide. Life is always flowing and going somewhere; we must be able to go with the flow. Don't stagnate and make memorials out of what God might be finished with.

We will not find peace while living in the past. God's power is available for us to live today; yesterday is gone, and we must let it go mentally and emotionally.

FILL YOUR THOUGHTS WITH FAITH

Although we have already discussed worry, I want to say a few more things regarding excessive thinking about the future. We would all love to know what the future holds, but nobody knows except God and those to whom He reveals coming events. He may, from time to time, give us supernatural insight into what the future holds, but generally speaking, we must live by faith daily.

Having faith means that we don't see or have any natural proof of what tomorrow may hold. We believe for good things, we expect good things, and we wait on God. We may be disappointed occasionally, but in Christ we can always get quickly reappointed. We can shake off the disappointment or discouragement and move on with what God is doing.

I was pondering just this morning the future of our ministry. We have been in ministry since 1976, and many things have changed during those years. I realize that things will not be the same ten years from now, but I don't know exactly what they will be. Dave and I are getting a bit older, and we realize that we will not always be able to maintain the heavy travel schedule that we have now.

When I try to look into the future with my thoughts, I must admit I don't really see anything definite. I intend to keep doing what I am doing and prayerfully helping more and more people. I just believe whatever God does, it will all be good. I believe it is important for many of our readers to realize that even ministers and authors don't always have exact direction from the Lord; we walk by faith just like everyone else. I trust that God will always take care of us, that He will always do the right thing. God does not make mistakes—people do. Often we make ours from excessive personal planning that becomes so important to us we miss what God wants to do.

Making plans for the future is part of our thinking process. If we go overboard, we can cause ourselves a lot of misery. We expect things to go the way we have planned, then when they don't, we are unhappy and lose our peace.

God's plan is always better than ours, so we should be careful about making too many of our own. I always say, make a plan and follow your plan, but be ready to let it go quickly if God shows you something else. God should always have the right of way and the right to interfere with our plans at any time.

We cannot live without making plans; if we tried to live without a plan, most of us would do nothing. But there are people who are obsessive about making plans, and I have noticed they seem upset a good part of the time. Why? Simply because they are not in control, but God is. Make plans in areas that you need to, but don't plan your future so precisely that you create problems for yourself. One of the best pieces of advice we can receive is to live one day at a time.

These verses of Scripture teach us that God will get His way in the end, so be careful about excessive planning:

- The plans of the mind and orderly thinking belong to man, but from the Lord comes the [wise] answer of the tongue. Proverbs 16:1
- A man's mind plans his way, but the Lord directs his steps and makes them sure. Proverbs 16:9

Our minds can come up with what seem to be great ideas, but in reality they will not work because they are our plans, not God's. The Bible says that there is a way that seems right to man, but the end of it is death (see Proverbs 16:25). That does not mean we will literally die because of our plans, but it does mean they won't add to our lives, they will subtract from them. They will cause trouble and not minister peace and joy; they won't work.

We should thank God that our plans don't always work, once again remembering that God is smarter than we are, and His plans are better. I want His will in my life more than I want my own, and I am sure you feel the same way.

How much mental time do you spend planning what you will do tomorrow, or even the rest of your life? If it is too much, then I suggest you spend more time telling the Lord that you want His will, asking Him to make His plans come to pass for you.

The Word says that if we will roll our works on the Lord, He will cause our thoughts to become agreeable to His, and our plans will succeed because they will actually be His plans (see Proverbs 16:3).

What does it mean to *roll our works on the Lord*? I believe it means that we genuinely want His will, not our own, and that we avoid getting into works of the flesh by trying to make things take place according to our design.

I am grateful that I can usually discern when *I* am trying to make something happen and when God is behind it, making it happen. When God is involved, things flow, there is a certain holy ease about the project. He gives favor and opens doors; He provides. When it is all me, I struggle, there is not enough of anything, and I certainly have no peace or enjoyment.

No matter how strongly I want a thing to happen, I have learned it does no good to keep pushing a project in which God is not involved. Our works of the flesh produce no good fruit. Therefore, we should roll our works on the Lord and trust Him to put right thoughts into our minds, thoughts that will be in agreement with His will so they produce good things.

TRUST IS BETTER THAN KNOWLEDGE

We usually think we would like to know the future, yet in many cases if we did know all the future holds, we would be miserable and even afraid to go forward. Trusting God enables us to handle life one day at a time. God gives us what we need. We do not have everything we need right now for our future because it is not here yet, so if we did know the future, we would all feel overwhelmed.

I have discovered that I lose a lot of peace by what I know. Knowing is not all it is cracked up to be. Some things are better left alone. For example, I don't want to know if someone doesn't like me and has been talking unkindly about me; all it does is make me unhappy. Sometimes we are quite peaceful and then we receive some information, and suddenly we lose our peace over what we just learned.

I would love to know all the wonderful, exciting things that are going to happen in my future, but I don't want to know the difficult or disappointing ones. However, I realize both will be in my future. Just like everyone else, I will have good and bad times. I really believe I can handle whatever comes if I take it one day at a time, but knowing it all now would be too much. This is why God withholds information from us and tells us simply to trust Him.

Trust really is better than knowledge. Trust ministers peace, and that is very important. I suppose we can ask ourselves this question: Do I want peace or knowledge? I choose peace. How about you?

SET YOUR MIND ON THINGS ABOVE

The Word admonishes us to think about things above, not things on the earth. This does not mean to sit and think about heaven all day, but it does mean to think about what God would think about.

He thinks of high things, not low things; good things, not bad things. We can think about anything we choose to, but we must remember that we reap what we sow. Thoughts are definitely seeds that will always produce a harvest in our lives.

The Word says we are to "aim at and seek the [rich, eternal treasures] that are above, where Christ is, seated at the right hand of God" (Colossians 3:1). When we do this, we will indeed be raised with Christ to a new way of living. Verse 2 says to "set your minds and keep them set on what is above (the higher things), not on the things that are on the earth." This clearly means that we seek whatever we think about. Whatever we fill our minds with is what we are looking for, desiring, and will more than likely end up with. Remember, where the mind goes, the man follows.

Set your mind on eternal treasures where Christ is. The mind has a tendency to wander. Our powers of concentration are not too strong. This is partially due to the age in which we live. We have literally thousands of messages coming at us on a regular basis. Just driving down the highway is like driving through an encyclopedia. We might view hundreds of various types of advertisements on billboards and posters in a short drive.

We live in the age of information. As many as five or six things can be advertised during one commercial break on a television program, and this occurs numerous times in one hour. Most of the time, commercials are so overwhelming and even frustrating to me that I will not watch regular television programs. I either watch noncommercial stations or videos that I own. I want peace of mind, not so much information coming at me at one time that I cannot possibly take it in.

The Bible says to set our minds and keep them set. That basically means, think on right things and keep thinking on them—don't give up quickly. For example, if you think about starting an exercise program, you will need to keep your mind set to do it, otherwise you will quit when you get tired or sore.

Satan steals from us by getting us to change our minds about doing right things. He shows us what is difficult about everything we try to do. We have to remember that the Holy Spirit empowers us to do difficult things and to tell the devil so. Believe that you can do whatever you need to do for as long as you need to do it.

We can live the good life, but not if we don't set our minds and keep them set on good things. Be careful when choosing what to think about, for your thoughts help determine your future. God has a plan for you, but so does the devil! With whom will you agree?

Any thought that does not minister peace is one we should cast down and reject. God is the God of peace, not confusion and turmoil. Jesus is the Prince of Peace; He left His peace for us to enjoy.

If we begin to feel upset in any way, we should examine what we are thinking about. Sometimes thoughts are so vague that we are almost unaware that we are thinking them. We might, for example, have an underlying bitter thought about someone who has hurt us. Several times a day, this little vague thought comes to us and we don't think about it long, but it keeps coming back, and by the end of the day we have actually spent quite a bit of time dwelling on something we should not have on our minds.

Recently an individual aggravated me by seeming to be always in disagreement with me. No matter what I liked, this person never liked it, making simple decisions much more difficult. I just wanted to decide something and go on, but this individual always had to make a big deal out of things that were minor issues to me.

Although each time this occurred, I consciously made a decision to forgive the offensiveness and let it go, I found myself feeling irritated several times a day when I thought of this person. My mind reviewed events where we had disagreed, and I even began to anticipate the same behavior in the future meetings. I needed to show this individual another project and found myself dreading it because I "thought" I would face the same opposition as in previous encounters.

I finally got rather violent with the devil. Realizing that he was responsible for injecting these negative thoughts in my mind, I began saying out loud, "I get along quite well with _____, and we are able to make quick decisions together. We like a lot of the same things and enjoy harmony with one another."

Although I have never experienced agreement and harmony with the individual I am talking about, I desire to do so in the future, so I am calling those things that are not into existence as if they already existed. As I've mentioned, Romans 4:17 teaches us that God does this same thing: He "gives life to the dead and speaks of the nonexistent things that [He has foretold and promised] as if they [already] existed." We, too, can declare in faith what we believe is God's will for our situations because He created us in His image and encourages us to practice doing what He does.

It certainly is not going to help me in any way to keep thinking and saying what I have experienced in the past; it will only create more of something I don't want.

What if, even after making this good confession, my experience does not change with the person in question? I will continue to war against negative thoughts about this individual, because those thoughts make me feel bad inside, they steal my peace, and it is not God's will that I think bitter thoughts. I will continue to fight the good fight of faith, knowing that my reward will come from God.

THE MIND IS AMAZING

No matter what upsetting circumstances are going on in life, if we can get them off of our minds, they no longer upset us—it is as if they do not exist for us. When we recall them, they once again become part of our reality. No wonder Satan continually brings up things that steal our peace. He even uses other people to remind us of things we want to forget.

If we want to enjoy peace, we need to be willing to tell people that we don't want to talk about certain things. Recently I made a phone call to another minister I know, and he began telling me about a minister we both know, sharing details of a messy divorce situation, lies, and immorality. He explained the situation but then obviously wanted to go on and on, talking more about it. I started losing my peace and was feeling irritated, so I simply said, "Well, you have told me what I need to know, so let's go on to something else."

Was I rude? I don't think so. Once I would have listened as long as he wanted to talk and participated myself. But those were also days when I did not enjoy a peaceful life and didn't seem to know why. I have found that being a garbage dump for other people does not promote peace for me, and I want peace more than I want to know what is going on in everyone else's life.

Don't let Satan use other people to steal your peace through giving you upsetting information you don't really need, and make sure that the enemy doesn't use you to upset other people in the same way.

The mind is an absolutely amazing organ. Thoughts affect our emotions, our health, our futures, our attitudes, our relationships, and much more. Certainly we should be careful concerning them.

What we think about literally becomes our reality. We can think of something that is not even true, but our thoughts will make it real for us. I can imagine that someone is ignoring me and feel hurt when in reality he didn't even see me. The pain is the same to me although my mind manufactured it all.

Make sure your thoughts are not deceiving you. Find out what the truth is, knowing that the truth will set you free. Paul said,

For the rest, brethren, whatever is true, whatever is worthy of reverence and is honorable and seemly, whatever is just, whatever is pure, whatever is lovely and lovable, whatever is kind and winsome and gracious, if there is any virtue and excellence, if there is anything worthy of praise, think on and weigh and take account of these things [fix your minds on them]. Practice what you have learned and received and heard and seen in me, and model your way of living on it, and the

God of peace (of untroubled, undisturbed well-being) will be with you. (Philippians 4:8–9)

If we follow this advice, we will please God and enjoy much more peace. Having peace with God and with yourself is the foundation of having peace in life. But there is still more—you must have peace with the people around you. Only then will you enjoy the full, abundant life that God's Word directs us to enjoy.

Peaceful relationships are the real evidence of living a Spirit-led life. In the next section of this book, I will share with you seven ways to keep peace with others.

Part 3

BE AT PEACE
WITH OTHERS

*So then, whatever you desire that others would do to and for you, even so
do also to and for them, for this is (sums up) the Law and the Prophets.*

—JESUS, *Matthew 7:12*

ESTEEM OTHERS AS HIGHER THAN YOURSELF

The only way we can ever hope to have peace in our relationships is if we are willing to humble ourselves and esteem others the way Jesus does. This means that we are not to think we are too good, or too important, to be the ones who initiate the act of making and maintaining peace with someone else.

I realize that the things I will be suggesting in these next few chapters will sound easier to do than they actually are. Your heart may say *Amen,* but your flesh may cry out, "I cannot do this" when the time comes to act. However, humility inspires harmony in relationships.

Humility has an enemy called *pride.* Pride is the enemy of us all. While we reviewed in previous chapters that it is important to love ourselves and to be at peace with who we are, we must never consider ourselves as more important than anyone else. In fact, the real test of humility is to regard others as a prize, *better than ourselves.* These verses hold important keys to our keeping peace with people we encounter:

Do nothing from factional motives [through contentiousness, strife, selfishness, or for unworthy ends] or prompted by conceit and empty arrogance. Instead, in the true spirit of humility (lowliness of mind) let each regard the others as better than and superior to himself [thinking more highly of one another than you do of yourselves]. Let each of you esteem and look upon and be concerned for not [merely] his own interests, but also each for the interests of others. Let this same attitude and purpose and [humble] mind be in you which was in Christ Jesus: [Let Him be your example in humility]. (Philippians 2:3–5)

Inspired by the Holy Spirit, the apostle Paul was telling us how to avoid strife through the true spirit of humility by regarding each other as better than *and* superior to ourselves. That is a difficult challenge because our flesh wants to shout, "But what about me?"

Yet, this Word clearly exhorts us to be of the same humble mind that Jesus displayed: to think of others as better than ourselves, to be more concerned for their interests and welfare than for our own, and to do nothing from conceit or empty arrogance. If we are obedient to this instruction, if we humble ourselves to tend to the needs of others, we will live in harmony and therefore be pleasing the Lord. Jesus taught us to respect all men and treat them with kindness.

Sometimes a person who does everything fast will look down on a slower person, even showing irritation. This kind of arrogance often shows up in people who are waiting in a line to be served at a fast-food restaurant. And a person who learns quickly may become impatient with someone who has to hear more than once how to do something. Truly humble people demonstrate patience, and even an *eagerness* to help the person who is weak where they are strong.

But we all have real faults, and this Scripture tells us very plainly how to handle the faults of others:

Brethren, if any person is overtaken in misconduct or sin of any sort, you who are spiritual [who are responsive to and controlled by the Spirit] should set him right and restore and reinstate him, without any sense of superiority and with all gentleness, keeping an attentive eye on yourself, lest you should be tempted also. Bear (endure, carry) one another's burdens and troublesome moral faults, and in this way fulfill and observe perfectly the law of Christ (the Messiah) and complete what is lacking [in your obedience to it]. For if any person thinks himself to be somebody [too important to condescend to shoulder another's load] when he is nobody [of superiority except in his own estimation], he deceives and deludes and cheats himself. (Galatians 6:1–3)

I have personally read and meditated on these Scriptures hundreds of times. I have a natural temperament that avoids humility, so I need all the scriptural help I can get. I do want to please God, and I am willing to do things His way, no matter how difficult it is. Reading these Scriptures reminds me that while misconduct should be confronted in a loving way, I will also have times of needing simply to bear and endure the troublesome faults that others have. Humility allows us to be patient with the mistakes of others. As we walk in love and pray for people, God will intervene and deal with their faults. We reap what we sow: If we sow mercy, we will reap mercy when we need it.

Even though we find it difficult at times to bear with the weaknesses of others, the Word of God actually strengthens and enables us to do God's will. When you are being tempted to be prideful, study and meditate on the Word, asking the Holy Spirit to do through you what you certainly cannot do by sheer willpower. Remember, pride is a sin, and it is the culprit behind all broken relationships.

The signs of pride include an unwillingness to admit fault, to take responsibility for one's actions, and to initiate making peace. Pride wants to do all the talking, and none of the listening. Pride is stubborn; it does not want to be instructed, it wants to instruct others.

Pride was Lucifer's sin; he said he would lift himself and his throne above God's! Therefore, we see that pride manifests in one's esteeming himself above the value of another, but God says we are all equal in His eyes. Lucifer, of course, was not equal with God, but as far as human relationships are concerned, no one is better than another.

Avoid Unrealistic Expectations

We all have personal standards that we expect other people to meet, and we are disappointed when people fail to act the way we hoped. But is it really what they do that hurts us, or is it our own unrealistic expectations that set us up for the pain we feel when they don't perform to our standards?

God's Word tells us to expect things from God, but not from man. But how can we have relationships and not expect anything from people? In reality, there are some things we have a right to expect, but there are also expectations that we place on people that are not rightfully their responsibilities to fulfill. For example, my joy is not my husband's responsibility—although I thought it was for many years. If he was not doing what made me happy, I became angry. *I* thought he should be more concerned about my happiness and do things differently. It was *what I thought* that caused the problem, not what he did.

Dave and I have very few arguments now that I know my personal joy is my own responsibility, and not his. Dave should do things for me that make me happy, just as I should try to please him, but there were many years in my life when it would have been practically impossible for anyone to keep me happy. My problems were in me; they were the result of abusive treatment in my childhood. I was filled with bitterness, resentment, rage, anger, and self-pity.

There was no way I could ever be truly happy until I dealt with those things. Dave could not deal with them; I had to. I was placing responsibility on Dave to make up for pain he had not caused. I was literally trying to punish him for the unfair abuse that someone else had perpetrated.

Over time, I noticed that no matter had badly I acted, Dave remained happy. It irritated me but also served as an example. I eventually became very hungry for the peace and joy I saw in his life, which were not dependent on any of his circumstances. In other words, he never made me responsible for his joy. If he had been dependent on me to make him happy, he would have never enjoyed life, because I gave him no reason to rejoice.

Are you perhaps trying to make someone else responsible for things that only you can do anything about? Are you blaming people for your problems when Satan is actually your true enemy? Let us take responsibility and stop expecting people to do for us what we should, in reality, be doing for ourselves or trusting God to do.

If I give someone some of my time by doing a favor for him or her and then expect to receive the same thing in return, I am setting myself up for disappointment. He or she may not know of my expectation. When people don't know what we are expecting from them, it is unfair to become angry when they don't meet our requirements.

The Bible says when we give a gift, we are to expect nothing in return from people. It is God who returns to us what He wants us to have according to our investment and heart attitude (see Matthew 6:1–4).

We often think people should be able to read our minds when we should be willing to clearly communicate what we expect from them. If I have a certain expectation for return of a favor I am willing to grant, I should say in the beginning, "I will be glad to do this-or-that for you, and then would you be willing to do thus-and-so for me?"

I can say to Dave, "Well, I expected you to stay home tonight." But if I did not communicate my desire to him ahead of time, it is not fair later to blame him for something he did not even know I wanted. I agree that some people should frequently be more thoughtful than they are, but we should also be willing to ask for what we want and humble ourselves by being quick to forgive those who do not fulfill our wishes.

If you truly want to have peaceful relationships, examine yourself and ask God to show you if you have expectations for people that you should not have.

We all have times when perhaps we have worked really hard or endured a difficult trial and need some special blessing to balance things out. I have learned over the years to ask God to give me encouragement when I need it. True, He frequently uses a person to do so, but I put my expectations in Him as my source, and not on people.

I ask God to provide encouragement when I feel that I have reached a place in life where I need something special to happen. I spent many years getting angry with people when I had times like this because I looked to them to make me feel better. It never produced anything but strife and offense. People are not our source, God is.

Go to God, and if He wants to use people to bless you, He will; if not, trust that whatever He chooses is what is best for you at the present time. Even if God should choose not to give the encouragement immediately, you can trust that His timing is perfect in your life.

Accept What Others Have to Offer

We expect people to give us what we would give them. We also expect people to love us the way we would love them, but this produces disappointment—and quite often, even more serious problems. We need to appreciate what other people are willing to do for us and receive their offerings with thankfulness.

One of the ways I show love is through communication. I say

uplifting things to people or spend time talking with them. My husband, on the other hand, is not a big talker. I have often wanted him to sit and talk for long periods of time, but he says what he wants to say and then prefers to be quiet. I will often go over and over the same thing, talking about it in different ways; Dave hates to do that. I have expected Dave to talk to me in the way I want him to, but he is not able to comply. It would be unnatural for him. Dave and I do talk and have good conversations, but I like to analyze things and people while he absolutely loathes doing that.

Another way I show love is to buy people things, so naturally I would like it if Dave bought me more gifts. He will let me buy whatever I want that we can afford, and he will buy me anything I ask him for, but he is not the type to go out shopping and bring surprises home to me on a regular basis. He is more logical, and his logic says, "Why should I spend all day shopping for a gift for you when you will probably take it back and exchange it anyway? Why not just let you go get what you want to start with?" I, of course, like most women, would like him to spend the day shopping for me just to know he did it.

One of the major ways Dave does show love for me is by protecting me. That is very important to him. He feels he is my covering and should make sure I am safe. For years, some of the things he did while trying to protect me irritated me immensely.

For example, Dave might tell me to make sure I bend my knees when I pick something up off the floor. He does that so I don't injure my back as I have in the past. I, however, don't want to be told how to bend over, so it has irritated me. When I get out of the car, he reminds me to watch for traffic. He is making sure I don't get hurt, but I have felt as though he thought I was dumb and couldn't cross the street without his advice. (I am sure you can see that my main problem was that I just plain did not want to be told what to do.)

After several years of his protectiveness becoming a bone of contention between us, I read an article explaining that not everyone shows love in the same way, and it set me free. I now realize that

Dave is showing me love in his way, and I received it wrong because it was not my way.

One of our daughters had a similar experience with her husband. She is very affectionate, like most women, and would like lots of pretty words, hugs, kisses, flowers, and candy. Her husband is not like that at all, so for years she felt that he was not showing her love. She even shared publicly in one of our conferences that she was very unhappy for a long time because of how she viewed her situation. She read the same article I did and realized that he did indeed love her very much. He showed his love by being a good provider, by taking care of things around the house, making sure the walk was shoveled during snow or ice so she didn't get hurt, and other things like that.

This does not mean that women have to settle for having no affection, but it does mean that women are different from men, they approach life differently, and we cannot expect our spouses to give us what we would give them.

Men are providers and protectors; God has designed them that way, and it only causes trouble when wives constantly try to make their husbands be something they are not. Should men show affection? Absolutely! But most of them will never demonstrate their affection as women do. Of course, there are men who are very affectionate and some women who are not, but I am making my statements based on what most women experience.

I am sure my husband would like it if I enjoyed sports with him, simply because it is something that really gives him pleasure. But I don't like playing or watching sports very much, and he has accepted that. I don't think he feels that I don't show him love because I don't watch football or play golf every week. I do play golf occasionally, and I do listen when he shares about sports he enjoys, but my enthusiasm level is certainly not what his is. He knows I love him, and he accepts me the way I am.

Being accepted by those we love is very important because we all want to receive acceptance. But are we giving it to others?

Remember, according to God's Word, we should esteem others as a prize—just the way they are—especially if we want to enjoy peace in our relationships with them.

I believe a humble attitude and a willingness to accept what demonstrations of love others offer to us may really help a lot of people, as it did me. Realize how your family and friends show love for you, and stop concentrating on how they don't. Be positive and not negative.

DON'T GRIEVE THE HOLY SPIRIT

We've already studied in previous chapters how stress causes a great deal of diseases. We know that the symptoms are real, but how many bottles of medicine are sold to combat emotional disorders when the root cause is actually a lack of peace in an individual's life?

I wonder how many cases of stress and depression are the result of strife between relationships in the home or on the job. We treat the symptoms of stress, but we often ignore the sin of pride as the underlying cause of our lost peace. Our general health is much better when we live in peace. Humility, always esteeming others as higher than ourselves, will keep us full of peace and free from grieving the Holy Spirit.

Ephesians 4 teaches us that we grieve the Spirit of God ("offend or vex or sadden Him") when we are not getting along with each other—when we lack harmony and unity. Paul exhorted us to let go of all bitterness, wrath, passion, rage, bad temper, anger, animosity, quarreling, clamor, contention, slander, evil speaking, abusive or blasphemous language, malice, spite, ill will or "baseness of any kind" (see vv. 30–31). If we are living in those conditions, no wonder the Holy Spirit is grieved! Yet many homes are filled with these demonstrations of strife every day.

But it is quite plain; in essence, the Word says we are to stay in peace at all times. The power of peace binds us together. The presence of the Holy Spirit produces peace, and Paul encouraged us to "be eager and strive earnestly to guard and keep" it (Ephesians 4:3).

The thought of grieving the Holy Spirit makes me very sad. I am willing to humble myself and resist strife when I remember that what I do affects the Holy Spirit. When He is grieved, we also feel that way because He lives in us.

AVOID BLINDNESS TO YOUR OWN FAULTS

One of the ways to maintain godly humility and promote peace in our relationships is to take a good, long, honest look at our own faults. Self-deception is one of our biggest problems as human beings. We easily and quickly see what is wrong with others but rarely, if ever, see what is wrong with us. We judge others, and the Lord tells us there is no justification for this: "Therefore you have no excuse or defense or justification, O man, whoever you are who judges and condemns another. For in posing as judge and passing sentence on another, you condemn yourself, because you who judge are habitually practicing the very same things [that you censure and denounce]" (Romans 2:1).

Why would we judge someone else for the same thing we are doing? Because we look at others through a magnifying glass but see ourselves through rose-colored glasses, a tinted glass that makes everything look lovely whether it is or not.

In our thinking, there is absolutely no justification for the wrong behavior of others, but for us there always is. We always seem to have some valid reason why we have behaved badly that excuses us from being responsible. For example, someone might be short-tempered with us, and we feel it was inexcusable for him or her to treat us that way. We might have treated someone the same way on another day, but we had done so because we felt ill or had a bad day at work.

In reality, we should practice being harder on ourselves than others simply because the Word tells us we will not be asked to give an account of their lives, but of our own: "Why do you criticize and pass judgment on your brother? Or you, why do you look down upon or despise your brother? For we shall all stand before the judgment seat of God" (Romans 14:10).

I read this Scripture often because it reminds me how God views my critical judgment of other people. Second Corinthians 13:5 says we are to examine ourselves, but we are usually examining others, which produces nothing but judgmental attitudes and eventually trouble.

Paul said to examine ourselves before God, not unto condemnation, but in order to recognize areas of need in our own lives, and to ask God for His help. But nothing will change if we are blind to the truth of our own shortcomings. Psalm 51:6 says, "Behold, you desire truth in the inner being; make me therefore to know wisdom in my inmost heart."

Jesus has paid for our freedom to see the truth, yet it does us no good until we are truthful with ourselves, about ourselves. We fear looking at ourselves; our pride keeps us from wanting to see our own selfish tendencies. The way we evade facing this needed truth about ourselves is by finding fault with other people instead.

But when we judge others, we are setting ourselves up as gods in their lives. We have no right to judge others; they are God's servants. James 4:12 says it very plainly: "[But you] who are you that [you presume to] pass judgment on your neighbor?"

Can you remember a time, or times, in your life when God has strongly convicted you of some fault? Perhaps some situation exposed it. Times like this tend to humble us, at least for a while.

I had always been short-tempered with people who gossiped about me, not admitting that there were times when I also gossiped about others. Then I got caught, and a friend who heard what I had said confronted me. I had no way out and was terribly humbled. For a while after that, I was very patient with other people who said things about me, but eventually my pride crept back in, and I had to be humbled all over again.

God tells us to humble ourselves, but if we don't, He will do it for us. He either corrects us privately, or if we persist, He will do it publicly. We either fall on Jesus (the Rock) to be broken, or the Rock falls on us to break us—the choice is ours.

If God begins to deal with us about some wrong behavior, there is no point at all in trying to avoid Him. When God admonishes me for my behavior in a relationship, it is particularly difficult for me if I feel the other person does the same thing that God is asking me to change. I have told God more than once, "This is not fair. What about the other person?" He always reminds me that *how* and *when* He corrects another is His business. All I need to do is receive my chastisement from Him without complaint or comparison.

I remember one particular time when God was strongly dealing with me about not being rude to my husband. However, I felt Dave was also being rude to me, and I told God so. I was so frustrated about God confronting me and not Dave also, that I went to Dave and asked him if God was correcting him about anything.

He pondered for a moment, and then with an innocent look on his face, he said, "No, I don't believe He is." I look back now and those events amuse me, but they sure were not funny at the time.

Being willing to be first to do whatever is right is commendable behavior. Being willing to do what is right, even if no one else ever does what is right, is something that God may call upon us to do. We also may have to do what is right *for a long time* before we will get right results, and we may have to treat people in our lives right (humbly love them) a long time before we begin reaping the good seeds we have sown.

CORRECT WITH SINCERE LOVE

Remember, we have a right to pray for people but not to judge them. Should we ever try to correct another brother or sister in the Lord, or someone in our families? Yes, as we read in the beginning of this chapter, there may be times when God will use us to confront someone for misconduct, but once again it must be with humility, not having an exaggerated opinion of our importance or spirituality.

Paul was an apostle, and therefore God used him to bring correction to the churches quite frequently. But he said, "By the grace of God given unto me, I warn you not to estimate and think of yourself more highly than you ought to" (see Romans 12:3). I have always been struck by the fact that Paul said he corrected people because of God's grace in him to do so, not just because he had an opinion and wanted to express it.

When we do anything by God's grace, it has God's power on it and therefore produces good results. When we try to correct people, but God has not given us the assignment to do so, we only cause trouble.

I quickly learned in the early years of my marriage that I am not my husband's teacher, nor have I been assigned the job of correcting him. There have been rare occasions when God has used me in that way with Dave, and each of those times he has received the correction. The times I just decided I was going to tell him a thing or two only initiated a small war between us.

When we do correct people, it should be because we truly love and care about them, not just because we want to tell them what is wrong with them and act superior. I do have an assignment from God that requires frequent correction of people, both in my teaching and among my staff. I try to maintain a truthful attitude about myself also, lest I become bossy with them.

I can be the boss and not be bossy. I always share with people what they are doing right as well as wrong, and I also try to admit my own faults with them as well because I find this puts people at ease.

BE WILLING TO BE WRONG

Most of us have an out-of-balance craving to be right about everything. My personal belief is that the need to be right rises from insecurity, which is also a manifestation of pride. If we have peace with God and are secure in ourselves, why do we need to be right all the time? Why can't we be wrong about something without feeling wrong about ourselves?

It is amazing, the fleshly feelings we have when we try to sit quietly and let someone else think he is right when we are convinced we're the one who's right. Dave and I both have rather strong personalities in many ways and neither of us enjoys saying, "I was wrong." We both do it at times, but we are still in the process of learning to enjoy it.

First Corinthians 13 says love doesn't demand its own way. That means there are times when we will have to give up what we think is our right to be right. It is amazing how many arguments we can avoid if someone is willing to say, "I think I'm right, but I may be wrong." Even if one party has the humility to say he could even *possibly* be wrong, it seems to dissipate the argument.

Sometimes we argue over things that don't even make sense—things so unimportant that they should be left entirely alone. Dave and I used to argue over directions on how to get to a place we were going; he wanted to go one way, and I thought another way was a little bit shorter. It would have been better to take a little longer to get there, if that ended up being the case, rather than argue about it. Most of the time there is more than one right answer, and peace is much more important than having your own way.

The Word says that a servant of the Lord must "have nothing to do with trifling (ill-informed, unedifying, stupid) controversies over ignorant questionings, for you know that they foster strife and breed quarrels" (2 Timothy 2:23). Staying out of strife is not a suggestion; it is a command from the Lord.

We lose our power when we lose our peace. We hinder the flow of our anointing, which is one of the most precious treasures we have, and we also hinder our blessings from flowing in abundance. Remember the example I gave in the beginning of the book about

Abraham and Lot? Abraham was so determined to stay out of strife that he allowed Lot to choose the best part of the land for himself, while he (Abraham) took what was left. God blessed Abraham and rewarded him for his right choice by telling him he could have all he could see as he looked north, south, east and west.

We can be prideful or peaceful. Pride says, "I am right" and has no willingness to even consider it might be wrong. Humility says, "I may be wrong, and it is not that important whether I am right or not."

I believe you can see why humility is the basis for any successful relationship. Even if only one person in the relationship will treat the other with loving humility, the relationship will flourish, because God promises to lift up the one that is humble (see Psalm 147:6). The Word also says that the one "who is of a humble spirit will obtain honor." In this light, we should never fear the consequences of adapting ourselves to the needs of someone else. In the next chapter, we will look at the rewards of being Peacemakers by remaining flexible and encouraging others.

ADAPT YOURSELF TO THE NEEDS OF OTHERS

The Word says, "If possible, as far as it depends on you, live at peace with everyone" (Romans 12:18). First Peter 3:11 makes this very clear: "Let him turn away from wickedness and shun it, and let him do right. Let him search for peace (harmony; undisturbedness from fears, agitating passions, and moral conflicts) and seek it eagerly. [Do not merely desire peaceful relations with God, with your fellowmen, and with yourself, but pursue, go after them!]"

Peaceful relationships seem to be fading away in our society. The divorce rate is still climbing, and the percentage of failed marriages is said to be even higher among Christians than other people in the world. What is wrong? Is it the stressful society in which we live, or is selfishness still on a rampage?

The Word says that in the last days will come "times of great stress and trouble [hard to deal with and hard to bear]. For people will be lovers of self and [utterly] self-centered" (2 Timothy 3:1–2). They will love money, be greedy, hard-hearted, disobedient, immoral, lacking self-control, and they will have no desire to make peace.

We are living in those times. These are days of great moral darkness, and we, as believers in Jesus Christ, must let our light shine out in the darkness. In practicality, that means we must let our behavior emulate that of Jesus and not be sucked into the world and its system. If people treat us badly, we cannot return evil for evil, but rather forgiveness and love so that others will see God's love in the way we treat people.

Unity among people is pleasant. It releases blessings from God and the anointing power of His presence (see Psalm 133:1–3). Unity, harmony, and peace in relationships won't just come to us; we must go after them with all of our might. We must not wait for someone else to make the first move; we must be Peacemakers; we must make and maintain peace.

One usually must be spiritually mature before he will choose aggressively to be the peacemaker. Jesus said the Peacemakers will be called "the sons of God" (Matthew 5:9). As I have mentioned before, He said "sons," not children, indicating maturity. We are called to lay aside childish behavior and make and maintain peace as responsible sons and daughters of God.

Not all people are as easy to get along with as others. It seems we all have some people assigned to us in life who are like sand-paper. They always seem to grate on us and make a habit of being difficult. They are never happy, no matter what we give or do for them. They regularly find fault and rarely, if ever, encourage us in any way. They are takers and not givers.

Then there are the people who have irritating habits. We love them; we may even be married to them, yet they have one or more idiosyncrasies that continue to rub us the wrong way. An example is those who feel they must give their opinion on everything, whether anyone asks for it or not. Then there are the people who dominate all conversations, to whom we rarely, if ever, get to express ourselves. Even when we try, they interrupt us. They may not even realize they are making conversation difficult; they may be doing something as simple as slurping their soup or popping their chewing gum, but the distraction throws off our concentration and frustrates us.

My point is that we all get opportunities to hold our peace and to be Peacemakers. I dare say that every person in this world has some challenging people in his or her life. Of course, we must remember that we are also challenges to others. Someone struggles with us, with our personalities and habits, just as we struggle with others.

ARE YOU REAPING WHAT YOU HAVE SOWN?

We like the law of sowing and reaping if we are reaping good seeds we have sown, but we will also reap from the bad seeds we cast along our paths. I remember a time when I felt Dave was being particularly crude and rough in the way he was speaking to me. I immediately felt offended and began to complain to the Lord. He quickly reminded me that I had talked to Dave the same way for years and was only reaping on seeds I had sown in the past.

Actually Dave rarely talked to me in that brisk way, whereas I had probably spent many years being grumpy with him. I had improved and had forgotten about all the years I had spoken that way to him. We want other people to be patient with our faults, but we are not always willing to give others the same mercy and grace we want to receive.

Facing truth is one of the most beneficial things we ever do in life, but it must be truth about ourselves that we face. Truth sets us free; self-deception keeps us in bondage.

Why is it so painful to see ourselves as we really are? Simply because of pride. When we see ourselves in reality, the way others see us, our pride is hurt and we are embarrassed.

When someone talks unkindly about me, is he sowing seeds to reap unkindness, or am I reaping on what I have sown in the past? When we have an appointment and the other person is late, is he sowing seeds that will cause others to be inconsiderate, or are we perhaps reaping on times when we have been late for other appointments? These are questions we must ask ourselves.

We must be honest with ourselves and not go through life blaming others for everything that goes wrong in our relationships.

Pride causes us to be blind to our own faults, but God's Word encourages us to be careful when we think we stand, lest we fall. In other words, we shouldn't think more highly of ourselves than we ought to because this type of pride will also cause our own downfall (see Proverbs 16:18).

DON'T FORCE YOUR CONVICTIONS ON OTHER PEOPLE

It is arrogant of us to try to make other people agree with our convictions. For example, I try to eat reasonably healthy meals, and I have studied nutrition and its effects on the body. Consequently, I have strong opinions about how we should take care of ourselves. I do eat sweets, but only small amounts, and I am usually concerned when I see anyone regularly consuming large amounts of sweets and other foods that I know to be unhealthy.

I have tried to tell people that they are eating poorly, and they have not received my advice well, to say the least. I even had one person say, "If we are going to spend time together, I don't want you telling me what to eat all the time and making me feel guilty when I eat something you don't approve of."

The person went on to say, "I know I don't eat right, but I am just not at the place yet in my life where I am ready to do anything about it. I have lots of things wrong with me that I feel are more urgent than my appetite. So I am concentrating on what I feel God is dealing with me about, and I have no time to pay attention also to what you are dealing with me about."

The person sounded pretty harsh and actually did not display a good attitude toward me, but I got the point, and I have been less likely ever since to tell anyone how he or she should eat. We all tend to put our convictions on others; we think if they are priorities for us, they must be priorities for everyone.

The fact is that people have a right to make their own choices, even wrong ones. God will actually protect people's right to go to hell if that is what they choose to do. In other words, even as much as God wants them to spend eternity with Him, He won't force them, and we cannot force people to do things we want them to do either.

Romans 14 shares examples of how people were in a quandary about whether or not they should eat meat that had been offered to idols. Some thought it would be a sin, and others said the idols were nothing anyway and therefore could not harm the meat. Some could not eat because of their weak faith, and others ate because of their strong faith. Paul told them to let them each be convinced in their own hearts and not try to force their personal convictions on others. God seems to meet each of us where we are at in our faith. He begins with us at that point and helps us grow gradually and continually.

GIVE PEOPLE FREEDOM TO BE THEMSELVES

One of the most devastating things one can do to a relationship is try to make the other be what he or she can never be. We must accept people and not reject them when they don't change to suit us. We all seem to look at the way we do things as the standard for everyone, which is, of course, another manifestation of pride. Instead, we should see that God created us all differently but equally. We are not alike, and we all have the right to be who we are.

I am not speaking at this point about faults that God will deal with in time; I am speaking of our inherent, God-given traits that vary from person to person.

I talk a lot; Dave is quiet. I make decisions really fast, and he wants to think about things for a while. As I've mentioned, Dave loves all kinds of sports, and I don't really like any of them—at least not enough to put much time into them. Dave wants each item in a room to stand out, and I want everything to blend. I am sure you could tell similar stories about personal differences you have in your relationships with others.

I am a serious person (sometimes too serious), but I know people who seem to be serious about nothing. There are people I can say almost anything to and they are not easily offended, and then I know others who are very sensitive and I have to be more careful around them. I am blunt and straightforward, so sometimes I struggle with those who have tender personalities.

Why does God make us all different and then put us together and tell us to get along? I am convinced that it is in the struggle of life that we grow spiritually. God purposely does not make everything easy for us. He wants us to exercise our "faith muscles" and release the fruit of the Spirit, including love, patience, peace, and self-control.

If everyone pleased us all the time, if our faith was never stretched and our fruit never squeezed, we would not grow spiritually. We would remain the same, which is a frightful thought. There are two kinds of pain in life: the pain of change, and the pain of remaining the way we are. I am more fearful of remaining the same than I am of changing.

Dave and I argued and lacked peace in our relationship until we agreed to accept each other the way God had created us. I cannot say things were perfect after that, but they certainly improved. People cannot change people; only God can. We discovered it would be wiser to accept and enjoy each other while God was making whatever adjustments He wanted to make in His timing.

I learned that all people have God-given variations in their temperaments and therefore realized I was expecting people to be something they couldn't. I was asking for a response from them that they did not know how to give.

Some people are gifted with thoughtfulness, and others rarely think about doing things for other people. They are willing to do thoughtful acts if someone suggests it, but they don't take initiative on their own. The person gifted with thoughtfulness might also be impatient, while the person who is not very thoughtful (he will always forget your birthday) is extremely patient in every situation. We all have good qualities, but none of us is gifted in them all.

Accept people where they are, and trust God to change what needs to be changed in His timing, His way. Rejection is one of the greatest emotional pains we endure in life. I don't want to be the source of that kind of pain in anyone's life ever again. I finally realized I have more than enough faults of my own; I don't need to magnify anyone else's.

Tell people the good qualities you recognize in them; don't point out what you think they need to improve. Compliment, don't find fault. Accept, don't reject. Be positive, not negative. Be encouraging, not discouraging. You and I will never lack for friends if we will practice giving people the freedom to be themselves.

I honestly believe acceptance is something that all people crave. We cannot endure a person who constantly wants to turn us into something we don't know how to be. To be around such a person for too long is like living in prison.

We can easily fall into the trap of trying to change our children, as well as spouses, friends, and coworkers. We should merely encourage others to become all God has intended them to be. We must not expect to live our unfulfilled dreams through the lives of our family or friends. Everyone has a right to his or her own life.

Be Adaptable

One of the major ways to avoid strife and stay in peace is to be adaptable. We always want others to adapt to us, but they want us to adapt to them. Until someone decides to be adaptable as unto the Lord, strife and contention will rule, or in reality, the devil will rule because he is the one who instigates the turmoil to begin with.

The Word says, "Readily adjust yourself to [people, things] and give yourselves to humble tasks. Never overestimate yourself or be wise in your own conceits" (Romans 12:16). This Scripture has been very helpful to me. It is amazing how peace increases when we make the simple act of adapting or adjusting to someone else. This principle was once foreign to me. I wanted everyone else to do the adapting, and it never occurred to me to try adapting to other people's preferences.

When I tried, my flesh screamed out against it, because we are inherently selfish and our flesh always wants what it wants when it wants it. However, God calls us to follow the leading of the Spirit, not our flesh. The flesh was legally nailed to the cross with Jesus, and we have been resurrected to a brand-new life. We are called upon daily to put off the old man and put on the new man. This literally means to ignore the pleadings of the flesh and follow the Spirit of God.

Paul talked about buffeting his flesh, keeping it under discipline and self-control. This is all part of pursuing peace. For example, Dave and I planned to watch a movie tonight. We agreed to take our showers and prepare for the evening so we could begin the movie. I got ready, and Dave was sitting on the couch, reading a travel brochure about hotels around the world. I kept asking him to get ready because it was getting later and later. He kept saying "Uh-huh, okay" but was not moving. I could feel my flesh getting irritated, so I made a conscious decision to say nothing more and remain in peace no matter what happened.

Once I would have simply followed my feelings, and the entire evening would have been ruined. I would have nagged him until he either got up or got mad. I finally realized, somewhere along the way, that getting my way is highly overrated.

In other words, relieving the pressure the flesh feels when it does get its own way is not worth the pressure we endure from arguing and losing our peace to get it. When the flesh rules, everyone loses, except Satan.

An adapter is a device used to bring compatibility between two totally different parts. We use electrical outlet adapters when we travel to foreign countries. The outlets in the walls are different from the plugs on our electrical appliances, so we always take our adapters. One side plugs into our appliance and the other into the wall outlet, thus bringing the two into compatibility.

When we enter any type of relationship, we need to become willing to adapt simply because no two are ever exactly the same. Dave and I have recently become friends with a married couple. We like a lot of the same things, and it appears it will be a great relationship; however, we do have differences and will therefore need to adapt to one another. I am also certain from my experience with other relationships that the longer we know one another, the more things we may need to adapt to in each other.

What happens when one person in a relationship is willing to adapt, and it seems the other person never does? This, of course, makes it more challenging, but it has been a great help to me personally to remember that I am responsible to God only for my part, not what the other person does or does not do. We are not liberated to do wrong simply because someone else chooses to do wrong.

Be Happy for People When They are Blessed

I love to be around people who are really happy for me when I am blessed or have something wonderful happen in my life. Not everyone is like that. We should pay heed to the Scripture that says to rejoice with those who rejoice and weep with those who weep (see Romans 12:15).

I received a very special gift a while back, and it was interesting to see how different people responded. Some said, "Joyce, I am so happy for you. It really blesses me to see you blessed." I knew they were sincere, and it increased my joy. It also made me want to pray that God would do something awesome for them too.

Another friend said, "I wish someone would do something like that for me." Actually this particular person almost always responds in a similar fashion when I receive nice things. Even when my husband does lovely things for me, the individual will say, "My husband just doesn't seem to know how to do things like that." These responses indicate a spirit of jealousy or some deep-seated feeling that she is not getting what she deserves in life.

At one time I was like that: I pretended happiness for people when God blessed them in some special way, but inside I didn't really feel it. At that time in my life, I compared myself to others and always competed with them because the only way I could feel good about myself was if I was ahead of or at least equal to others in possessions, talents, opportunities, and literally anything else you could think of.

I am grateful that God has worked in my life, and I can be genuinely happy for others when He blesses them. I must be honest, though, and say I still sometimes have a little problem if the blessing comes to someone I might consider an "enemy." You know the type—someone who has hurt you in some way. I am not responding perfectly yet, but at least I have made progress.

I love the friend I just mentioned, and in many ways she meets my needs. I know this friend loves me and this is just a small character weakness, so I let it go. But I also know it prevents me from wanting to share what God is doing in my life because I know she cannot be truly happy for me. I also believe it prevents her from being blessed. Dave and I both feel strongly that we will not receive blessings until we can be truly happy for the blessings of others.

All of these areas are ways in which we can adapt to the needs of others. When we can adapt ourselves to both their needs and their celebrations, we will enjoy lasting peace with them. If we are struggling in our ability to adapt to the needs of others, we must be careful to avoid foolish, unproductive comments that will quickly tear apart even close relationships. Next, we'll talk about how idle words can steal our peace.

BEWARE OF IDLE TALK

The Bible teaches us to beware of idle talk—vain, useless words that do not minister life to either the speaker or the hearer. Believers are to speak words that are full of God's truth, that build up and encourage, but idle words cause life to drain out of relationships with one another. The Word says, "He who guards his mouth keeps his life, but he who opens wide his lips comes to ruin" (Proverbs 13:3).

Some people really seem to know the Word of God; they appear to have good relationships with God, yet when we are with them, we sense death instead of life through the words they speak. There is something about them that just doesn't seem right. Many of these people leak life and have nothing left but death because of their idle talk. They have received life from God, but they drain it away through unguarded, careless comments.

I believe that idle words can affect our health and even the length of our lives, but it is our spiritual lives that are quickly emptied when we indulge in vain, useless, idle talk. Other than obvious sin, idle words cause the most damage to our lives.

The Word says, "But I tell you, on the day of judgment men will have to give account for every idle (inoperative, nonworking) word they speak. For by your words you will be justified and acquitted, and by your words you will be condemned and sentenced" (Matthew 12:36–37). Imagine having God judge every idle word that we speak. This Scripture is not talking about unclean words, evil words, negative words, or even slanderous words. It speaks of ineffective, unnecessary words; idle words are those that have no value and are the faithless things we simply did not need to say.

What does the phrase mean, "They shall give account thereof" (Matthew 12:36 KJV)? I believe it means that we pay for them. They actually bring a curse with them, and in some ways, we endure the effect of it. Idle words steal our lives. The Word says clearly, "Death and life are in the power of the tongue, and they who indulge in it shall eat the fruit of it [for death or life]" (Proverbs 18:21).

You have probably heard the phrase, "You will have to eat your words before it's over," and this Scripture backs up the statement. We do eat our words! What we say not only ministers life or death to the hearer but also to us who speak them.

We can literally increase our own peace and joy by the things we say or the ones we don't permit ourselves to say. God's Word encourages us to think about what words we will use before we speak:

- The mind of the wise instructs his mouth, and adds learning and persuasiveness to his lips. (Proverbs 16:23)
- Be not rash with your mouth, and let not your heart be hasty to utter a word before God. For God is in heaven, and you are on earth; therefore let your words be few. (Ecclesiastes 5:2)
- Let every man be quick to hear [a ready listener], slow to speak, slow to take offense and to get angry. (James 1:19)

Words are containers for power, positive or negative. Words actually are a tremendous responsibility, and we should be more careful how we use them. Proverbs 6:1–2 says, "If you have given your pledge for a stranger or another, you are snared with the words of your lips, you are caught by the speech of your mouth."

Many relationships are destroyed because people speak foolish words that they don't even mean. People blurt out hurtful words that are very damaging. Wrong words cause a lot of problems because they are not easily retracted or erased from our memories.

As individuals, we are often uncomfortable if we are with people and nobody is talking. We seem to feel someone should be saying something all the time. During these times when we simply try to fill up the air space with words, we may speak idle words that cause problems. We can chatter on and on about things that don't even deserve discussion. Idle people with lots of idle time usually say lots of idle things.

Paul gave instructions about widows whom the church leaders were to support. He said younger widows should not be put on this list because they might become idlers and spend their time talking about things they should not mention. I believe Paul was assuming that younger women would have enough energy to work and be active. If they had nothing to do because the church was supporting them, it would lead to trouble. He wrote:

> But refuse [to enroll on this list the] younger widows, for when they become restive and their natural desires grow strong, they withdraw themselves against Christ [and] wish to marry [again]. And so they incur condemnation for having set aside and slighted their previous pledge. Moreover, as they go about from house to house, they learn to be idlers, and not only idlers, but gossips and busybodies, saying what they should not say and talking of things they should not mention. (1 Timothy 5:11–13)

I have been practicing thinking before I speak, and it is amazing to me how many times I realize that what I am about to say simply does not need to be said. It won't do any good; it does not build up or add to anyone. In many instances, what I was about to say could have been downright harmful, or at least useless. I believe forming this habit is adding peace to my life and the lives of those around me.

Idle words are one of the easiest ways to break unity and sabotage the power of peace. Apologies don't quickly repair the bad impression that heated, foolish words can leave. We can confess our sins, but how can we ever make amends for idle words spoken against other people? How can we repair someone's reputation that we have destroyed with foolish accusations? We may go to the person and ask forgiveness, but we cannot take the words back. Their message has already entered people's ears, and we have no way to eliminate them. You can pay someone back for something you steal, but you cannot repay the damage done by idle, careless words.

People who talk a lot (like me) are more apt to make mistakes with their mouths than quiet people are. Those of us who talk a lot will need to exercise even more caution than others. With much speaking, the tongue becomes heated, and in being overheated, it loses gentleness. Proverbs 15:4 says, "A gentle tongue [with its healing power] is a tree of life, but willful contrariness in it breaks down the spirit." We should strive to keep a gentle, wise tongue, for idle words are the opening through which our power for life leaks away.

Guard Your Heart

Out of the heart the mouth speaks. If we permit wrong thoughts to dwell in our hearts, we will ultimately speak them. Whatever is hidden in our hearts, our mouths will sooner or later express openly. Satan may make an evil suggestion to us, he may try to plant a wrong thought; however, we need to be diligent to guard our hearts.

There is too much at stake not to use diligence in keeping our hearts full of God's truth. Our outer lives are only visible representations of our inner lives. If a tree is rotten, it will bring forth diseased and rotten fruit, and if it is good, it will produce good fruit.

We've seen that we must cast down wrong thoughts and bring them into subjection to God's Word (see 2 Corinthians 10:5). If we are thinking things that are contrary to God's Word, we must renew our minds with proper thoughts. We should think on good things, excellent, and noble things (see Philippians 4:8).

If the attitudes of our hearts are not in line with the heart of God, neither will the words of our mouths reflect His Word. Although you may sometimes say things in the heat of emotion, don't excuse yourself by saying that you did not mean what you said. Take responsibility before God, and ask for His grace to change if you are speaking idle words that are not full of faith or edifying to others.

Another example of idle words is those we speak to ourselves that upset us and get us in a bad humor. For example, we may have been dealing with a particular upsetting issue, which we have prayed about and have even cast our care on God. By doing so we have enjoyed peace even though we have an unpleasant situation. But then someone asks us about it, and in talking about it, we give gruesome details and discuss how unfair and painful the entire thing is. Soon we find ourselves upset once again.

We can actually upset ourselves by how we choose to talk about our situations. When we are filled with life, we are filled with peace; when we leak life, we experience a loss of peace.

SAY THINGS THAT EDIFY

Speaking idle words can become a bad habit. Thankfully, we can break bad habits and form good ones. Let us strive to form a habit of speaking words that edify people. Words of edification minister life, not death. Make a commitment to spread good news, and let all bad news stop with you. When someone tells you some kind of an unclean, unkind, or negative story, don't spread it to anyone else.

If you have an opportunity to stop people before destructive words escape their mouths, do so. To have these leaks in us completely stopped, we must get rid of our curiosity.

Most people are full of curiosity; even Christians are nosey. People tend to enjoy knowing all that is going on in other people's lives. Being delivered from this morbid curiosity, we will sin less. We will have less opportunity to speak idle words if we know less.

I must admit I have always been a curious person; I've said already that once I liked to be "in the know." But I discovered that I could be very peaceful and thoroughly enjoying my life and then find something out that immediately stole my peace. I then wish I had never asked a question or listened to what I just heard, but it was too late.

I have often paid for my curiosity with a loss of peace. I may have heard a negative or judgmental comment about me or someone else I love, and then suddenly I lost my peace. If only I had not heard it, if only someone had been wise enough not to speak it—but it is too late. The words have done their damage and cannot be retracted. We can help one another stay strong and enjoy the peace of God by not speaking idle words.

Our challenge is to "make every effort to do what leads to peace and to mutual edification" (Romans 14:19 NIV). The *Amplified* translation says we are to "eagerly pursue what makes for harmony and for mutual upbuilding (edification and development) of one another." I have made a point to repeat, throughout this study, that we must pursue peace. It seems that we must pursue all good things. The flesh has a natural negative bent; without restraint it will always go in the wrong direction, just as water will always flow to the lowest point unless a dam is built to prevent it from doing so.

Edifying others not only increases their peace and joy, it also increases our own. We feel better when we are saying kind things, things that minister life. We are to help develop one another, not destroy one another.

There are times when we think good things about other people we are with or know, yet plain laziness prevents us from opening our mouths to say the good things that are in our hearts. Be aggressive in saying good things and passive concerning saying evil things.

I am not naturally an exhorter, but I have developed a habit of looking for good and expressing it. Some people have this gift; they are called to be encouragers. It is, of course, easy and natural for these people to do what God has gifted them to do, just as it is easy for me to teach and preach the gospel.

For a long time, I simply made an excuse for not being exhortative by thinking, *I'm just not that way. I just don't think about it.* It even seemed uncomfortable for me to try to do, but God corrected me and told me to start doing it on purpose. There are many things we can choose to do on purpose that will help to increase our peace immensely. Saying good things to people is only one of them.

Establish a boundary in your own heart, and determine that you will not cross the line and speak careless, destructive words to or about others. As you will see in our next chapter, boundaries are important to protect peace in all of our relationships.

ESTABLISH BOUNDARIES WITH PEOPLE

To enjoy peaceful lives, we should learn how to establish and maintain boundaries. Without boundaries, we have no ownership of our lives. We need to learn that even though people may be good at heart, without boundaries most will go farther than we would like them to, and they may even try to control us. Boundaries protect us.

Having an unlisted telephone number is a boundary. If I didn't have one, many people would call me all the time, asking me to meet their needs, and my own life would fall apart. We cannot be available to people all the time and enjoy peace in our lives. Saying no when we need to is not wrong or unchristian.

We are not offended to see the boundaries of fences on someone's property. They communicate "You can come this far, but no farther." Signs that say "Keep Out" are boundaries telling us "This is private property, and you are not welcome here." We accept boundaries in other areas of life yet often fail to establish them in our own lives.

Home owners who have boundaries on their properties are usually strict about maintaining them. People who put up fences might become angry with neighbors who violate their boundaries. People don't want their neighbor's dogs to do their business in their yards. People usually don't want the neighborhood children playing in their yards. People don't want their neighbors' daily newspapers collecting in front of their houses. When people purchase property, they pay for surveys to make sure their boundary lines are what they think they are, so they get all they are paying for.

We want to know our property boundaries—so why do we care more for a piece of property than we do our own personal lives?

Like many people, I was guilty of not establishing and maintaining boundaries in relationships for many years, but after seeing how this adversely affected my health and peace, I made some drastic changes. People don't always like boundaries, but we are definitely wise to establish them.

ESTABLISH BOUNDARIES TO PROTECT YOUR PRIVACY

We live very close to all of our children and our eight grandchildren. We wanted to live close because most of us in the family travel, and living near each other allows us the opportunity for quick visits. I can go to a son or daughter's house with my coffee cup in hand and chat for thirty minutes and return home. This helps keep our relationships strong and healthy.

When we first made this decision, I was a bit concerned about how I would handle the grandchildren wanting to go to Grandma and Grandpa's house all the time. This is certainly a normal desire for a grandchild. I knew I would not be happy if they just started showing up whenever they wanted to, so I talked with my children, and we agreed they would not let their children come over without asking or calling first. To some people that might seem strange, but it was vitally necessary for me because of my busy schedule.

Dave and I and our children talked about our boundaries, and as long as everyone respects them, we get along great. It is not wrong to have personal boundaries; it protects the privacy to which we are entitled.

What should you do when people don't understand the boundary you have set? Most of the time, when this is the case it is simply because it is not a boundary they need in their lives, so they don't understand why you do. People have different needs because of the differences in their personalities, as well as lifestyles.

We should respect each other's needs, not judge and criticize them. Some people are just plain selfish, they want to do whatever they want to do, whenever they want to do it, with no regard or consideration for anyone else. This, of course, is a wrong attitude, and being forced to respect other people's boundaries is actually good for these types of people. Selfish people can certainly steal our peace if we allow them to do so.

As I stated, everyone has different needs and boundaries. This is true even of our four grown children. One of our daughters wants people in the family to call her before stopping by, and the other says, "Come by anytime, the door is always open." We improve our relationships with others by respecting their boundaries. Respect is vital for good relationships.

Everyone in life has a right to privacy. There may be things we don't want people to know or see. No matter how close we are to someone, we all have a right to and a need for privacy. Even in a marriage, we need a certain amount of privacy. For example, I don't like for anyone to get into my purse without my permission, not even my husband. It is not because I am hiding anything—there is nothing in my purse that would be a problem for anyone to see—but it is my private space to keep my personal things, and I want others to respect my right to have that space.

I never get into Dave's wallet unless he asks me to. If I had an emergency and needed money, I would do it, but I don't go through his private things. I don't go through his briefcase, because that is another area where people keep things that are special to them. Once again, it is not because people are hiding something, it is simply to respect their privacy. By doing so, we are respecting their rights as persons.

I had a relative once who came to my house, and without asking, ate things out of the refrigerator. Often the person ate the last of something, not caring whether or not we had any plans to use it ourselves. This is rude and unacceptable behavior. I had to talk to this person about it, though this individual really should not have even put me in the position to need to say something.

Sometimes we pressure others and cause them work because we don't respect their privacy properly. Some people ask questions they should not ask, some are nosey, and some are just unwise. I am a very straightforward individual and I ask lots of questions, but I also try to use wisdom and not breach anyone's privacy. I would not ask someone how much money he or she made, for example. I would never ask someone who was obviously over-weight how much he or she weighed. I would not ask someone how much he or she paid for an outfit of clothing unless it was someone to whom I was very close and whom I knew I would not offend. If someone is wearing what appears to be a large diamond, I would not normally ask if it was real or fake.

Because I am straightforward, I usually tell people, "If I ask you something you don't want to answer, just tell me, and I won't be offended." I am very open about my life and sometimes need to be reminded that not everyone is that way.

Be clear about what you want in relationships, and be ready to confront people lovingly when they do not honor your boundaries. The way you begin relationships is the way they continue, so if you don't approve of something, don't be afraid to speak up. When you let something go and don't deal with it, people view it as approval and usually get worse.

Very often people don't confront others, which is another way of saying they don't establish boundaries. Confrontation fre-quently offends people simply because unbridled human nature wants to do whatever it wants to do without concern for others. This is not healthy for any relationship or person. We all need to hear people say in various ways, "You can go this far and no farther."

We need to let people know what we are and are not willing to do. For example, grandparents should be able to say, "I will baby-sit once in a while, but not all the time." If they want to do it more, that is fine, but they should not be made to feel as if they are bad grandparents if they don't choose to. Once again, we should remember that we all have different lifestyles and tolerance levels, and no one should be shamed because he or she doesn't desire to do what someone else does.

My daughter's mother-in-law loves to watch the grandchildren. She does it all the time, many times for days at a time. I would not want to do that, not because I don't love my grandchildren—I do love them very much, and I minister to them in other ways—but my lifestyle would not permit me to spend most of my free time baby-sitting and at the same time remain happy. I would resent it.

Lots of people do many things they resent simply because they don't understand the importance of boundaries. Boundaries not only protect us, they protect other people and the longevity of relationships. Boundaries protect our peace!

Keep Wrong People Out of Your Life

Perhaps nothing affects us more than the people with whom we spend a lot of time. The Bible has a lot to say about what kinds of people we should not let into our lives.

For example, the Word tells us not to associate with someone who gets drunk or is a glutton or robber, who is guilty of immorality or greed, is an idolater, or is a person with a foul mouth (see Proverbs 23:20–21; 1 Corinthians 5:11). Why not? Simply because we are tempted to do what others do, and these behaviors lead to unhealthy ends. Have you ever decided you were not going to eat dessert and then changed your mind because others decided to eat it? Obviously I am not saying it is wrong to eat dessert; I am simply making the point that we are easily swayed by what others do.

If people have no measure of discipline in their lives, they may gossip and tell your secrets. Undisciplined people quite frequently live under the curse of a spirit of poverty, which literally affects every area of their lives. Prosperity or poverty is much more than merely a financial matter.

People who function under a poverty spirit will usually do everything poorly, or at best, mediocre; they never press into excellence. They are often late for appointments if they show up at all. They are in debt, and their possessions are in disarray. Things they own are dirty or in need of repair. They may have poor health and many broken relationships.

The people with whom we associate partially determine our reputations. I choose to associate with people of whom I am proud, not ashamed. Occasionally we spend time with people for the purpose of trying to help them, but we must have our boundaries so we make sure they don't eventually hurt us. Scripture warns us about associating with those who indulge in idle conversation: "He who goes about as a talebearer reveals secrets; therefore associate not with him who talks too freely" (Proverbs 20:19).

We can be sure if someone is talking to us unkindly about others, he will most likely talk the same way about us. I had many disappointments in relationships until I realized this truth and set boundaries on whom I choose for friends.

I once met someone I actually liked very much. We had a lot in common and could have been good friends, but I kept noticing that we never spent time together without this individual saying something derogatory about somebody. It actually made me afraid to go deeper in relationship because I felt sure this person would do the same thing to me. I might spend time with someone like that occasionally, but I would not let him or her get very close.

We should not be hesitant to establish boundaries to protect ourselves. If we want peace, we need to fellowship with people who work for and make peace too.

We should not develop relationships with people who have a spirit of rebellion. Paul said at the end of his message to believers in Thessalonica that they should not associate with anyone who refused to follow his instructions given in the letter (see 2 Thessalonians 3:14). In other words, avoid people who rebel against God's guidelines. In our society today, it seems that rebellion is rampant, and many think rebellion is cool, or a sign of freedom. However, this is the exact opposite of the attitude that God teaches us to have in His Word.

We are to submit to right authority in our lives, and those who refuse to do so have a serious problem. The Bible actually states that the spirit of rebellion at work in the world today is the spirit of antichrist (see 2 Thessalonians 2:7–8). We will never learn godliness from a rebellious person; instead, we will learn lawlessness. The following is a strong Scripture to which I have had to give much thought:

> But now I write to you not to associate with anyone who bears the name of [Christian] brother if he is known to be guilty of immorality or greed, or is an idolater [whose soul is devoted to any object that usurps the place of God], or is a person with a foul tongue [railing, abusing, reviling, slandering], or is a drunkard or a swindler or a robber. [No] you must not so much as eat with such a person. (1 Corinthians 5:11)

I believe the same guideline applies that I mentioned earlier: help people if you can, but don't let them hurt you. If we are spending time with people hoping to be able to help them, to be an example to them, or to minister to them, we certainly cannot do so by refusing ever to be near them. But we must influence them and not allow them to influence us. I often say we need to make sure we *affect* them, and they don't *infect* us.

Jesus ate with publicans and sinners, but He did so in order to help them see the light, and by His example, also see the life that was available to them. Jesus said we are the light of the world, and we should not put our light under a bushel. In other words, we cannot stay hidden all the time and do the world any good.

When I am with people I know have problems, and I don't want to have the same problems, I keep my heart guarded to a certain degree. Proverbs 4:23 says, "Keep and guard your heart with all vigilance and above all that you guard, for out of it flow the springs of life." In other words, I am especially careful not to adopt attitudes or opinions that are contrary to what Scripture tells me. I set a boundary, and I let people come close enough to try to help them, but not to hurt me.

Beware of Entanglements

It is unwise to become entangled in other people's problems. Some individuals are what I call *drains*. They add nothing to my life, and Satan uses them to drain me of needed strength. Hebrews 12:1 states that we are to avoid every encumbrance and the sin that so readily entangles us. It is not only sin that does this, but also messy circumstances in other people's lives. They weigh us down and steal the energy we need in order to pursue the call of God on our own lives.

Second Timothy 2:4 encourages us as soldiers in God's army not to get entangled in things of civilian life. The word *entangle* is the key thing to consider. Of course, we will always be involved with people, and many of them will have problems; we will also try to help them in the love and mercy of Christ. The Scripture does not say, "Don't have *any* involvement with these types of people"; it says not to get entangled.

To *entangle* means to complicate or confuse, to get into a snarl or a tangle. These difficult relationships bring pain into our own lives, just as trying to comb a bad tangle out of our hair brings pain.

We comb our dog daily so her hair does not become tangled. On occasion, when we have let it get messy, it has been very painful and time-consuming to get the knots out. Likewise, we should watch over our lives and relationships regularly to make sure we are not out of balance, that we are not getting entangled in things that will drain us of energy and never really help anyone else.

I love people, and the call on my life is to help them in whatever way I can; however, I finally had to learn that not all the people I try to help will actually receive help. Even the ones who claim they want it won't always take what we offer. They may want to entangle us in their problems, they want to talk about them, go over and over them, and be bitter about them, but they don't really want to move on beyond them.

For some people, their problems have become their lives, and they wouldn't know how to spend their time without them. Their problems become who they are: persons with problems to whom everyone is supposed to cater. This may sound a bit too stern if you are tenderhearted or are blessed with the gift of mercy, but when enough people have stolen your time, people who will never change, you understand what I mean.

I spent three years ministering almost daily to a relative I loved and desperately wanted to help. The person claimed to want help and even made progress for periods of time, but the person always fell back into the same pit. It cost money, time, effort, and at the end, nothing was different from how it had been the day we began.

I am not sorry I did what I did; I don't regret any of the investment because I believe God often uses us to give people opportunity. All people are entitled to opportunity, but what they do with it is up to them. This individual had literally every opportunity to have an awesome life and still made a choice that brought more destruction.

I knew very definitely when the day came that I was finished. The desire to be further involved totally left me. I received phone calls from others telling me I needed to help, to do something, to provide an answer for the person, but I was finished. I could not let this person make me feel guilty because I knew that I had followed God not only in trying to help but also in letting go. I had to establish a boundary that in this case said "Keep Out."

If I could have been emotionally driven or accepted a false guilt, I would have become entangled in something that God would not have given me the grace to withstand. When we do things without God's grace, we are doing them in the energy of our own flesh, and it not only frustrates us, it also confuses and defeats us.

I wasted a lot of my life trying to do things myself, independent of God's help and approval. I flatly refuse to do so any longer. I will not be entangled with people who want me to use my time and energy trying to help them, when they really don't want to change. I will not permit them to frustrate me and therefore steal my peace.

Remember that Jesus said to stop allowing yourself to be "agitated and disturbed" (John 14:27). Some of the people and circumstances in life that upset us will never change until we establish boundaries and keep them out.

Of course, we have helped thousands of people over the years. People who had serious problems have received what we offered and completely changed for the better. We have also learned to recognize the signs of those who will never change. They have had eternal problems, they talk about them incessantly, their problems are always someone else's fault, they are hurt if you try to get them to face the truth or take any responsibility, and they won't follow a program that someone designs for their recovery. As before, they say they want aid, but they somehow never end up applying it.

You should never feel guilty about placing a boundary around your life that keeps out these types of people. You are actually not using wisdom if you don't establish such boundaries. God's Word calls us to peace, and boundaries are one thing that will help us keep it.

FAMILIARITY BREEDS CONTEMPT

Establishing and maintaining proper boundaries prevents familiarity. This is very important because familiarity breeds contempt or disrespect. Think of how a person treats a new car. He admires it, thinks it is beautiful, washes it all the time, and expects everyone to be very careful when inside it. He allows absolutely no dirty shoes or food in the car.

But what happens when the car has been around for a few years? It is now dirty all the time, dented, full of empty soda cans and hamburger wrappers. What happened? The owner became familiar with it, took it for granted, and no longer showed it the same respect he did when it was new. He could have kept it looking and running as if it was new had he given it the attention he had in the beginning.

When people first come to work for our ministry, they think it is the greatest thing that has ever happened to them, and they are amazed at and extremely thankful for the opportunity God has given them. However, if they are not very careful, after time goes by they find themselves complaining about the very things they previously thought were wonderful. Why does this happen? One reason and one only: familiarity.

We find a great example of the dangers of familiarity in the Bible concerning the ark of God. When David was attempting to bring it home, a man called Uzza put out his hand to steady the ark on the cart that was carrying it, and God struck him dead because no one was supposed to touch it (see 1 Chronicles 13).

Uzza knew the strict guidelines concerning the ark, so why did he touch it? I believe it was because it had been stored in his father's home for quite some time, and he had become familiar with it. Therefore, he felt he could take liberties. His respect level had lowered without his even knowing it, simply due to his being around the ark too much. In this case, familiarity cost him his life.

Perhaps familiarity costs us more than we realize in our own lives. Perhaps we let godly relationships with people slip away because we have lost sight of their value in our lives.

It is the same thing that happens in a marriage, or a friendship, or with any privilege we are afforded. New things seem wonderful, but when we become familiar with them, we begin to have less respect for them, or even contempt. A new bride may hang on her husband's every word and agree with him about each thing he says, admiring him openly for his wisdom. After ten years of marriage, she may be argumentative about all of his opinions, and yet someone she barely knows can have the same opinion as her husband and she will respect and receive whatever he says. Have you ever said to your spouse, "I told you the same thing they did, and you argued with me"? I have had it happen to me.

The Lord once spoke to my heart, saying, "If you would show your husband one half of the respect you show your pastor, your marriage would be a lot better." I am ashamed to admit that He was absolutely correct. Why did I behave that way? Not because I didn't love my husband, but I had let familiarity lessen my admiration and willingness to receive advice from him. The pastor was a newer addition in my life at that time, and I had not known him long enough for him to seem familiar.

How can we live with someone and not become familiar? Certainly we will know very well those with whom we spend a lot of time. But losing sight of *why* we first admired a person is what breeds familiarity and destroys the peace in God-ordained relationships.

For this reason, many people in authority feel they cannot spend a lot of time with those under their authority. Their experience has been that most people will lose respect through familiarity. It takes a wise person, who is very spiritually mature, to work under someone's authority and also be close friends with him or her.

People usually admire and look up to "the boss," which is a good thing; we are to give respect and honor to whom it is due. It helps us serve people properly if we really respect and admire those over us. Being around them a lot, however, can cause us to begin to look at them as "Good ole Joe" or "My buddy Charlie," and something happens in the heart that eventually kills the relationship. Respect is a key in good relationships, and I feel the lack of it is one of the main reasons that relationships are destroyed.

We should not allow ourselves to become too familiar with the things and people in our lives that are now special. Some things I own are very special to me; I treat them as valuable, taking precaution that they encounter no harm. How we view things determines how we will treat them. Even more, the people in our lives who are special to us we should treat with great respect, handle them carefully, be appreciative, thanking God for their friendship. Don't let what is special become mundane. To keep from taking each other for granted, we can practice remembering how precious people are and focus on thankfulness for their presence in our lives.

It may even be healthy to think about how it would affect our lives if we lost certain persons' presence or friendship. *What if So-and-so and So-and-so were no longer in my life? What if suddenly they were gone?* It could help us keep in the forefront of our thinking how vital they are and assist us in treating them as such. I have done this with my husband, Dave. I have thought about how it would change my life if he suddenly was not in it. He is very valuable to me, and I intend to treat him with respect and honor.

Set Boundaries on Teasing

I am aware of a relationship between two men who really enjoyed one another that was ruined through excessive joking. The relationship began with tremendous respect and admiration; they were both fun-loving guys who enjoyed teasing people. As they became more and more familiar with one another, the teasing took on a more tense nature. At first, their jesting was cute and funny, but it soon became a point of rivalry, and I noticed they used the pretense of "I'm joking" to make crude comments to each another when they were upset.

They should have shown respect for each other by practicing honest confrontation during a disagreement, but instead one would make a comment to the other that he intended to bring correction, but he did it under the guise of joking. Then the other one would respond with similar statements. This bantering would go back and forth, all, of course, under the mask of "I'm joking."

When someone's character, physical appearance, or family members are the brunt of "the joke," it ceases to be funny.

The comments became more and more rude and crude until these two men began to disrespect each other and lost the desire to have a relationship. I certainly did not enjoy being around them; their way of dealing with one another was uncomfortable. I could tell there was underlying strife. I could tell that the "joking" was not really as funny as they were pretending it was. The Bible says in Ephesians 5:4 that we are to rid ourselves of all "coarse jesting, which [is] not fitting or becoming," because it causes problems between people that in turn grieve the Holy Spirit of God.

They could have teased one another and enjoyed it, but only with boundaries. Even something like having fun must have boundaries, or it becomes an evil thing. In other words, we need to know how far to go and when to stop. We can set boundaries on ourselves and never put someone else in a position of having to enforce his own boundaries.

I know within myself when I am spending too much, talking too much, working too hard, and not getting enough rest. I also know that when teasing becomes rude, it has gone too far. At that point, I need to apologize and stay within God-ordained boundaries, or I may ruin an otherwise great relationship.

Familiarity is often the root cause of coarse jesting. When we don't know someone really well, we are more careful what we say, but it seems the better we know an individual, the more the "real us" pops out and the importance we place on good manners diminishes. It is better to remain respectful in all relationships and always to treat everyone with courtesy.

FOLLOW THE HOLY SPIRIT

Our goal is to let the Holy Spirit of God lead us into what will produce good fruit in our lives, such as discipline, which is another way of saying we have boundaries in our lives.

Without boundaries, everything is out of control. God wants to be in control, but He won't force us. We discipline ourselves to follow Him, which means we learn to live within boundaries.

We cannot follow the Holy Spirit and also follow people. We will either be God-pleasers or people-pleasers. If we establish boundaries for others as well as ourselves, we are on the pathway to being led by God's Spirit.

If you really think about it, life is filled with boundaries. A bedtime is a boundary. It says, "I will stay up until this time and no later." That boundary allows us to get good sleep and feel healthy the following day; it provides much needed energy. If we frequently ignore our boundaries in this area, it will adversely affect our health.

Stop signs and traffic lights are boundaries, as well as speed-limit signs and the yellow lines in the middle of the road. These boundaries are set in place for our safety.

Don't look at boundaries as something to be despised, but as something that provides safety and security for all of us. If *boundary* is a word you are not familiar with, I suggest you learn all you can in this area. I highly recommend Dr. Henry Cloud and Dr. John Townsend's book titled *Boundaries*. It was very helpful to me as well as several people I know. Without boundaries, we will never enjoy peace in our lives.

If you have made a decision to pursue peace, then establishing and maintaining boundaries must become a priority to you. Boundaries will protect you from being easily offended, which is the next way to keep your peace.

LET GO OF OFFENSES

We must learn to pick our battles. There are simply too many conflicts in life to fight them all. We will have many major things to deal with, so the least we can do is practice letting go of all the little things that people do that irritate us. As we saw in the chapter on esteeming others, God may lead us to confront people for misconduct, or even for crossing our set boundaries, but there will be many little issues that we need to just ignore.

We are not alone in our dilemma; even the twelve disciples whom Jesus personally trained had relationship problems with each other. Peter asked Jesus how many times he must forgive his brother for the same offense (see Matthew 18:21–22). This indicates that someone, maybe one of the other disciples, continually irritated Peter in some way. It may have been as simple as a personality conflict or an irksome habit, but whatever it was, Satan used it to steal Peter's peace.

Jesus told him to forgive seventy times seven, which meant the perfect number of times. However many times it takes to remain in peace throughout our lives, that's how many times we are to overlook the offenses of others.

People should enter into close relationships with their eyes wide open, realizing there will be things about people that bother them. *After* we enter these relationships, we will have to *close our eyes* to many things. It will not do any good to concentrate on faults, because some of them may never go away. Some things change with people as the years go by, and others seem to remain forever.

"Love covers a multitude of sins [forgives and disregards the offenses of others]" (1 Peter 4:8). The Bible instructs us to make allowances for one another (see Ephesians 4:2). In other words, we are to allow people to be less than perfect.

I personally respond much better to people who allow me to be human than I do to those who expect me to be divine (perfect). I hate the pressure of trying to please someone in all things. It makes me uneasy and on edge, and I feel as if I must tiptoe around lest I offend in some minor thing. If I want to reap relationships that allow me to be myself, I must sow them.

I was recently speaking with my administrative assistant. We discussed the fact that it is impossible to spend as much time together as we do and never see each other's imperfect side. We must be generous with letting things go. That means we don't need to make a big deal out of every error and many times don't even need to mention them at all.

I have noticed in myself and others that even when we are willing to forgive, we want the person we are forgiving to *know* that we are forgiving him or her. We usually want to at least mention it.

You Will Be Tested Every Day

Why is it so hard to completely ignore offenses? We want to mention the fact that we overlooked their obnoxious behaviors so the people who offend us do not think they can treat us improperly and get away with it—it is a type of self-protection. But God wants us to trust Him to protect us as well as to heal us from *every* hurt and emotional wound, *every day*.

I wonder how weary we would be at the end of each day if God mentioned every tiny thing we do wrong. He does deal with us, but I am quite sure He also overlooks a lot of things. If people are corrected too much, it can discourage them and break their spirits.

We should form a habit of dealing only with what God Himself prompts us to address, not just everything we feel like confronting, or every little thing that bothers us. I am the type of person who would not be inclined to let anybody get away with anything.

I don't like feeling someone is taking advantage of me, partially because I was abused in my childhood and partially because I am human, and none of us embraces disrespect. In the past, I was quick to tell everyone his or her faults, but I have learned that is not pleasing to God.

Just as we want others to give us mercy, we must give it to them. We reap what we sow—nothing more or less. Even God may withhold His mercy from us if we are unwilling to give mercy to others.

We are to be Peacemakers, not Peace Breakers. Always remember that it takes two people to fight. If you respond with harsh words, you will stir up anger, but if you respond to an offensive statement with "a soft answer," you will "turn away wrath" (Proverbs 15:1). Someone has said that anger is one letter away from danger. Just add a *d*, which could well represent *devil*, in front of anger, and you see the trouble with rage.

I believe that our lives can be full of peace if we simply decide to do what is right in every situation that comes along. There is a right and a wrong way to handle the storms of life. But until I was filled with the Holy Spirit and began to learn about the power that is available to me as a believer to do the right thing, I never handled offenses right.

Jesus' economy is upside down from what the world teaches us. He says that we can have peace in the midst of the storm. Now just think about how awesome that would be, if *no matter what happened*, you could remain full of peace.

You can keep your peace in an unexpected traffic jam. You can keep your peace when you have to wait in the grocery store line, while the person in front of you doesn't have any prices on his products, the clerk runs out of cash-register tape, and she's new, and she doesn't know what she's doing anyway, and she is fumbling around trying to get the tape in the register, and you are in the biggest rush you have faced all week.

Even then, you can keep from losing your peace, from getting a headache or an ulcer, and from blowing your whole witness by acting like a fool. Even then, you can just stay steady because you have the power living in you to stay in peace.

Jesus said that He gives us power even to "trample upon serpents and scorpions, and [physical and mental strength and ability] over all the power that the enemy [possesses]" (Luke 10:19). He promised that nothing will harm us in any way. If we have the power over the enemy, surely we can overlook the offenses of others. He gives us the energy we need to treat people right.

Understand that every time you are tempted to be offended and upset, your faith is being tried. The Word says,

> [You should] be exceedingly glad on this account, though now for a little while you may be distressed by trials and suffer temptations, so that [the genuineness] of your faith may be tested, [your faith] which is infinitely more precious than the perishable gold which is tested and purified by fire. [This proving of your faith is intended] to redound to [your] praise and glory and honor when Jesus Christ (the Messiah, the Anointed One) is revealed. (1 Peter 1:6–7)

Peter was saying, "Don't be amazed at the fiery trials that you go through, because they are taking place to test your quality." Every relationship test is an opportunity to glorify the work of God in you as a testimony to those watching you endure the offense.

Why do you think that in school you had to take final exams before passing to the next grade? You didn't graduate to the next level just because you showed up at school every day. You got a diploma only when you took the final exams and showed that you could answer the questions.

The Bible says that God will never allow more to come on us than what we can bear. But with every temptation, He also provides the way out. Remember, the only time we will not find the strength of God in our lives to do what is before us is if we're trying to do something that God never told us to do. He never told us to hold offenses against others. In fact, forgiveness is a very big issue with God.

Jesus said,

> For if you forgive people their trespasses [their reckless and willful sins, leaving them, letting them go, and giving up resentment], your heavenly Father will also forgive you. But if you do not forgive others their trespasses [their reckless and willful sins, leaving them, letting them go, and giving up resentment], neither will your Father forgive you your trespasses. (Matthew 6:14–15)

Don't Ask Yourself for Advice

Solomon said that he took counsel with his own mind, and in essence he concluded that it was like "searching after wind" (see Ecclesiastes 1:17). Our minds say to be upset if someone offends us, but God says to let it go.

I often share a teaching that I call "Shake It Off," which is based on the time Paul was on the island of Malta. He was helping some people build a fire when a poisonous serpent crawled out and attached itself to his hand. At first, when the people saw it they thought that he must be wicked to have such an evil thing happen to him. They watched, waiting for him to fall over dead.

But the Bible says that Paul simply "shook it off."

We can learn so much from that. When somebody offends or rejects us, we need to see it as a bite from Satan and just shake it off. If we hear that somebody has been talking about us, we need to shake it off. When we are sitting in a traffic jam and begin to feel upset, we need to let it go.

Frustration won't stop on its own. It keeps raising the pressure higher and higher, as if somebody is tightening the screws on our nerves. But when you feel that happening, you can literally shake it off and refuse to give in to it. Sometimes we make things bigger than they need to be; we blow them out of proportion. We can choose to let offenses go before they take root in us and cause serious problems.

Jesus told the disciples that if they entered towns that didn't receive them, they should just go to the next town. He told them to shake the dust off of their feet and move on. He didn't want the disciples to dwell on the rejection they had experienced; He wanted them to stay focused on sharing their testimony of His working in their lives.

Likewise, as we follow the Spirit, we can shake off offenses and hold on to our peace. When others see that we are able to remain calm even when "the serpent" bites us, they will want to know where that peace is coming from in our lives.

When we are in a state of upset, we cannot hear from God clearly. The Bible promises us that God will lead us and walk us out of our troubles, but we cannot be led by the Spirit if we are offended and in a dither.

We can't get away from the storms of life, or the temptation to be irritated at someone. But we can respond to offenses by saying, "God, You are merciful, and You are good. And I am going to put my confidence in You until this storm passes over" (see Psalm 57:1). We cannot prevent feeling negative emotions, but we can learn to manage them. We can trust God to give us grace to act godly even in an ungodly situation.

One day we were looking for a parking place, and a car was backing out, so Dave waited so he could get the spot. He had his blinker on, clearly showing that he was waiting to park. Well, a guy behind us on a bicycle was very put out because we had stopped. He was ranting and raving, and he pulled around Dave, but we held our peace and smiled at him. But while this guy was railing on us, somebody else took our parking place!

I can remember when that kind of thing might have really irritated us, but we've been through so many trials that we could shrug and say, "Bless you, hope you enjoy that parking place!" And we found another one. We've learned not to let offensive people steal our joy anymore. You might say that we have learned not to let offensive people offend us.

What good does it do to get upset at someone who takes your parking place? You can get all mad and bothered, but the other person will still have your spot. And you probably will never see that offensive person again as long as you live, so why let it steal your peace, even for a few minutes?

As soon as you lose your peace, the devil wins. If getting you offended works once, believe me, he will set you up with the same opportunity over and over.

Later, Dave said that person who took our place actually helped us. We didn't know that we were in the wrong block, and if we had parked there we would have been far from where we wanted to go. What Satan means for our harm, God intends for our good. Doing what is right leads to peace and joy.

Righteousness, peace, and joy in the Holy Ghost are a progression. If we don't know who we are in Christ, then we won't realize that we have His strength in us to do the right thing. Then we won't have peace, and if we don't have peace, we won't have joy. So if you have lost your joy, you need to back all the way up and find out where it was that you lost your peace, and then do what is right in that situation.

People without Christ, who don't live in the kingdom of God, don't have the power to keep from being offended. When they have a problem, they only have one choice, which is to get upset. But we have a choice. We can believe that Jesus is in our situation with us, and even though sometimes it feels as if He is sleeping through our storm, we can know that He is able to tell the storm to be still—and when He does, it will stop.

DON'T CRY OVER SPILLED MILK

If you are going to walk in peace, you have to be willing to be adaptable and adjustable to people and circumstances. When I lived in the "explode mode," it never failed that one of my children spilled something at the dinner table—every night. And every night I had a fit.

They would tip over their cups and start crying as soon as they saw their milk running under the bowls. I learned that when you spill something, you have to try to get to it before it gets to the crack in the table, because milk will sour quickly in there with all that other hidden dirt! And then eventually you will have to take the whole table apart and scrape dried milk and foodstuff out of its crevices with a table knife. (Now I have a table with a glass top, but everybody scratches it! You see, there is always something you will have to put up with and let go of in life.)

I used to shout at the kids, "Can't we ever have one meal in peace?" I didn't realize we could have had a meal in peace if I stopped shouting at everyone. I could have brought peace to our table every night if I had just cleaned up and shut up.

So, if you have wondered how to have peace, I can tell you that it will come if you will quit making a big deal about everything. You will have to be willing to let go of getting distraught over accidents or not getting your way.

One night I was under the table because whatever the kids had spilled had made it to the crack in the table before I got there, and the liquid was running down the center table legs. I was having a fit, and the kids were upset, and somebody kicked me in the head, and that made me even madder. I knew it was an accident, I knew he or she didn't do it on purpose. Poor Dave had to be weary from sitting down to dinner after working hard all day and having to endure my outburst. (And I couldn't figure out why he wanted to go to the driving range every night and hit golf balls, so I'd throw a fit about that too.)

So there I was, under the table, saying, "Every night some-body's got to spill something, and we just need some peace around here. . . . " And the Holy Ghost came unto me (right under that table), saying, "Joyce, once the milk is spilled, no matter how big of a fit you have, you are not going to get it to run back up the table legs, across the table, and into the glass." And He said, "Joyce, you need to learn how to go with the flow."

There are some things that we can do something about, but there are a whole lot of things that we can't do anything about. If it is something we can't do anything about, then we need to let it go and keep our joy. We need to hold our peace, do what is right, and let God work on our behalf.

When Jesus said, "Stop *allowing* yourselves to be agitated and disturbed; and do not *permit* yourselves to be . . . unsettled" (John 14:27, italics mine), He was saying that we must control ourselves.

For many years, I argued, "God, I don't want to act like that, but I just can't help it." The Bible says that self-control is a fruit of the Spirit, who dwells in us. We don't have to give way to unbridled emotions. God will give you power to do whatever you need to do, as often as you need to do it. God will help you manage your emotions. Be sure to read my book *Managing Your Emotions* if you frequently lose your peace through emotional responses to life's trials. Whether it is to help us not get upset over spilled milk or to forgive an offense, the Lord will give us grace as often as we need it.

The only way we will have peace is if we let little offenses and irritations go. Why not save some time and grief and just forgive people right away? When we are upset, we are much less likely to be led by the Spirit of God. We are not sensitive to His touch when we don't maintain a quiet inner life, which we will look at next.

MAINTAIN A QUIET INNER LIFE

To enjoy more peace in our lives, we need to practice just being still and staying calm even when we feel like spilling out everything we think and feel. Many relationships break apart because everyone wants the last word. Sometimes, simply holding our peace is the right thing to do.

Although we have already talked about the importance of not speaking idle words, there is also great value in learning to entrust our battles to the Lord. Knowing He will fight for us fills us with deep peace that passes understanding, like the peace Daniel felt when he was thrown into the lions' den. David wrote some words that may express Daniel's feelings:

He has redeemed my life in peace from the battle that was against me [so that none came near me], for they were many who strove with me. God will hear and humble them, even He Who abides of old—Selah [pause, and calmly think of that]!—because in them there has been no change [of heart], and they do not fear, revere, and worship God. (Psalm 55:18–19)

If we will spend time meditating on God's promises, considering the great things He has done in our lives, it will fill us with a deep peace that will cause us to be calm even when others seem full of fear, rage, or anxiety. Our peace will bring peace to others. The Word teaches that we will win the respect of other people by how we live our lives: "Make it your ambition and definitely endeavor to live quietly and peacefully, to mind your own affairs, and to work with your hands, as we charged you, so that you may bear yourselves becomingly and be correct and honorable and command the respect of the outside world" (1 Thessalonians 4:11–12).

God wants us to have a disposition that will bless others; we are ambassadors of Christ, Peacemakers who should demonstrate the calm, soothing presence of Jesus. God created us in His image, and our lives should be filled with the fruit of His indwelling presence.

Many people believe that if Jesus walked into a roomful of strife, it would take Him only a few minutes to bring peace to whatever the circumstances were. He had a soothing nature; He was clothed with meekness. He wasn't out to prove anything. He wasn't concerned about what people thought about Him. He already knew who He was, so He didn't feel the need to defend Himself.

In fact, even when Pilate brought charges against Him, Jesus made no answer (see Matthew 27:14). Other people got upset with Jesus and tried to start all kinds of arguments with Him, but His response was always peaceful and loving. His mellow disposition was the result of a quiet inner life, and a confident relationship with His Father. Inner peace produces outer peace.

Jesus was the fulfillment of Isaiah's prophecy:

Behold, My Servant Whom I have chosen, My Beloved in and with Whom My soul is well pleased and has found its delight. I will put My Spirit upon Him, and He shall proclaim and show forth justice to the nations. He will not strive or wrangle or cry out loudly; nor will anyone hear His voice in the streets; a bruised reed He will not break, and a smoldering (dimly burning) wick He will not quench, till He brings justice and a just cause to victory. And in and on His name will the Gentiles (the peoples outside of Israel) set their hopes. (Matthew 12:18–21)

God wants us to enjoy the same inner peace that was visible in the life of Jesus, and He expects us to bless others with the same grace. First Peter 2:15–16 confirms, "For it is God's will and intention that by doing right [your good and honest lives] should silence (muzzle, gag) the ignorant charges and ill-informed criticisms of foolish persons. [Live] as free people, [yet] without employing your freedom as a pretext for wickedness; but [live at all times] as servants of God."

The *Living Bible* (TLB) paraphrases this verse: "It is God's will that your good lives should silence those who foolishly condemn the Gospel without knowing what it can do for them, having never experienced its power."

Meditate on God's Goodness

Peter's letter called for believers to show respect for everyone and especially to love other Christians. We are to honor those in government and submit ourselves not only to those in authority over us who are kind, but also to those who are unjust (see 1 Peter 2:17–18). Keep in mind, the reason God asks us to do this is so that we are a testimony of His love to people who have never experienced His power. God does not delight in our suffering in these types of situations, but He does delight when we behave in a godly manner and glorify Him with our attitudes during them.

I know how difficult this sounds, but our peace must come from the confidence that the Lord will fight our battles for us. Hebrews 13:6 says, "So we take comfort and are encouraged and confidently and boldly say, The Lord is my Helper; I will not be seized with alarm [I will not fear or dread or be terrified]. What can man do to me?"

We are to keep our minds on God, who works "wonders in the earth" and makes wars cease. The Lord says, "Let be *and be still,* and know (recognize and understand) that I am God. I will be exalted among the nations! I will be exalted in the earth!" (Psalm 46:8–10, italics mine).

If we spend time meditating on the wonders that God is doing in the world and exalt Him above all of our differences with other people, we will enjoy a calm joy deep within our hearts. Then, when squeezed by the pressure of relationships and the trials of everyday life, we will emulate the soothing fruit of the Spirit.

We have outer lives and inner lives; there's more to us than what we see when we look in the mirror. There's another whole life going on inside each of us, and this inner life needs to learn to be still and know that God will work everything out for our good.

We know that people can pretend one thing on the outside and have something else totally different going on inside. And the Bible makes it very clear that our inner lives are more important than our outer lives to God, because He looks at our hearts. It was really life-transforming for me to realize that I might be fooling a lot of people, but I wasn't fooling God.

For me to act as if everything were okay while I had strife in my heart was not pleasing to the Lord. I decided I had to find a way to make things right inside of me. Real peace cannot be faked. Even though we may hide our real attitudes from people, we cannot hide them from God, because He lives *in* us.

Keep God's Temple Full of Peace

First Corinthians 3:16 says, "Do you not discern and understand that you [the whole church at Corinth] are God's temple (His sanctuary), and that God's Spirit has His permanent dwelling in you [to be at home in you, collectively as a church and also individually]?"

The Scripture teaches us that when we are born again, we become the home of God. Isn't that about the most awesome thing you can imagine? We are God's home, we are His dwelling place, and we should want Him to be comfortable living in us.

No one is comfortable living in a house of strife, and the Holy

Spirit is especially grieved when we are not in peace. All those years I spent in turmoil were wasted. The peace I enjoy now is so inspiring that I want to reach everyone in the world with the good news of its availability through Jesus.

Before I learned how to enjoy the inner life of peace, I was always angry; if not with somebody else, with myself. I found out that if I wanted to have peace, I had to choose peace.

When I read in First Peter 3:11 that we weren't to just "*desire* peaceful relations*" (italics mine), we are to pursue peace with everyone, I realized that this meant we aren't to just wait for peace to happen.

I believe a lot of people *desire* to have peaceful relations, but they are waiting for the other persons to act right so they can feel peaceful. I always remind people that they don't need a wishbone; they need backbone. We have to *make* peace happen.

Practice Being Still

I found out that in many instances, Dave and I could have peace if I adapted myself a little bit, or if I chose *not to say something that I really wanted to say*. I discovered that simply being still made peace happen.

See, in the beginning, I wanted peace, but I wanted Dave to give it to me. I wanted my children to give it to me. I wanted God to give me peace, and so I was always praying: "Oh, God, give me peace." But then I realized that Jesus had already left His peace with me, so begging God to give it to me was futile. I just needed to use the peace that was available deep within me.

I had enjoyed days when I was peaceful, I had plenty of money, nobody was bothering me, everybody was doing what I wanted, I was getting my way, I felt good, and the house was clean. But that was the kind of peace that the world gives us, and we don't need the power of the Holy Spirit to have peace on days when everything is going well.

The peace that Jesus said He left for us is a deep sense of knowing that even though everything isn't all right today, things will work out in the end. We believe *this too shall pass*. That peace is from the power of the Holy Spirit, and it equips us to have peace when it doesn't make any sense to have peace. As Spirit-filled believers, we have the strength of the Holy Spirit not to worry even when there are plenty of things to worry about.

Calming down is something you do on purpose. You can get upset without trying to, but if you're going to calm down, you will have to work at it. Keeping quiet is a powerful way to calm down. Often to have peace, as I just mentioned, I have to *not say* something that I really want to say. And I'm a talker, so usually it is *hard* for me not to make the point or have the last word. But I have learned that the fruit of peace is a greater reward than the temporary satisfaction of putting in my two cents. I'm learning that (as I said in chapter 16), being right is highly overrated. We usually strive to be right, but is it worth all we go through for the momentary, fleshly satisfaction we get from it?

Calming down is a decision. It has nothing to do with feelings. It is an act of obedience, and we do it to honor God because He lives in our house, and He's saying: "I want it—I want some peace in this house. I want it quiet in here. I want you to be full of peace."

What is normal for a Christian? Are we supposed to be all stirred up and anxious while trying to figure out something? Are we to be angry while wild thoughts and wicked imaginations go on inside of us? No. But it's amazing how many people live that way; they go to church on Sunday and think that's all it takes.

Having a right relationship with God is going to take a commitment of your time, and you're going to have to dedicate your inner life—not just church attendance, a few good works, and a little bit of your money—to the Lord. A quiet spirit is probably the greatest sacrifice we can offer up to God.

Watchman Nee, author of *The Spiritual Man,* was a gifted preacher of the gospel in China during the early 1900s. He wrote the following excerpt about how Christians are to have quiet spirits:

"To aspire to live quietly" (1 Thess.4.11). This is the duty of every Christian. Modern Christians talk far too much. Sometimes their unuttered words surpass in number those that are spoken. Confused thought and endless speech set our spirits to wandering away from the control of our wills. A "wild spirit" often leads people to walk according to the flesh. How hard it is for believers to restrain themselves from sinning when their spirit becomes unruly. An errant spirit invariably ends up with an error in conduct.

Before one can display a quiet mouth he must first possess a quiet spirit, for out of the abundance of the spirit does the mouth speak. We ought to carefully keep our spirits in stillness; even in time of intense confusion our inner being should nevertheless be able to sustain an independent quietude. A placid spirit is essential to anyone walking after the spirit: without it he shall quickly fall into sin. If our spirit is hushed we can hear the voice of the Holy Spirit there, obey the will of God, and understand what we cannot understand when confused. Such a quiet inner life constitutes the Christian's adornment which betokens something manifested outwardly.*

The thing we need to do when we are in trouble is hear from God. That's why it's so important that when we have some trial, some turmoil going on outwardly, we manage to keep our spirits quiet. If we get all stirred up inside, we are not going to hear from God. We cannot understand Him when we are confused and then cannot obey the will of God.

We will have peace when we learn to maintain an inner quiet. That's not a job we can give to God; we have the job of leaning on

*Watchman Nee, *The Spiritual Man,* Vol. 2 (New York: Christian Fellowship Publishers, Inc., 1968), 180–181.

the power of the Holy Spirit by faith to maintain a quiet spirit. Then we can hear from God and obey the leading of His Spirit. I share more about how to do this in my book titled *How to Hear from God*.

When we get disturbed in the flesh, we release idle words that cause damage. But being still isn't just refraining from speech; it is about living every day in a calm state of confidence in God that encourages the Holy Spirit to thrive in our house.

The serenity of God's presence makes us attractive to others and is a powerful testimony of God's work in our lives. I just love peace. I'm addicted to peace. Paul knew the value of peace, as we see when he was training Timothy, a young preacher. When he was giving Timothy instructions on how to handle his ministry, Paul told him, "Be calm and cool and steady, accept and suffer unflinchingly every hardship, do the work of an evangelist, fully perform all the duties of your ministry" (2 Timothy 4:5).

That is good advice for all of us. If we are calm and steady, people know they can depend on us. God can depend on us. No one has to wonder what we might be like one day from the next. When our unsaved friends see the calm and steady faith we have, they will be open to our testimony of the gospel. Stability is the fruit of living a peaceful life.

STABILITY RELEASES ABILITY

I believe that stability releases ability. I think a lot of people have ability because God has given them gifts, but they're not stable Christians, and so God cannot use their gifts publicly in ministry. They would end up hurting the cause of Christ because of their unpredictable behavior.

We can't be stable just when we're getting our way. We have to be stable when we're having trouble and trials, when people are coming against us, and when people are talking about us. Paul knew a lack of stability would hurt Timothy's witness and anointing; it would prevent him from hearing from God. We don't enjoy life unless we develop an ability to remain stable in the storm.

When we're upset, we are usually not listening. People don't hear because they don't get quiet enough to hear what God is saying. God isn't going to yell at you. He usually speaks in a still, small voice, and to hear Him, we must maintain an inner calmness. Actually, peace itself is a guideline for what God is approving and disapproving of in your life. We must all learn to follow peace if we intend to follow God.

You have to choose purposely to stay calm, to put your confidence and trust in God, and to be a ready listener for His voice. Then you have to be willing to make whatever adjustments are necessary to have peace in your life.

Some people might say, "Well, it's not fair for me to always be the one who's changing and adjusting to keep harmony with everyone else." It might not be fair, but God will bring justice in your life if you do what He's asking you to do. It might not be fair, but it will be worth it.

Just because somebody else is hard to get along with, we don't need to be hard to get along with too. We have to stop letting somebody else's bad behavior steal our joy.

I've mentioned that in the early years of our marriage, when I threw temper tantrums and didn't talk, Dave just stayed calm and happy. He went around the house singing and whistling; he went to play golf and watch football and play with the kids; he continued to enjoy life. When I was about to blow my cork in another room, he was steady and stable, and even though it made me so mad that I couldn't get him upset, he eventually won me over by the peace that he always maintained.

Unhappy people want to make other people unhappy; it irritates them to be around someone happy. But people who are full of peace can positively affect unhappy people. I saw Dave's example and became hungry for what he had. I know, without a doubt, if Dave had not had that stability in his life, I wouldn't be in ministry today.

I needed an example of peace because I grew up in a house of strife. I actually did not even know how to remain peaceful when I did not like my circumstances. Even someone preaching it to me would not have been enough; *I needed to see it*. His example was very important for what God had planned for me.

So, if you are in a relationship with somebody who is like I was—angry, upset, out of control, throwing temper tantrums, making bad choices—you can influence him or her to receive the grace of God to change if you will be stable in the power of the Holy Spirit.

It won't do any good to leave gospel tracts around the house or play my teaching tapes real loud. It won't help to leave books opened with underlined passages for that person to find. The Word says that we win people over, not by discussion, but by our godly lives (see 1 Peter 3:1). Of course, sometimes God uses our verbal witness to help others, but He uses our example even more.

Dave didn't preach to me: His life was a sermon. He lived his confidence in God in front of me. And his stability is one of the things that I still appreciate in him.

I grew up in a home where I never knew from one minute to the next what was going to happen. Somebody could be happy one day and ready to hit me the next day, and I didn't even know why. I lived through a lot of violence and anger, where ranting and raving was a daily event.

Perhaps you live in such a home now, but God can change it if you will abide in Him. Isaiah 32:17–18 promises this: "And the effect of righteousness will be peace [internal and external], and the result of righteousness will be quietness and confident trust forever. My people shall dwell in a peaceable habitation, in safe dwellings, and in quiet resting-places."

First Peter 3:2 gives us guidelines on how to live our lives to win over those who do not know about the grace of God. Though it is written in light of women with their husbands, the same principles apply to all relationships that we have with others. It says to conduct ourselves with reverence toward others, "to respect, defer to, revere, . . . esteem, appreciate, prize, and, in the human sense, to adore" and enjoy those whom God has given us to love. People's attraction to us will not be based on our outer lives, our hairstyles, or our pretty clothes.

Instead, we will draw people to us by "the inward adorning and beauty of the hidden person of the heart, with the incorruptible and unfading charm of a gentle and peaceful spirit, which [is not anxious or wrought up, but] is very precious in the sight of God" (1 Peter 3:4). We are true sons and daughters of God if we do right and let nothing terrify us, if we "don't give way to hysterical fears or [let] anxieties unnerve" us (v. 6).

Our circumstances won't change until we change. Remember, we are to keep our minds stayed on God, and He will keep us in perfect peace. And whoever heeds wisdom will "dwell securely and in confident trust and shall be quiet, without fear or dread of evil" (Proverbs 1:33).

Watchman Nee said that we should keep our spirits in a position of "being light and free all the time—keeping in mind that the outer man is different than inside." We can have raging storms taking place around us and still enjoy perfect peace on the inside.

I realize that I have already given you a lot of information on how to keep peace in your life, but in the next chapter I will share one more Peacekeeper that will keep you in God's will for the rest of your journey.

AGGRESSIVELY PURSUE PEACE

The main point I hope you remember from this study is to aggressively pursue peace. Through Jesus Christ, God has provided everything you need to enjoy a life of peace. The Word tells us, "*Strive* to live in peace with everybody and pursue that consecration and holiness without which no one will [ever] see the Lord" (Hebrews 12:14, italics mine).

The word *strive* has been translated in various Bible versions as "follow," "pursue," and "make every effort." It's important to understand that God expects us to interact with people. I know believers who withdraw from everyone, who don't think it is important to go to church or spend time with people. But that is not the heart of God. He wants us to find peace *with* people, not away from them. In fact, the Lord tells us to look after each other, helping each other to be built up in faith, as these next Scriptures command:

> And let us consider and give attentive, continuous care to watching over one another, studying how we may stir up (stimulate and incite) to love and helpful deeds and noble activities, not forsaking or neglecting to assemble together [as believers], as is the habit of some people, but admonishing (warning, urging, and encouraging) one another, and all the more faithfully as you see the day approaching. (Hebrews 10:24–25)

God gives His blessings as a free gift, yet we receive or appropriate them through faith. If we don't release our faith in the promises of

God, they will not help us. We can encourage each other to remain faithful. We can pray for each other when our own faith weakens. Above all, we can encourage each other to aggressively pursue peace.

An aggressive peacemaker remains on watch to see that no one in the body falls away from God's grace. Hebrews 12:15 charges us to "exercise foresight and be on the watch to look [after one another], to see that no one falls back from and fails to secure God's grace (His unmerited favor and spiritual blessing), in order that no root of resentment (rancor, bitterness, or hatred) shoots forth and causes trouble and bitter torment, and the many become contaminated and defiled by it."

People could conceivably have money in the bank and yet live as those with none simply because they never went to the bank to get it. Jesus arranged for us to enjoy peace, but we must pursue it. Actually it is important to remember that God's Word says in Psalm 34:14 that we are to *"seek, inquire for, and crave peace and pursue (go after) it!"* (italics mine). When I saw this Scripture and then this similar one in 1 Peter 3:10–11, it was life-changing for me:

> For let him who wants to enjoy life and see good days [good—whether apparent or not] keep his tongue free from evil and his lips from guile (treachery, deceit). Let him turn away from wickedness and shun it, and let him do right. Let him search for peace (harmony; undisturbedness from fears, agitating passions, and moral conflicts) and seek it eagerly. [Do not merely desire peaceful relations with God, with your fellowmen, and with yourself, but pursue, go after them!]

When I first understood this Scripture, I realized that even though I prayed for peace regularly, there was something else I needed to *do*: I needed to pursue it, go after it in a strong way.

I began to study peace and examined what types of things caused me to lose my peace. I decided that I was absolutely unwilling to live my life frustrated and upset.

THINGS DON'T CHANGE OVERNIGHT

I would like to be able to tell you that things changed overnight; however, they didn't. I had to study the subject of peace for quite a long time and practice principles of peace until they became habit for me.

We form addictive habits throughout our lives. We learn to respond in certain ways and do so without even thinking about it. We must break these habits and form new ones, and this takes time. I want to *stress* that becoming a peacemaker and developing peaceful ways will take time, otherwise you may become discouraged in the beginning and just give up. I encourage you to stick with your pursuit until you experience victory, because it is well worth it.

One of the habits I had to break was getting upset whenever I did not get my way. I examined my pattern to understand why I always reacted like this. I realized that I had watched my father respond this way for years, while I was growing up. He was a very angry and controlling man and always got furious when things did not go his way.

As I have said before, my childhood home was filled with turmoil. It was our normal atmosphere. I doubt that I ever really enjoyed peace as a child. My alcoholic father was abusing me sexually, and he was violent toward almost everyone. My life was filled with fear: fear of being hurt, of someone's discovering what my father was doing to me, of no one's ever discovering it and helping me, of the fact that somehow it might be my fault, of making mistakes because I always got into trouble when I did. Fear! Fear! Fear! That was what life was to me.

I never learned peaceful ways as a child, but thank God we become new creatures when we enter a personal relationship with God through putting our faith in Jesus Christ (see 2 Corinthians 5:17). I share more about the story of God's redemptive work in my life and my father's in my newly revised book *Beauty for Ashes*. It bears our testimonies that we clearly receive a new beginning through faith in Jesus Christ; we can have our minds renewed and learn how to think and respond correctly to every situation in life.

God has blessed me with a strong personality. It helps me in many ways, but it can also be a great hindrance because I don't give up easily. In other words, if I have my mind set that something should be a certain way, it is not easy for me to let it go and trust God. Now, when I need to press through to the finish of something and refuse to give up, my personality is a benefit. But when I really cannot change a thing and need to let go and let God work, I have often found it difficult, to say the least. This is why I often say that it is so important to change what we can change, let go of what we cannot change, and have the wisdom to know the difference.

You might say, "Well, Joyce, I was not raised in a home filled with turmoil, and I don't even have the kind of personality you do. But I still don't have peace! So, what is my problem?" Satan works hard all of our lives to make sure we don't have righteousness, peace, and joy. He finds ways to steal from everyone.

We have examined many of the ways he will steal our peace in great detail, but the important thing is to be determined to have peace no matter how long it takes, or what it requires.

Crave peace, pursue and go after it! I love that statement. Each time I hear or read it, I feel a surge of determination within me to enjoy the life of peace that Jesus died to give me.

SATAN STEALS PEACE

Satan relentlessly attempts to steal everything God has provided for His children through Jesus Christ. Peace is one of the biggies; it is one of the things he works extra hard to prevent us from enjoying. Remember, *we have peace*—Jesus provided it—but *we must appropriate it*. Satan does everything he can to keep us from doing so, beginning with deception; he wants us to think that peace is not possible, that it is not even an option.

How can we remain peaceful while life seems to be falling apart around us? He screams into our ears when we have a challenging situation, "What are you going to do? What are you going to do?"

We frequently don't know what to do, nevertheless, Satan pressures us for answers that we don't have. He tries to make us believe it is our responsibility to solve our problems when the Word of God clearly states that our job as believers is to believe. We believe, and God works on our behalf to bring answers to meet our needs.

A good example appears in Exodus 14. The Egyptians were pursuing the Israelites; all the horses and chariots of Pharaoh, his horsemen and army were in pursuit of God's people. When the Israelites found themselves stuck between the Red Sea and the Egyptian army, it seemed hopeless. They could see no way out, so naturally, they became fearful and upset. They began to complain and make accusations against their leader, Moses. "Moses told the people, Fear not; stand still (firm, confident, undismayed) and see the salvation of the Lord which He will work for you today. For the Egyptians you have seen today you shall never see again. The Lord will fight for you, and you shall hold your peace and remain at rest" (Exodus 14:13–14).

It may have sounded foolish to the Israelites to stand still, hold their peace, and remain at rest, but that was God's instruction to them—it was their way of deliverance. When we remain peaceful in tumultuous circumstances, it clearly shows that we are trusting God. We often say, "God, I trust You," yet our actions show that we do not.

The lies of Satan steal our peace; however, the truth sets us free. Satan's lie is that we have to take care of ourselves: The truth is, God will take care of us as we place our trust in Him. When I began to practice this "peace principle" of simply trusting God, I actually felt guilty, as if I were not doing my part. I felt obligated to worry and try to figure out how to solve the current problem. This, of course, is exactly what Satan wants. He desires more than anything to bestir us to action that is useless. Then we end up exhausted and discouraged.

To enjoy a life of peace, you will need to examine your own life to learn what your "Peace Stealers" are. Satan uses some of the same things on everyone, but we also have things that are particular to each one of us. For example, one person may be very disturbed by having to do two things at one time, while another person may actually be challenged and energized by multitasking and doing several projects at once. We are all different, and we must learn to know ourselves.

My husband is not the least bit concerned about hearing that someone is talking unkindly about him, but he is easily disturbed when a driver does not stay in his lane of traffic or cuts in front of us. I am just the opposite. Although I would not appreciate unsafe driving, it does not disturb me as much as hearing I am being accused unjustly.

When our children are going through hard things, Dave says it is good for them and will help build their character; on the other hand, I want to rescue them. Since we are all different, Satan uses different things on each of us, and he usually has studied us long enough to know exactly what buttons to push at what time.

I can endure things better when I am not tired, and the devil knows this, so he waits to attack until I am worn-out. I learned by pursuing peace what Satan already knew about me, and now I try not to get overly tired because I know I am opening a door for Satan when I do.

It will be virtually impossible to enjoy a life of peace if you don't study to know what your Peace Stealers are. Keep a list of each time you get upset. Ask yourself what caused the problem, and write it down. Be honest with yourself, or you will never break free.

You may have things on your list like this:

- I didn't get my way.
- I had to hurry.
- I became impatient and got angry.
- Financial pressure upset me.

- I was too tired to deal with anything.
- I had to deal with a certain person who always frustrates me.
- A friend embarrassed me.
- I was in a traffic jam.
- A very slow clerk waited on me.
- A friend disappointed me.
- I got a stain on my dress.

You will have a lot of different things on your list, but it will help you to realize what bothers you. Remember, we cannot do anything about things we don't recognize. That the truth sets us free is a wonderful fact from God's Word that has truly been life-changing for me. Of course, truth must be faced in order for it to help anyone. This is often the painful part. Why does truth hurt? Simply because we don't like to see ourselves as we really are, and we have spent a lifetime developing systems of escape through making excuses and blaming others for our problems.

For many years, every time I became upset, in my mind it was always someone else's fault. I thought, *If Dave would just act differently, then I would not get upset. If life was not so challenging, then I could live peacefully. If my children would behave better, I could enjoy peace.* In my mind, my loss of peace was never my fault; it was always something and someone else's fault.

Only when I took responsibility for my reactions and decided to pursue peace did I begin to see change. Excuses and blaming others does us no good at all. If this has been your pattern, as it was mine, I strongly encourage you to ask the Holy Spirit to reveal the truth to you *about you,* and it will be the beginning of enjoying a life of peace.

PEACE EQUALS POWER

I have learned through my experience as well as God's Word that peace is power. That is one of the big reasons that Satan tries to steal our peace all the time. He wants all of God's children to be weak and powerless, not strong and powerful.

Maintaining your peace is your power over Satan. Consider this Scripture: "And do not [for a moment] be frightened or intimidated in anything by your opponents and adversaries, for such [constancy and fearlessness] will be a clear sign (proof and seal) to them of [their impending] destruction, but [a sure token and evidence] of your deliverance and salvation, and that from God" (Philippians 1:28).

We see that remaining peaceful is a clear sign to Satan of his upcoming defeat. *Peace is power!*

We studied in an earlier chapter that the Bible teaches us that staying calm and giving a "soft answer turns away wrath" (Proverbs 15:1). In other words, if someone is angry and yelling, answering him or her calmly and gently will change the situation and stop the possibility of an argument. How awesome! But in order for this to work, one of the people in the situation must be willing to humble him- or herself and respond the opposite of how he or she might feel like responding. Someone has to choose to be a peacemaker in every situation.

Even when a person is sick, staying peaceful and calm will help him or her recover more quickly. Just think of the instructions given to a woman in labor. I was told to "Breathe deeply," "Don't get tense," "Don't be fearful," "Stay calm," and that if I relaxed, the labor would be easier. In other words, when difficult situations face us, becoming upset only makes them worse—it does not help. Being upset steals our power; it does not release it.

The Word states that "the servant of the Lord must not be quarrelsome (fighting and contending). Instead, he must be kindly to everyone and mild-tempered [preserving the bond of peace]" (2 Timothy 2:24).

Why is a servant of the Lord required to be a peacemaker? I believe the Lord instructs us to avoid quarrels because they not only hurt our own witness to the world, but they also cause us to lose our power. We need to walk in this world with power—power against the forces of darkness. Satan seeks to stir up strife between people because we walk in power only when we walk in peace.

Second Timothy 2 continues to tell us clearly how a peacemaker is to train in the skill of keeping peace with others:

> He must be a skilled and suitable teacher, patient and forbearing and willing to suffer wrong. He must correct his opponents with courtesy and gentleness, in the hope that God may grant that they will repent and come to know the Truth [that they will perceive and recognize and become accurately acquainted with and acknowledge it], and that they may come to their senses [and] escape out of the snare of the devil, having been held captive by him, [henceforth] to do His [God's] will. (2 Timothy 2:24–26)

I realized that often Dave and I got into arguments or experienced turmoil right before we went out to minister to people or conduct a seminar. It took a while for us to see Satan's plan, but finally we understood that the devil was "setting us up to be upset" so he could steal our power.

Proverbs 17:1 says that a house full of sacrifices with strife is not pleasing to the Lord. In other words, we could make all kinds of sacrifices of time and effort to try to help people, yet God is not pleased unless we stay in peace.

Pursuing peace means making an effort. We cannot maintain peace simply by our own fleshly effort; we need God's help, and we need grace, which is His power assisting us and enabling us to do what needs to be done. The effort we make must be *in Christ*. So often we just try to do what is right without asking for God's help, and that type of fleshly effort never produces good fruit. The Bible calls this a "work of the flesh." It is man's effort trying to do God's job.

What I am saying is, be sure you lean on God and ask for His help. When you succeed, give Him the credit, the honor, and the glory because success is impossible without Him. Jesus said, "Apart from Me [cut off from vital union with Me] you can do nothing" (John 15:5).

It takes most of us a long time to believe this Scripture enough to stop trying to do things without leaning on God. We try and fail, try and fail; it happens over and over until we finally wear ourselves out and realize that God Himself is our strength, our success, and our victory. He doesn't just give us strength—He is our Strength. He does not just give us the victory—He is our Victory. Yes, we make an effort to keep peace, but we dare not make an effort without depending on God's power to flow through us; failure is certain if we do.

The Lord blesses Peacemakers, those who work for and make peace. Peacemakers are committed to peace; they crave peace, pursue peace, and go after it. Jesus promised: "Blessed (enjoying enviable happiness, spiritually prosperous—with life-joy and satisfaction in God's favor and salvation, regardless of their outward conditions) are the makers and maintainers of peace, for they shall be called the sons of God!" (Matthew 5:9).

Peacemakers take the first step in working things out when disagreement, disharmony, or disunity exists. They work toward peace; they don't just hope or wish for it, they don't even just pray for it. They aggressively pursue it in the power of God.

Make a commitment to pursue peace from this day forward: to discover all you can about what your Peace Stealers are, to know yourself and face the truth that will set you free.

Call yourself a peacemaker, one who works for and makes peace with God, himself, and others.

About the Author

Joyce Meyer is one of the world's leading practical Bible teachers. A #1 *New York Times* bestselling author, she has written more than seventy inspirational books, including *Look Great, Feel Great*, the entire Battlefield of the Mind family of books, and many others. She has also released thousands of audio teachings as well as a complete video library. Joyce's *Enjoying Everyday Life*® radio and television programs are broadcast around the world, and she travels extensively conducting conferences. Joyce and her husband, Dave, are the parents of four grown children and make their home in St. Louis, Missouri.

*Study Guide available for this title.